Liberalism and the 'Politics of Difference'

For D. P.

Liberalism and the 'Politics of Difference'

Andrea T. Baumeister

Edinburgh University Press

© Andrea T. Baumeister, 2000

Edinburgh University Press Ltd
22 George Square, Edinburgh

Typeset in Melior
by Tradespools Ltd.,
and printed and bound in Great Britain
by MPG Books Ltd, Bodmin

A CIP Record for this book is available from British Library

ISBN 0 7486 0909 1 (paperback)

The right of Andrea T. Baumeister
to be identified as the author of this work
has been asserted in accordance with
the Copyright, Designs and Patents Act 1988.

Contents

Acknowledgements

I would like to thank my colleagues at the University of Stirling for their continued support and encouragement throughout the process of writing this book. Here special thanks go to Stephen Ingle who kindly agreed to 'trade' sabbatical leave with me to help me complete this book.

I am particularly grateful to John Horton, Noël O'Sullivan, Stanley Kleinberg, Ricardo Blaug, and Luke Swaine, who have read and commented upon earlier drafts of part of the text. Their astute comments have saved me from many errors and led to many improvements. Although I fear I have not done justice to the worries they have raised.

I would also like to thank my editor Nicola Carr, who has remained good-natured and patient throughout the many extended deadlines.

Finally, I am grateful to my partner David, who never complained about 'lost' weekends and whose practical support has been invaluable.

Section 2 of Chapter 2 draws upon ideas set out in A. T. Baumeister, 'The New Feminism', in N. O'Sullivan (ed.) *Political Theory in Transition* (London: Routledge, 1999). Parts of Chapter 3 were originally published in A. T. Baumeister, 'Cultural Diversity and Education: The Dilemma of Political Stability', *Political Studies*, Vol. 46, No. 5, Dec. 1998, pp. 919–36. Chapter 7 develops and expands upon an argument first developed in A. T. Baumeister, 'Two liberalism and the politics of difference', *Journal of Political Ideologies*, Vol. 3, No. 3, 1998, pp. 307–24.

Andrea Baumeister

Preface

One of the most striking features of recent political discourse has been the rise of cultural pluralism and the 'politics of difference'. For liberalism this emphasis on difference and particularity has frequently been rather problematic. Indeed, since the onset of Romanticism, critics have rejected the liberal preoccupation with universalism as a failure to acknowledge the significance of those characteristics which distinguish particular groups from one another. To assess the basis of this critique, Part I will outline the rise of this regard for the particular. Whereas Chapter 1 explores the tensions between the emphasis of Enlightenment liberalism upon universalism and immutable standards, on the one hand, and the regard for plurality which informs the views of the Romantics and subsequent critics of liberalism such as Nietzsche on the other, Chapter 2 provides an overview of the contemporary 'politics of difference' and the challenges it poses for modern liberalism. Here some of the most sustained and influential critiques have come from feminist scholars. Through their critique of the liberal conception of the individual, feminists have developed important theoretical frameworks for assessing the nature, role and political implications of difference and identity in general. Indeed the emphasis upon our particular characteristics, experiences and perspectives has not only been central to contemporary feminist thought, but also informs the concerns of an increasing number of religious, ethnic and national minorities currently campaigning for recognition. These demands for the support of particular identities and cultures have drawn attention to the potential difficulties inherent in the individualistic and difference blind manner in which liberals have traditionally defined citizenship. To gain a clearer understanding of the nature of these challenges and to assess the degree to which these demands question principles central to liberal conceptions of citizenship, Chapter 2 develops a number of important distinctions. Not only is it helpful to categorise groups in terms of the nature and origin of the particular group, the character of the specific rights they demand, and the manner in which these rights are to be exercised, it is also vital to clearly identify the type of multicultural politics implicit in the wide array of demands voiced by various minorities. Here a distinction has to be drawn between instances of thin multiculturalism, where the various protagonists continue to subscribe to a shared set of liberal values, and cases of thick multiculturalism, which are characterised by a fundamental conflict of values and, hence, frequently entail a genuine difficulty on the part of the various protagonists to truly understand and appreciate each others values, cultures and perspectives.

Liberals have sought to respond to the challenges of thin and thick multiculturalism in a variety of ways. Part II considers liberal attempts to accommodate the demands of difference and particularity by establishing an impartial point of view, which can provide the basis for a new consensus based upon liberal principles. According to this school of liberal thought, the state can only claim legitimacy if it can secure the free and willing assent of those it governs. In a culturally and ethically diverse society such assent can only be assured if the state can be shown to respect the different moral, religious and philosophical beliefs of its citizens. Advocates of this strand of liberal thought maintain that the liberal state can and should be neutral between these competing conceptions of the good, and therefore can potentially win the assent of most, if not all citizens in modern liberal democratic societies. Probably the two most prominent examples of this approach can be found in the works of John Rawls and Jürgen Habermas. Chapter 3 focuses upon Rawls's conception of political liberalism, which seeks to establish an impartial point of view by removing all controversial questions from the political sphere. This strategy, however, implies a sharp distinction between the political and the non-political which ultimately cannot be sustained. Such a distinction not only ignores the complex interrelationship between the political and the non-political, and thus fails to take into account the concerns raised by well-established feminist critiques of traditional liberal conceptions of justice, it also disregards the profound diversity of values within contemporary liberal societies. The latter difficulties are clearly illustrated by the controversies that surround the question of education in a Rawlsian society. While it is vital to the success of political liberalism that children are educated to understand and appreciate the role of the individual and society that underpins the notion of citizenship in a Rawlsian society, such an education will foster a set of values and attitudes which are at odds with the conception of the good of at least some non-liberal life-styles and may indeed threaten the long-term viability of such ways of life. In the light of the difficulties which surround Rawls's approach,

Chapter 4 turns to Habermas and his idea of discourse ethics. While Habermas's context responsive conception of impartiality is better placed than Rawls's political liberalism to capture the concerns that inform thin multiculturalism, Habermas, like Rawls, fails to take into account the fundamental diversity of values associated with thick multiculturalism. For Habermas worldviews which fail to share the liberal commitment to critical rationality and autonomy are incompatible with practical discourse in a constitutional state. In the final analysis the consensus which Rawls and Habermas seek is only possible if those conceptions of the good which do not share the liberal commitment to autonomy are excluded from the political arena. Yet under these circumstances the liberal state may fail to gain the assent of a significant number of citizens. The liberal quest for impartiality therefore appears to be misplaced.

Although liberals such as Habermas acknowledge that individuals may be entitled to special cultural and social rights, many of the demands voiced by minorities seeking recognition cannot readily be conceptualised in terms of personal cultural rights. Instead they appear to imply corporate cultural rights to be exercised by the collective as a whole. Part III examines the work of liberals who acknowledge the special status of collectivities and who have attempted to develop distinctly liberal accounts of group rights. Chapter 5 focuses on the work of three prominent liberal writers – Will Kymlicka, Chandran Kukathas and Joseph Raz – whose approaches to the question of group rights are informed by a commitment to the traditional liberal values of individual liberty and equality of respect. Contrary to the widely held view that group rights are incompatible with the liberal emphasis on individual freedom, autonomy and equality, both Kymlicka and Raz argue that these liberal ideals actually entail certain group rights. However, while Kymlicka bases his theory firmly within the liberal tradition of neutrality, Raz views the liberal commitment to individual freedom and autonomy as a perfectionist ideal. Chandran Kukathas, however, rejects the concern with group rights which informs the work of Kymlicka and Raz. While, like Kymlicka, Kukathas endorses a version of liberal neutrality, he believes that the demands by minority groups and cultural communities do not warrant a special theory of group rights. On the contrary, for Kukathas legitimate demands for self-government can be accommodated via a robust account of the individual right to freedom of association. The discussion in Chapter 5 suggests that despite the marked differences in the approaches adopted by Kymlicka, Kukathas and Raz all three theories are potentially problematic for both liberals and non-liberal minorities. While liberals and advocates of thin multiculturalism are liable to express concern about the impact of the demands and expectations of the collective upon individual autonomy and liberty, groups whose claims fall within the realms of thick multiculturalism will regard the emphasis on individual liberty and autonomy as a potential threat to their long-term viability. However, liberal conceptions of group right need not necessarily be grounded in a commitment to individual rights and equality of respect. Chapter 6 considers an alternative approach to the question of liberal group rights developed by Charles Taylor and Michael Walzer. According to Taylor and Walzer, the liberal state can actively pursue particular goals and support specific conceptions of the good, provided it respects the basic rights of citizens who wish to pursue a different way of life. While the account offered by Taylor and Walzer can readily accommodate the aspirations of at least some national minorities, in the eyes of liberals and advocates of thin multiculturalism both theorists disregard the internal heterogeneity of cultural groups and thus fail to pay sufficient attention to the role internal power relations play in the formation of cultural identity. Furthermore, their vision of the liberal state as a political community united by common meanings based upon a shared language, history and culture, neglects the fundamental diversity of values associated with thick multiculturalism and thus fails to offer effective protection to cultural and ethnic minorities within the political community.

In the light of the difficulties inherent in the quest for impartiality and the search for group rights, Part IV examines the distinctive approach to cultural diversity associated with the liberal value pluralism of writers such as Isaiah Berlin and Stuart Hampshire. This strand of liberal thought rejects the preoccupation with 'universal reason' which characterises the liberal Enlightenment project in favour of a vision of human excellence which echoes the Romantic regard for diversity. For value pluralists such as Berlin and Hampshire morality is characterised by numerous, conflicting values which cannot be combined in a single life or a single society. Consequently, human identities and cultures are by their very nature diverse; each expressing a distinct set of values and virtues. Given this inherent diversity political life is characterised by the inevitable conflict among incommensurable cultures and values. Chapter 7 explores the implications of such a robust defence of 'diversity'. It concludes that value pluralism gives rise to a liberalism which is aware of its own historical contingency and which recognises the tensions and conflicts inherent in its own values. This allows liberal value pluralists to acknowledge the significance of group membership and ensures that this strand of liberal thought is well placed to

PREFACE xi

accommodate the demands associated with both thin and thick multiculturalism. However, a value pluralist perspective is not without its dangers for both liberals and advocates of diversity. While the open and dynamic conception of the political community central to a value pluralist perspective grants this position the flexibility to acknowledge and respond to a wide variety of different concerns and perspectives, it does not privilege any particular viewpoint or guarantee a specific outcome. Hence neither liberals nor advocates of diversity can be certain that their concerns will win out in the process of political debate and negotiation. Chapter 8 considers the implications of these dilemmas for both liberals and their critics. For liberals the 'politics of difference' raises important questions regarding the nature of diversity, the conception of the self and the role of the political. The emphasis upon universal values and the shared aspects of our identity characteristic of the Enlightenment tradition, has led many liberals not only to underestimate the significance and complexity of diversity, but has given rise to a 'flight from the political'. If liberalism is to respond adequately to the challenge of a 'politics of difference', it must acknowledge diversity as an inherent and positive aspect of identity and accept the primacy of the political as a sphere in which the conflicts that inevitably accompany diversity can be negotiated. While many of the prominent liberal responses can accommodate some aspects of the 'politics of difference' and many thus appeal to certain minorities currently campaigning for recognition, only liberal value pluralism acknowledges the wider implications of a commitment to genuine diversity. The dangers inherent in value pluralism serve as a reminder that in a society characterised by genuine diversity, tensions and uncertainties are ultimately inevitable.

Part I: The Rise of the Particular

The Rise of the Particular

For many modern advocates of cultural pluralism and the 'politics of difference' the vision of human excellence at the heart of liberalism is deeply flawed, since it fails to acknowledge the significance and pervasiveness of particularity and diversity. While these concerns have of late been voiced with renewed vigour, they reflect a number of long-standing worries about the limitations of the liberal tradition. Indeed the debate between liberals and the advocates of diversity can be traced to the Enlightenment, many of whose themes and preoccupations still dominate liberal thought today. Since the onset of Romanticism, critics have sought to assert the value and pervasiveness of diversity in the face of the cosmopolitanism of the Enlightenment and its search for universal values and principles of justice. These tensions between early Enlightenment liberals and their critics anticipate many of the themes of the contemporary debate surrounding the 'politics of difference'. Whereas Chapter 1 explores the tensions between Enlightenment liberalism and the Romantics, Chapter 2 provides an overview of the contemporary 'politics of difference' and the challenges it poses for modern liberalism.

Chapter 1: The 'Drive for Diversity'

In the latter part of the twentieth century liberalism has undoubtedly been subject to a remarkable renaissance. Indeed for some commentators the collapse of the former 'Soviet Block' and the fall of the Berlin wall signalled the victory of liberal democracy over its traditional socialist/marxist challengers.[1] Yet, while these developments may have given liberals a renewed sense of confidence, the tensions and heated debates within contemporary liberal democracies suggest that, although some of the old challenges may have receded, a new range of questions has emerged.

Probably the most significant of these debates has centred upon identity, group membership and difference. At the political level, this debate has in part been fuelled by the ever more vocal demands of an increasing number of minority groups for the recognition and support of their particular identity and culture. What characterises these demands is the desire to maintain and perpetuate 'difference' by ensuring the continued survival and flourishing of the distinct values and way of life of particular groups. Thus many liberal democracies have found themselves confronted not only with the more familiar demands of established national minorities, like the Catalans in Spain,[2] for greater regional autonomy, but have also had to respond to the campaigns for cultural recognition and support by ethnic and religious minorities. Such demands for recognition have been associated with campaigns for the legal protection of minority beliefs and practices, public funding for minority institutions, access to the national media and the establishment of institutional mechanisms for influencing public policy in relation to issues of particular significance to a minority. For example, members of the Muslim community in Britain have campaigned for the extension of British blasphemy laws so as to cover Islam and have sought to obtain funding for Muslim schools. In a similar vein Christian fundamentalists in America have demanded the legal right to withdraw their children from those aspects of the public school curriculum which they regard as incompatible with their beliefs.[3] Finally, in Canada, New Zealand and Australia indigenous people have campaigned for greater control over resources and policies which affect their way of life.[4]

At first glance, liberalism, with its emphasis upon toleration, autonomy and self-determination, may appear to be well placed to respond sympathetically to such demands. However, while minorities campaigning for such measures tend to regard them as vital to the protection of their identity, in practice liberal democracies have frequently found it difficult to accommodate the expectations of cultural and religious minorities. These difficulties are not entirely surprising. Although liberalism advocates tolerance in the face of diversity, this tolerance is grounded in the recognition of the universal capacities all human beings share. Thus the traditional liberal conception of citizenship has rested on the belief that differences, be they in terms of gender, race or ethnicity, should not affect our standing as citizens. Whereas all individuals may differ with regard to their social background, history, biology and the beliefs and values they subscribe to, liberals have tended to view these differences as merely contingent and inconsequential compared to the features all human beings hold in common. It is these shared, universal criteria which provide the basis for formal legal and political equality. Hence difference and particularity are to be relegated to the private sphere. In the political arena citizens should transcend their differences and act on the basis of the common good or 'general will'. However, many of the groups currently campaigning for greater recognition have been highly critical of the liberal emphasis on universal criteria and the subsequent exclusion of difference and particularity from the political sphere.

At a theoretical level this unease with universalism has given rise to a systematic critique of the liberal conception of citizenship. Here some of the most sustained attacks have come from feminist scholars. Rather than regard differences as merely contingent, many contemporary feminists have asserted the moral and political significance of those characteristics which distinguish women from men. This regard for women's moral and political voice has recently given rise among feminists to a wider concern with the nature, role and political implications of difference and identity in general. Thus in the eyes of critics like Young, Honig and Mouffe[5] liberalism's preoccupation with abstract universalism amounts to a failure to acknowledge the significance of those characteristics which distinguish particular groups from one another.

While these concerns have of late been voiced with renewed vigour, they reflect a number of long-standing worries about the limitations of the liberal tradition. Indeed the debate between liberals and the advocates of diversity can be traced to the Enlightenment, many of whose themes and preoccupations still dominate liberal thought today. Since the onset of Romanticism, critics have sought to assert the value and pervasiveness of diversity in the face of the cosmopolitanism of the Enlightenment and its search for universal values and principles of justice. These tensions between early Enlightenment liberals and their critics anticipate many of the themes of the contemporary debate surrounding the 'politics of difference'.

Enlightenment, Romanticism and Cultural Diversity

Reason and the 'drive for generality'

It is widely recognised that the term Enlightenment refers to a rather diverse set of ideas, which was subject to complex tensions and disagreements among its champions. Indeed in as far as it is possible to speak of a common purpose and shared enterprise this appears to spring more from a recognition of a common enemy – the status quo and those who supported it – and a preoccupation with certain questions and problems rather than substantive agreements in terms of philosophical doctrine and practical goals. For instance, Voltaire and Diderot, two of the most influential French *philosphes*, disagreed on 'atheism, politics and above all the best strategy for progress'.[6] Furthermore, the expression and development of the Enlightenment varied across Europe, reflecting the distinct national contexts within which its ideas evolved. It has therefore become commonplace to speak of the French, German or Scottish Enlightenment.

However, despite this diversity, it is possible to identify a number of pivotal themes which forged Enlightenment thought. Central to one of the most influential strands of Enlightenment philosophy was an emphasis on the use of reason to critically examine all issues. For writers such as Voltaire and d'Alembert 'ignorance, mysticism, superstition and general irrationalism' were the true enemies of Enlightenment.[7] This outlook had its roots in the philosophy of Descartes, whose rationalistic method and basic assumptions deeply influenced many of the French philosophers. Not surprisingly, the preoccupation with reason shaped the conception of human nature central to the work of many figures of the Enlightenment. According to Enlightenment thinkers, such as the German philosopher Immanuel Kant, all men are equally endowed with the capacity to reason, and reason is identical in all men. From this perspective reason provides a universal standard of intelligibility and accountability, which should 'constitute the decisive criterion of validity or of worth in all matters of human concernment'.[8] Thus Kant urges his readers to follow the law of practical reason which demands that they '[a]ct only on that maxim through which you can at the same time will that it should become a universal law'.[9] For him this law of practical reason – the categorical imperative – provides a universal standard of morality which can be recognised by all human beings. This strand of Enlightenment thought, therefore, aimed to simplify human life and to provide man with an uncomplicated, immutable and uniform standard applicable to every rational being. As John Gray[10] notes, associated with this emphasis on universal reason was the belief in the 'evanescence of particularistic allegiances, national and religious, and the progressive levelling down, or marginalization, of cultural difference in human affairs'. This perspective is evident in Kant's view of the Enlightenment as 'a singular stage within a universal developmental account of human history'.[11] For Kant the goal of this development is the full realisation of the ends of reason. While he acknowledges that at first sight it may appear an absurd proposition to write a *history* according to an idea of how world events must develop if they are to conform to certain rational ends',[12] Kant maintains that:

A philosophical attempt to work out a universal history of the world in accordance with a plan of nature aimed at a perfect union of mankind, must be regarded as possible . . .[13]

Hegel perpetuates this Enlightenment view, when he describes history as a rational and necessary process of development, whose final goal is the establishment of a rational community. As these accounts of history suggest, many Enlightenment liberals believed that critical rationality and conscious reflection would enable mankind to overcome national and cultural disagreements and would permit humanity to establish universally acceptable, fundamental values and principles of justice. Consequently, Enlightenment thinkers such as Kant emphasise the importance of autonomy, conceived in terms of a distancing from or a transcending of our particularistic allegiances. In the context of citizenship this emphasis on universality gave rise to what Iris Marion Young refers to as 'the drive for generality'.[14] The ideal of 'generality', which has its roots in the philosophies of Rousseau and Hegel, demands that citizens transcend their differences and act on the basis of a common interest or 'general will'. Thus, whereas Rousseau recognises that a man's private will or interests may well be contrary to the 'general will', he stresses that:

the general will alone can direct the forces of the state in accordance with that end which the state had been established to achieve – the common good; for if the conflict between private interests has made the setting up of civil society necessary, harmony between those same interests has made it possible. It is

what is common to those different interests which yields the social bond . . .
And it is precisely on the basis of this common interest that society must be
governed.[15]

To achieve this, the proponents of the ideal of 'generality' invoke a
sharp distinction between the public and the private realm. Here the
public realm is identified with normative reason, whereas difference,
particularity and affectivity are firmly relegated to the non-political
private sphere.

Montesquieu and the fact of human diversity

While this strand of Enlightenment thinking proved to be highly
influential in the development of modern liberal thought, by no means
all Enlightenment philosophers endorsed the preoccupation with
'generality' and 'uniformity'. Montesquieu, for instance, is keenly
aware that the various philosophical and religious systems that have
tried to establish which ultimate goal man should seek have provided
widely varying answers to the question of what ends man should
pursue. This recognition of diversity leads him to emphasise the
unique character of different civilisations and traditional ways of life.
For Montesquieu '[m]en are governed by many things: climate,
religion, law, the maxims of government, the examples of past things,
customs, [and] manners'.[16] Not only do men differ from one another,
the conditions in which they live diverge widely. Consequently,
different societies will pursue different goals and ends. Thus, for
example, laws 'should be so adapted to the people for which they are
created, that it should be a great coincidence if the laws of one nation
suit another'.[17] Montesquieu firmly rejects the idea that there can be a
single set of values suitable for all men everywhere'[18] or one generally
acceptable solution to social and political problems. However, despite
this emphasis on diversity, Montesquieu nonetheless 'did not doubt
the universality of *ultimate values*.'[18] By nature all men desire
security, justice, social stability and happiness. However the means
they employ to achieve these goals differ 'according to natural
environment and social conditions and . . . institutions, habits, tastes
[and] conventions'.[20]

Here Montesquieu distinguishes between the social mores and legal
traditions of different societies, which quite properly and necessarily
diverge widely in line with the varying conditions and circumstances
in which human beings find themselves, and the underlying fundamental human values which are universal. Montesquieu therefore
retains the Enlightenment conviction that different ways of life could

be judged and perhaps graded in terms of such universal principles as political "liberty" and "natural" principles of justice'.[21] From this perspective cultural diversity is merely an inescapable fact of life akin to differences in human shapes, sizes and pigmentation. Although Motesquieu accepts the plurality of life-styles, he does not regard diversity as a source of value.[22] Consequently, while his work challenges the view that cultural differences can be progressively eliminated, he does not question the validity of underlying universal standards.

Romanticism and the excellence of diversity

Yet it is precisely this commitment to universal standards and the conception of human excellence that accompanies it which is challenged with the emergence of what is frequently referred to as Romanticism. Whereas Enlightenment thought emphasised the significance and desirability of universal reason, the Romantic movement aimed to highlight the value and pervasiveness of diversity. As Lovejoy[23] notes, for the thinkers of the Romantic period human life is not merely characterised by a diversity of excellences, but this diversity constitutes the very essence of excellence itself. The roots of this romantic regard for diversity can be found in Fichte's celebration of will over discursive thought. For Fichte values, principles, morals and political goals are not objectively given by nature, God or reason, but are determined or created by the agent himself. Thus '[e]nds are not discovered at all, but made, not found but created.'[24] While for the philosophers of the Enlightenment politics and ethics are akin to the natural sciences, the Romantics view the political and ethical as analogous to artistic creation. This emphasis by Romantics such as the young Friedrich Schlegel, Teich or Novalis on the creative aspect of the human self gives rise to the assertion that the good life consists of developing one's own distinctive life and particular values. The Romantics therefore urge us to give the fullest expression to and take delight in our unique and different characteristics, be they in terms of our individual identity, family membership, nationality, race or gender. We should acknowledge our own particularity. After all the situation in which you find yourself is,

the best for you; you will be as it were out of your native element if you try to be anything different. A modern man should be profoundly modern, a German proudly German, an Englishman distinctively English.[25]

Thus, for example, Herder[26] in his attack upon what he perceived to be the hollow cosmopolitanism and universalism of the French philosophers, stresses the unique character and value of diverse and incommensurable cultures. In demanding that we abandon the natural bonds of language, history, habit and tradition which bind us to a specific culture and community, the cosmopolitanism of the Enlightenment asks us to shed those characteristics that make us most human. This hostility to universal prescriptions leads Herder also to reject the Kantian conception of history. While for Kant earlier epochs are merely steps in the general progress towards the final goal of history, Herder urges us to value every period for its own sake and not to view it simply as a 'precursor or prelude to later periods'.[27] Although Herder does not rule out the notion of progress, he feels that every epoch and culture possesses its own unique ideals and standards, each displaying a 'new and notable side of mankind'.[28] As Berlin notes, for Herder:

The conception of history as a single universal process of struggle towards the light, the later stages and embodiments of which are necessarily superior to the earlier, where the primitive is necessarily inferior to the sophisticated, is an enormous fallacy.[29]

Given that the values and ends pursued by different societies are frequently incommensurable, Romantics such as Herder view the Enlightenment vision of a perfect society in which most if not all genuine human values are reconciled as simply misconceived. The values and virtues of ancient Greece are not a mere precursor or stepping-stone to Roman culture. The ends pursed by these two cultures may well differ, but this is not to suggest that one is inferior to the other. It merely highlights the extent to which values and ends are incommensurable.[30] To gain an insight into the rich diversity of human excellences, Herder, like many Romantics, urges us to cultivate our appreciation and understanding of all cultures. While cultures differ, our faculties of sympathetic insight, which we employ to understand one another at an individual level, also enable us to understand the values and virtues of foreign cultures.

The impact of the romantics

This conflict between the Enlightenment ideal of universal reason and the romantic assertion of difference has in many ways continued to shape our cultural climate and intellectual debates.[31] For instance, in the face of the universalism and abstraction advocated by thinkers such as Kant and Hegel, Kierkegaard[32] asserts the significance of the particular and the subjective. For Kierkegaard the Hegelian view of history as a rational and necessary process loses sight of the concreteness of human existence. He therefore rejects the 'illusions of objectivity' inherent in the idea of an abstract, 'impersonal knowing self', in favour of an emphasis upon subjectivism. The individual is constituted not by what he knows, but by what he wills; that is the choices he makes with regard to his life-style and outlooks. However, while Kierkegaard shares Kant's regard for autonomy, he does not view autonomy in terms of the dictates of abstract practical reason. In place of the Kantian abstract self, Kierkegaard asserts that the individual who chooses is a concrete self; a self that stands in 'reciprocal relations' with its actual social and cultural surroundings.[33] Consequently, whereas Kant asks us to transcend our particular attachments, Kierkegaard views 'things like marriage, having a job and undertaking civic and institutional responsibilities' as 'intrinsic to personal fulfilment in the required sense.'[34]

The romantic reaction to the Enlightenment also provides the foundations for Nietzsche's influential reassessment of the Enlightenment tradition.[35] Rather than regard the ideas invoked by the Romantics as antithetical to the Enlightenment, Nietzsche views these ideas as the impetus for a new and deeper realisation of the process of enlightenment.[36] For Nietzsche,

it is precisely the spirits the Germans so eloquently conjured up . . . now fly on the broadest wings above and beyond their former conjurors as new and stronger genie of that very Enlightenment against which they were first conjured up.[37]

In the process of redefining Enlightenment, Nietzsche offers a profound critique of the principles of 'universality' and 'generality', central to many of the earlier conceptions of Enlightenment. Just like Kant before him Nietzsche views Enlightenment as emancipation from alien guidance. However, while for Kant the main impediment to this emancipation lies in our readiness to accept the guidance of figures of authority, such as priests and doctors, Nietzsche argues that the idea of a universal rational standard, championed by philosophers such as Kant as the very essence of Enlightenment, constitutes merely another obstacle on the road to emancipation. While the advocates of universal reason thought to 'furnish the rational grounds of morality', their pride and ignorance lead them to ignore the 'the real problems of morality – for these come into view only if we compare many moralities'.[38] For Nietzsche the 'rational grounds of morality' advocated by thinkers such as Kant offer little more than an endorsement of, or faith in, the prevailing morality. Thus the advocates of 'universal reason' fail to recognise the historical specificity of their own principles. In Nietzsche's opinion the notion of a universal rational standard can be traced to the ascetic ideal central to Christianity. In an attempt to transcend the limitations of human existence this ascetic ideal constructs a dichotomy between the 'real' and the 'apparent' world. While the 'apparent' world is identified with all that is transient, contingent or animalistic – growth, death, wishing, longing etc. – the 'real' world is conceptualised as a source of unitary value which provides the overarching goal and purpose of human existence. The aim of human existence is to subject the 'apparent world' to the rule of the 'real world' by way of a universal law. In a similar vein advocates of the principle of universal reason such as Kant draw a distinction between universal reason and the multitude of human desires and life-styles. While reason is viewed as essential and real, and provides a common standard and goal for all of humanity, the multitude of human desires and life-styles is regarded as merely contingent and apparent. For this tradition of thought the overarching goal of human existence is to subject this diversity to the universal rule of reason. Nietzsche argues that by suggesting that all human beings must obey this universal rule of reason, philosophers such as Kant, rather than show humanity the road towards emancipation, merely make man subject to yet another 'guardian'. Thus Kant, for instance, demands that we simply obey the dictates of the categorical imperative. For Nietzsche, his attempt to construct a universally applicable coherent system of rational principles gives rise to an inability to appreciate and respond to genuine diversity and deep value-conflicts. Since Nietzsche rejects the idea of an ultimate, unitary source of value, he regards such value-conflicts as inevitable. Hence, in place of the principle of universal reason he offers us a picture of human history characterised by a 'plurality of styles of reasoning' and the recognition of a plurality of values.[39]

The tension between the emphasis of Enlightenment liberalism upon universalism and immutable standards on the one hand, and the regard for plurality which informs the views of the Romantics and subsequent critics of liberalism such as Nietzsche on the other, foreshadows many of the themes of the contemporary debate between liberals and their challengers. Thus just as the Romantics asserted the importance of national differences in the face of Enlightenment cosmopolitanism, national, ethnic and religious minorities currently campaigning for recognition have sought to extend the principle of diversity by highlighting the significance of intra-national differences. In a similar vein Nietzsche's attempt to highlight the historical specificity and philosophical limitations of the Enlightenment conception of universal reason can be seen as a precursor to modern critiques of the liberal tradition.

Notes and References

1. For the view that liberalism has defeated its challengers, see, for example, F. Fukuyama, *The end of history and the last man* (London: Hamish Hamilton, 1992).
2. In Spain the move to a modern liberal democracy has been associated with an increasing recognition of the demand for greater autonomy on the part of national groups within Spain including the Catalans, the Basques and, more recently, the Andalusians (T. O. Hueglin, 'Regionalism in Western Europe', *Comparative Politics*, Vol. 18, No. 4, 1986, pp. 439–58). However, for liberal democracies not all demands for greater regional autonomy are unproblematic, since in certain cases such demands reflect a secessionist agenda. For example, the goal of many Quebec nationalists is secession. Consequently, their demands have placed a severe strain on the political fabric of Canada.
3. See, for example, the case of Mozert v. Hawkins, discussed in S. Macedo, 'Liberal Civil Education and Religious Fundamentalism: The Case of God v. John Rawls', *Ethics*, Vol. 105, April 1995, pp. 468–96.
4. For instance in Canada the indigenous people of northern Quebec secured under the James Bay and Northern Quebec Treaty of 1975 the right to participate, along with local government, in the formulation of policies and regulations concerning the development of the region.
5. I. M. Young, *Justice and the Politics of Difference* (Princeton: Princeton University Press, 1990); B. Honig, *Political Theory and the Displacement of Politics* (Ithaca: Cornell University Press, 1993); C. Mouffe, *The Return of the Political* (London: Verso, 1993).
6. L. G. Crocker, *The Age of the Enlightenment* (London: Macmillan, 1969).
7. R. Wokler, 'Enlightenment', in M. A. Riff (ed.), *Dictionary of Modern Political Ideologies* (Manchester: Manchester University Press, 1987) p. 75.
8. A. Lovejoy, *The Great Chain of Being* (New York: Harper & Row, 1960) p. 289.
9. I. Kant, *The Moral Law*, translated by H. J. Paton (London: Routledge, 1989).
10. John Gray, 'Agnostic Liberalism', *Social Philosophy and Policy*, Vol. 12, Sept. 1995, pp. 110–35, p. 112.
11. D. Owen, 'Kant Critique and Enlightenment', *unpublished paper* (University of Southampton: Department of Politics, 1998).
12. I. Kant, 'Idea for a Universal History With A Cosmopolitan Purpose', in *Political Writings* (Cambridge: University Press, 1991) p. 51.
13. Ibid. p. 51.
14. I. M. Young, *Justice and the Politics of Difference*.
15. J. J. Rousseau, *The Social Contract* (London: Penguin Books, 1968) p. 69.
16. Montesquieu, cited in I. Berlin, *Against the Current* (Oxford: University Press, 1981) pp. 134–5.
17. Ibid. p. 135.
18. I. Berlin, *Against the Current*, p. 143.

19. I. Berlin, *The Crooked Timber of Humanity* (London: John Murray, 1990) p. 72, my emphasis.
20. I. Berlin, p. 72.
21. B. Parekh, 'Moral Philosophy and its Anti-pluralist Bias', in D. Archard (ed.), *Philosophy and Pluralism* (Cambridge: University Press, 1996) pp. 117–34.
22. Ibid.
23. A. Lovejoy, *The Great Chain of Being*.
24. I. Berlin, *The Crooked Timber of Humanity*, p. 227.
25. A. Lovejoy, *Essays in the History of Ideas* (Baltimore: John Hopkins Press, 1943).
26. See I. Berlin, 'The Counter-Enlightenment' in *Against the Current*, pp. 1–24. As Berlin notes, Herder was not a nationalist, but believed that 'different cultures could and should flourish fruitfully side by side' (I. Berlin, *Again the Current*, p. 13). Nonetheless, his thought undoubtedly provided the foundation for the aggressive nationalism of his nineteenth-century followers.
27. H. Reich in Kant, *Political Writings*, p. 97.
28. Herder cited in A. Lovejoy, *Essays in the History of Ideas*, p. 170.
29. I. Berlin, *The Crooked Timber of Humanity*, pp. 37–8.
30. Although Herder celebrates differences between societies, he does not appreciate differences within each of them. On the contrary, Herder argues that in order to preserve the 'distinct genius' of a particular society, a society should disallow all internal plurality that conflicts with its internal cultural integrity (see B. Parekh, 'Moral Philosophy and its Anti-Pluralist Bias').
31. I. Berlin, *The Crooked Timber of Humanity*.
32. For a selection of Kierkegaard's writing see, H. J. Blackham, *Reality, Man and Existence* (London: Bantam Books, 1965).
33. E. Craig (ed.), *Routledge Encyclopedia of Philosophy* (London: Routledge, 1998) p. 239.
34. Ibid. p. 239.
35. Nietzsche's relationship to romanticism is rather complex and has been subject to considerable debate. While Nietzsche is very critical of many elements of romanticism, numerous commentators have highlighted the continuity between his thought and aspects of romanticism. See Del Caro, *Nietzsche contra Nietzsche* (Baton Rouge: Louisiana State University Press, 1989).
36. D. Owen, 'Kant, Critique and Enlightenment'.
37. F. Nietzsche, *Daybreak* (Cambridge: University Press, 1982) p. 118.
38. Nietzsche cited in D. Owen, 'Kant, Critique and Enlightenment', p. 12.
39. D. Owen, 'Kant, Critique and Enlightenment', p. 16.

Chapter 2: The 'Politics of Difference'

One of the most striking features of recent political discourse has been the rise of cultural pluralism and the 'politics of difference'. For liberalism this emphasis on difference and particularity has frequently been rather problematic. Just as the Romantics asserted the importance of national differences in the face of Enlightenment cosmopolitanism, many of the new advocates of diversity have been critical of liberal universalism both at the political and theoretical level. While at a political level liberal democracies have been confronted with ever more vocal demands by national and ethnic minorities for the recognition and protection of their particular culture and identity, at a theoretical level liberalism has been attacked by the advocates of difference and diversity for failing to acknowledge the significance of those characteristics which distinguish particular groups from others. To assess the degree to which this 'politics of difference' challenges modern liberalism, it is vital to gasp the worries and demands which underpin this commitment to particularity.

At a theoretical level some of the most sustained and influential critiques of the traditional liberal response to difference and diversity have come from feminist scholars. Whereas the first generation of reforming feminists regarded the liberal conception of citizenship as a vital intellectual weapon in their fight for equal rights for women, many modern feminists contend that the preoccupation with abstract universalism which characterises liberal conceptions of citizenship constitutes a failure to acknowledge the significance of difference. Feminist critics fear that this neglect gives rise to a discourse in which what constitutes a proper person, a true individual, is representative of men's experience and reasoning rather than women's. In the light of their critique of liberal universalism feminists have not only explored the significance of differences between men and women, but have also emphasised the impact of race, class and sexual orientation upon the lives of women. This preoccupation with the wider ramifications of difference and identity has led feminists such as Spelman, Harris, hooks and Flax[1] to reject the unitary vision of the self, central to traditional liberal conceptions of citizenship, in favour of a conception of identity as multiple, contingent and context bound. This is not to suggest that all modern feminists have been hostile to the concerns which lie at the heart of the traditional liberal emphasis upon universality and formal equality. On the contrary feminists such as Young readily acknowledge the potential appeal of liberalism's commitment to universality and the equality of moral worth of all persons.[2] However, according to Young the scope and character of these values must be redefined to ensure that the claims of difference and particularity are recognised.

This emphasis upon the significance of our particular characteristics, experiences and perspective has by no means been unique to feminist debates. In recent years many liberal democracies have been confronted by the ever more vocal demands of an increasing number of religious, ethnic and national minorities for the recognition and support of their particular identity and culture. These demands have drawn attention to the political significance of group membership and thus underline the limitations inherent in the individualistic and difference-blind manner in which liberals have traditionally defined citizenship. To assess the impact of these challenges upon liberal conceptions of citizenship, it is important to draw a number of distinctions. Not only is it helpful to categorise groups in terms of the nature and origin of the particular group, the character of the specific rights demanded, and the manner in which these rights are to be exercised, it is also vital to clearly identify the type of multicultural politics implicit in the wide array of demands voiced by various minorities. Here a distinction has to be drawn between instances of thin multiculturalism, where the various protagonists continue to subscribe to a shared set of liberal values, and cases of thick multiculturalism, which are characterised by a fundamental conflict of values and hence frequently entail a genuine difficulty on the part of the various protagonists truly to understand and appreciate each others values, culture and perspectives. Whereas the demands by feminists for the recognition of women's distinctive experiences and perspectives constitute a prime example of thin multiculturalism, the attempts by numerous religious minorities to shield their children from the impact of a broadly liberal education highlight some of the difficulties inherent in thick multiculturalism. Although both thin and thick multiculturalism entail a recognition of the political significance of particularity and difference, the demands and challenges inherent in these two types of multicultural politics differ notably. Yet if liberalism is to accommodate the 'politics of difference' it must respond to the fears and aspirations inherent in both thin and thick multiculturalism.

The Feminist Challenge

Feminism and liberalism

Historically feminism and liberalism are closely related. As Richard Evans observes, the liberal Enlightenment tradition had equipped feminists with 'a whole battery of intellectual weapons' including 'ideas of reason, progress, natural law, the fulfilment of the individual, the beneficent power of education and the social utility of freedom from restrictions and equality of rights'.[3] For instance, the notion of universal reason, central to the thought of liberal Enlightenment philosophers such as Kant, provided early feminist thinkers with a powerful argument to challenge those social conventions which excluded and marginalised women. If, due to their capacity for rational thought, all human beings deserve equal rights and respect, then women, as beings capable of reason, are surely entitled to the same rights and privileges as men. Thus, in their attempt to secure equal rights for women, many early feminists like Catherine Maculay endorsed the liberal view of differences between individuals as merely contingent and ultimately inconsequential. In the final analysis men and women shared the same faculties and capacities. Consequently women's apparent failure to develop their rational faculties was not an indication of deep-seated biological differences between men and women, but simply reflected the social norms and pressures placed upon them.[4] To remedy this situation and to encourage women to develop their full potential, feminists such as Mary Wollstonecraft[5] demanded equal access to education for women. For many early feminists education was a vital stepping-stone in their campaign for the extension of the franchise to women. Education would enable women to realise their rational faculties and would provide them with a foundation for autonomous action. Once women had attained rationality and autonomy they could not reasonably be denied the vote. After all, if the notion of self-sovereignty is to be meaningful it must surely include the right to self-governance in the political arena. Clearly '[t]he liberal language of individual rights and freedoms had tremendous resonances for women.'[6]

However, while many first wave feminists actively advocated liberal ideals and endorsed the liberal vision of a common citizenship, contemporary feminists have tended to be far more critical of the liberal project, both at the level of the individual and at the level of democratic citizenship. At the heart of this change lies a re-evaluation of the role of difference. This re-evaluation was undoubtedly fuelled in part by the apparent failure of women's enfranchisement to produce the radical transformation of women's lives anticipated by many first wave feminists. Whereas first wave feminists confidently predicted that women would use the vote to transform their position in society, the attainment of equal legal and political rights did not bring about a radical improvement in the position of women. Consequently, many second wave feminists have questioned the values which underpin the liberal notion of individual rights in general and the liberal conception of citizenship in particular. Thus, whereas first wave feminists like Maculay were keen to endorse liberalism's emphasis on universality and formal equality, many second wave feminists have argued that these commitments blind liberals to the significance of difference. Here numerous contemporary feminists have focused on the extent to which the notion of formal equality, central to the liberal conception of democratic citizenship, requires the exclusion of particularity. This exclusion of particularity is achieved by a sharp distinction between the public and the private sphere. Whereas the public sphere is seen as characterised by the general interest and the impartial rule of reason, particularity, affectivity and desire are assigned to the private sphere. In this context feminists have drawn attention not only to the fact that historically women have been assigned to the private sphere, but that this genderisation of the public/private distinction formed for many centuries the basis for excluding women from citizenship. Thus women were identified with the sphere of the particular and the affective; with nurture, reproduction, love and care and, consequently, were seen as lacking in the qualities required for public life. For second wave feminists this public/private division did not lose its potency with the advent of women's suffrage. If particularity is assigned to the non-political private sphere, then once women enter the 'male' public sphere the way in which they differ from men is seen as deviating from the norm. As Susan Mendus[7] points out, equality becomes then defined in terms of the removal of women's disadvantage or disability, with disadvantage being determined by a model which is intrinsically male. While a number of feminists have pointed to the failure to take effective measures to remove the social and economic disadvantages suffered by women, others have questioned whether the removal of differences is an acceptable political aim. This question has led some feminists to examine the impact of the liberal preoccupation with impartiality and formal equality upon conceptions of self and citizen.

Impartiality and formal equality

At the level of the self feminist theorists such as Pateman[8] have drawn attention to the manner in which liberals have attempted to abstract the individual from all social, economic and biological contingencies. Subsequently, the individual becomes disembedded and disembodied, giving rise to a unitary vision of the self – a self that is the same for all humanity. Hence morality is equated with impartiality; with recognising the claims of the other who is just like oneself. Thus, we are invited to view one another as abstract, autonomous beings, unencumbered by the particularities of our existence. To act morally is to follow the norm of formal equality enshrined in a system of justice based on a network of formal rights and duties. However, for many feminists such an account of the individual ignores the extent to which our identity is irrevocably shaped by the particularities and contingencies of our existence. Here a number of feminists have highlighted the impact our physical being has on our identity. As Pateman notes, if the individual is to be a universal figure, liberalism must ignore that 'humankind has two bodies, female and male'.[9] This, however, glosses over the fact that

there is a womanly capacity that men do not posses, and thus it implicitly denies that birth, women's bodies and feminine passions inseparable from their bodies and bodily processes have any political relevance.[10]

For feminists such as Pateman the tendency to regard the atomised individual as the norm has led liberal theorists either to view women and children as a deviant case or to ignore or deny the interdependence between women and children.[11] To many feminists liberalism's failure to acknowledge women's experiences has given rise to a discourse in which what constitutes a proper person, a true individual, is representative of men's experience and reasoning rather than women's. Thus, the liberal individual becomes synonymous with the independent, propertied male head of a household.

Since this conception of the individual shapes liberal notions of citizenship, the exclusion of the perspective of all but one group has important political consequences, not only for women, but for marginalised groups in general. Given that different groups have different experiences, histories and perspectives on social life, no one group can entirely understand the experiences of another. Hence no one group can speak for another. For feminist critics such as Young[12] to adopt, in the face of such profound diversity, a conception of citizenship based upon formal equality and impartiality is merely to privilege the dominant group. If all are given equal rights, but no one can speak for the other, the interests of the dominant group will prevail, since the members of the dominant group will be able 'to assert their experiences of and perspectives on social events as impartial and objective.'[13] Thus not only does the denial of difference allow privileged groups to ignore their own group specificity, it also disadvantages groups whose experience, culture and socialised capacities differ from this allegedly neutral standard. On Young's analysis the ostensibly neutral standards of the liberal public sphere merely reflect the experiences of white, middle-class, western males. Consequently the liberal appeal to formal equality and impartiality prevents the members of groups such as women, whose experiences and perspectives differ significantly from those of the dominant group, from participating in the public sphere.

The diversity of women

A number of feminists have sought to challenge this marginalisation of women's perspective by highlighting the political significance of women's traditional experiences as mothers and carers. While liberalism's emphasis upon formal equality and impartiality relegates these experiences firmly to the private sphere, feminists such as Elshtain, Dinnerstein and Ruddick[14] argue that the virtues of love, empathy, compassion and emotional sensitivity associated with women's traditional role as mothers and carers have potentially important political implications and are indeed capable of laying the foundations for a better society.[16] However, while such attempts to stress the political significance of women's experiences provide a forceful critique of liberal universalism and the liberal public/private distinction, an increasing number of contemporary feminists have argued that approaches such as 'the politics of maternal thinking' continue to endorse a unitary vision of individual identity and thus ultimately fail to take difference seriously. For writers such as Spelman, Harris, hooks and Flax[17] the emphasis these feminist theories place on the experience and identity of 'women as such' implies an unsustainable essentialism, which ignores the impact of race, class and sexual orientation upon the lives of women. As Harris notes, to maintain that the 'biological and social implications of motherhood shape the selfhood of all or most women',[18] rests upon two key assumptions: the supposition of a deep unitary self that is relatively stable and unchanging, and the belief that although there are significant differences between men and women, this self is the same for all women and for all men regardless of class, race or sexual orientation. For Harris such feminist essentialism is as unsustainable as earlier liberal claims to universality. Thus, just as liberalism's failure to acknowledge the significance of gender differences encourages theorists to regard the experiences of male adults as normative for humanity at large, so the focus on 'women as women' has given rise to a discourse in which the experiences of Western, white, middle-class women have been conflated with the experiences of all women. Consequently, just as liberal universalism defines difference in terms of a deviation from a standard that is essentially male, so feminist essentialism views differences among women as a divergence from a standard that is defined by the experiences of Western, white, middle-class women. For critics, feminist essentialism treats the experiences of women who are subject to multiple forms of oppression as merely 'addition' problems: black women suffer from sexism plus racism, while working class women are oppressed by sexism plus class structures. According to Spelman and Harris, such an approach not only forcibly fragments the experiences of black, poor and lesbian women, but also gives rise to the notion that the oppression women face 'as women' is best identified by studying the position of women who are not subject to other forms of oppression. This privileges the experiences of Western, white, middle-class women. For example the notion, advanced by many second wave feminists, that the solution to women's oppression was to be found in work outside the home, ignored the experiences of millions of women who had always worked outside the home, but for whom work had been a far from 'liberating' experience. In a similar vein the characterisation of the dominant feminine stereotype as passive and dependant, failed to recognise the experiences of black women who have struggled against images of matriarchy and sexual permissiveness.[19] Spelman and Harris conclude that instead of holding on to unsustainable notions of a deep, unitary and stable women's self, feminists must recognise that women are enmeshed in many and often contradictory discourses of sexuality, race and class. Hence not only should gender be viewed as a relational concept, whose characteristics and attributes can only be identified by comparing the situation of women with that of men, the construction of gender attributes will vary according to race, class and nationality. The task of feminist theorising is not to attempt to construct essences but to explore these contingent relationships.

The view of the individual which underpins the feminist politics advocated by Spelman and Harris implies a radical rejection of the disembedded and disembodied self central to the liberal conception of citizenship. Instead identities are to be viewed as multiplicitous, contingent and context bound. Thus 'the social agent is constituted by an ensemble of subject positions that can never be totally fixed in a closed system of differences'.[20] Differences are always relational, not inherent. Consequently identity is always defined in a specific context vis-à-vis specific others. This vision of a radically embedded, subjective self implies the rejection of the liberal view of an objective, rational, universal standpoint, which is accessible to all individuals and can generate universally applicable principles. If individuals are radically embedded, any conception of citizenship which demands that difference and particularity be relegated to the private sphere is unsustainable.

The dangers of fragmentation

While this vision of deep and radical diversity has been highly influential, not all second wave feminists have endorsed such an outright rejection of liberal principles. Indeed a number of feminists have expressed profound disquiet about the political implications of a commitment to 'radical otherness'. The basic worry here is that in the absence of any appeal to universally shared standards, an emphasis upon radical diversity will give rise to a process of fragmentation which may not only threaten the viability of a wider feminist politics, but may ultimately undermine the very notion of democratic citizenship. As Young[21] notes, whereas theorists such as Spelman have tended to regard the categories of class, race and nationality as relatively fixed, the stability of these categories is just as doubtful as the appropriateness of the category of 'women'. One possible response to this complex interaction between race, class, nationality and gender is to further distinguish between sub-categories. Thus one could, for example, sub-divide working class women further according to race, religion, nationality, ethnicity, region and sexuality, or distinguish between the different attributes of an African-American gender in relation to African-American men on the one hand and white men on the other. However, given that 'any category can be considered an arbitrary unity', such a strategy ultimately gives rise to an infinite regress which dissolves all 'groups into individuals'.[22] In the eyes of critics such a process of fragmentation is liable to undermine the wider sympathies essential to a shared sense of citizenship. While co-operation for the common good and general solidarity are widely regarded as important elements of democratic citizenship, a commitment to 'radical otherness' is liable to give rise to a focus on sectional interests.[23] Indeed, in the absence of shared norms and standards, understanding and co-operation across group lines is likely to prove difficult, if not impossible. From the perspective of traditionally marginalised groups this failure to generate wider sympathies is potentially rather worrying. In the absence of a general sense of solidarity, the dominant groups within society may feel little obligation to take into account the perspective and needs of less powerful groups. Such marginalisation is likely to be further reinforced by the process of differentiation, which may lead to the fragmentation of wider political movements such as, for instance, feminism. These fears have led some feminists to reassert the potential significance of the liberal universalist project. After all, as Anne Phillips notes,[24] historically the standards of impartiality implied by the liberal notion of a common humanity have been employed by many oppressed groups, including women, in their struggle for equality. Thus liberal notions of universality and formal equality have enabled oppressed groups to show that the manner in which they differ from the dominant group – be it in terms of gender, race or religion – does not constitute a legitimate ground for excluding them from citizenship. For Susan Moller Okin and Martha Nussbaum[25] such an appeal to universal standards is today still likely to be the most effective tool for securing equality for women worldwide.[26] As Nussbaum notes, the victims of oppression and domination frequently not only lack the intellectual and economic resources to challenge these injustices, but have often internalised the very values which oppress them. According to Nussbaum and Okin, such deeply entrenched discrimination can only be challenged effectively by an appeal to universal standards, which can be employed to hold local government, aid organisations and international bodies, such as the UN, to account for their failure to improve the position of women.

New feminist conceptions of citizenship

This awareness of the potential strength of the traditional liberal emphasis upon universality and equality has been reflected in some of the most influential contemporary feminist conceptions of citizenship. For example in Iris Marion Young's model of 'differentiated citizenship' the commitment to difference and diversity is tempered by a recognition of the appeal of liberal values and preoccupations.[27] Although Young stresses that each social group has its own unique experiences, histories and perspectives on social life, which can never be entirely understood or adequately represented by outsiders, she nonetheless retains a commitment to universality and the equality of moral worth of all persons. While the principle of equal moral worth provides a powerful argument in favour of the inclusion of all members of society in social and political life, the liberal commitment to formal procedural rules and basic rights safeguards minorities against the whim of the majority by setting limits to democratic deliberation and outcomes. However, while Young acknowledges the strength of liberal values and preoccupations, she contends that the traditional liberal conception of citizenship must be redefined to ensure that the claims of difference and particularity are recognised. Thus, although Young appeals to the value of universality at the point of inclusion, she stresses that,

[u]niversality in the sense of the participation and inclusion of everyone in moral and social life does not imply universality in the sense of the adoption of a general point of view that leaves behind particular affiliations, feelings, commitments and desires.[28]

On the contrary, given the specificity of each group in terms of its experiences, history and perspective on social life, equality in terms of the participation and inclusion of all groups, requires a specific set of rights for each group and for some groups a more comprehensive system than for others. Thus in place of the liberal emphasis upon formal equality, Young proposes a differentiated citizenship. Since dominant groups within society will always attempt to shape the public sphere in the light of their experiences and perspective, traditionally marginalised groups, such as women, the poor, ethnic minorities and the old, should be granted additional rights to group-specific representation at the various levels of government, thereby increasing their opportunities for political participation. Hence oppressed groups should be provided with the resources to organise themselves, should be invited to analyse and formulate social policy proposals and should have the right to veto specific policies which affect groups directly.

As Young's conception of a differentiated citizenship indicates, contemporary feminist attempts to reconceptualise citizenship are characterised by the rejection of the abstract unitary conception of the self central to traditional liberal notions of citizenship, in favour of a fluid, contextual conception of identity. It is this recognition of our particular attachments, concerns and perspectives which has led many feminists to reject liberal attempts to relegate difference to the private sphere. Consequently, whereas many contemporary feminists acknowledge the potential appeal of traditional liberal values, they contend that the scope and nature of these values must be reconceptualised to account for the political claims of difference and particularity. This emphasis upon the significance of our particular characteristics, experiences and perspective has by no means been unique to feminist debates. On the contrary, in recent years many liberal democracies have been confronted by the ever more vocal demands of an increasing number of religious, ethnic and national minority groups for the recognition and support of their particular identity and culture. These demands have drawn attention to the significance of group membership and thus have served to highlight the potential difficulties inherent in the individualistic manner in which liberals have traditionally defined citizenship.

The Claims of Diversity

Liberalism and group membership

Historically, liberal conceptions of citizenship have primarily focused on the relationship between the individual and the state. Individuals are incorporated into the state universally rather than consociation-ally. Hence individuals are not linked to the state through membership of a particular cultural community, but stand as singular citizens in the same direct relationship to the state.[29] Since individuals constitute the ultimate source of all moral value, the principal purpose of the state is to protect and promote individual rights and interests. This preoccupation with the relationship between state and individual citizen is probably most apparent in the liberal contract tradition. For contract theorists the state is the product of a process of deliberation among undifferentiated individuals and no account is taken of the customs, traditions and institutions which may constitute a particular people prior to the social contract. Thus, according to Locke, the state is a voluntary association established via a contract among individuals. It is instituted with the express purpose of protecting the rights of individual citizens and these rights set clear limits to the legitimate powers of the state. Hence government can only claim to be legitimate if it has the consent of the governed.[30] As Locke notes:

Men being, as has been said, by Nature, all free, equal and independent, no one can be put out of his Estate, and subjected to the political power of another, without his own *Consent*. The only way whereby anyone divests himself of his Natural Liberty, and *puts on the bonds of Civil Society* is by agreeing with other Men to join and unite into a Community for their comfortable, safe and peaceable living amongst another, in a secure Enjoyment of their Properties, and a greater Security against any that are not of it.[31]

While this preoccupation with the individual may be most apparent among liberal contractarians, it is undoubtedly an outlook that has shaped the liberal tradition in general. John Stuart Mill,[32] for instance, is primarily concerned with safeguarding individual freedom from encroachment by both the state and wider society. The strength and durability of this individualism is reflected in the work of contemporary liberals. For example, in John Rawls's[33] theory of justice the parties in the original position who work out the fundamental principles of justice are individuals. Rawls expressly denies these individuals all knowledge of their membership of specific groups and associations.

This vision of the character and role of the state has clear repercussions for the liberal picture of the nature and political significance of group membership. Liberals are inclined to regard religious, ethnic or national groups as private associations and therefore maintain that such groups should not play a formal role in the political process. Indeed some liberals have viewed groups and associations within the state with a degree of suspicion. As noted earlier, liberals have tended to associate citizenship with the adoption of the general point of view and the promotion of the common good or 'general will'. Group membership, however, is viewed as an expression of sectional, particularistic interests. If the common good is to be promoted, individuals must transcend such particularistic allegiances. In *The Social Contract* Rousseau, for instance, maintains that to ensure law is a genuine expression of the General Will, it is important that 'each citizen make up his own mind'.[34] For Rousseau associations or 'partial societies' pose a potential threat to the exercise of democracy and are therefore either to be eradicated or their potential influence has to be 'neutralised'. This sentiment is echoed by James Madison,[35] who advocates a system of checks and balances which seeks to guarantee individual liberty by ensuring that no particular faction can dominate the state. In this context some liberals such as Mill and Green[36] stress the importance of commonality. If democracy is to promote the common good, it must reflect a shared sense of political allegiance, which in turn requires a sense of belonging to one people or one nation. According to this strand of liberal thought, national and ethnic minorities should be assimilated so as to promote the cohesiveness of the state.

In line with this emphasis upon the common good, liberals have stressed the need for equal legal and political rights. For liberals all individuals have equal moral worth and hence should be 'treated as equal by government, with equal concern and respect'.[37] Hence liberals typically contend that each individual should have equal rights and entitlements, regardless of their sex, religion, race or other personal criteria. Thus, for Rousseau, law should be general – it should 'spring from all and apply to all'.[38] From this perspective the differential treatment of particular groups and individuals constitutes a threat to the viability and legitimacy of the state. Consequently, demands for special recognition on the basis of group membership are to be resisted. Among contemporary liberals this emphasis upon generality has given rise to a vision of the state as neutral arbiter. For modern liberal thinkers such as John Rawls and Ronald Dworkin[39] the state exists to ensure that there is a fair set of procedures which guarantees that all citizens are treated equally. Given that individuals subscribe to a wide variety of different conceptions of the good life, the state should remain neutral vis-à-vis competing conceptions of the good. Rather than support particular conceptions of the good the state should concentrate upon upholding the rules which ensure that all individuals are free to pursue their lives without undue interference from others. By focusing upon the rules of right conduct – on what is and is not morally permissible – contemporary liberal thinkers have given priority to considerations of the right over questions of the good. From this perspective, membership of particular religious, ethnic and national groupings constitutes an element of a particular individual's conception of the good and as such is secondary to considerations of the right.

Group rights

Yet recently this liberal vision of the nature and role of the state has increasingly been questioned as an ever larger number of religious, ethnic and national minorities have demanded recognition not as individuals but as members of particular groups. Numerous national minorities have sought to protect their distinct identity and culture by gaining legal protection and support for their national language. For instance, the Catalans in Spain, the Quebecois[40] in Canada and, to some degree, the Welsh in Great Britain have attempted to enshrine in law the use of their national language in schools, employment, the media and public life in general. Such campaigns have frequently been associated with wider demands for greater regional autonomy and, in the case of Quebec, secession. Another distinctive set of demands stems from the aspirations of indigenous people in New Zealand, Australia, Canada and the United States to gain greater control over the resources and policies which affect their way of life. Here the focus has tended to be on landrights. For example, in New Zealand, Maori have invoked the Treaty of Waitangi[41] to establish claims to ancestral lands, while in Australia the 1992 High Court Judgement in the Mabo case recognised the principle of indigenous land rights.[42] Similar legal challenges have been mounted in Canada.[43] Yet a different set of concerns has been voiced by religious minorities, who have expressed fears about the impact of educational provisions upon their ability to raise their children in accordance with their own religious beliefs. Thus in Britain sections of the Muslim community have campaigned for state funding for Islamic schools,[44] while in France Muslim girls have demanded the right to wear traditional headscarfs or hijab in the classroom.[45] In a similar vein in the United States members of the old order Amish obtained an exemption for their children from mandatory high school attendance,[46] whereas 'born again' Christians in Tennessee have sought the right to withdraw their children from a school reading programme, the content of which they regard as inhospitable to their beliefs.[47]

The emphasis these groups place upon group membership appears to challenge the individualism and egalitarianism central to the conception of citizenship advanced by many liberals. While liberals typically emphasise our shared or universal interests as fellow citizens, demands for recognition seek to highlight the political significance of those interests individuals possess by virtue of their membership of certain kinds of groups. Here proponents of diversity and particularity have stressed the impact of ethnicity, religion, nationality and gender upon the formation of individual identity and have pointed to the intricate links that frequently exist between the identity and well-being of individual members of groups, and the identify and well-being of groups as a whole. Hence, whereas liberals characteristically contend that each individual should have equal rights and entitlements, the 'politics of difference' has given rise to demands for group-differentiated rights. The groups to be protected via group-differentiated rights are usually taken to be those of which membership plays an important role in the individual's self-identification,[48] whose members 'think of themselves as a collective possessing a separate identity'[49] based upon their shared characteristics, and membership of which can at best only be cast aside with difficulty and at considerable cost in terms of the individual's sense of self.[50] This desire for group-differentiated rights has led to campaigns for both *personal cultural rights* and *corporate cultural rights*.[51] Personal cultural rights refer to group rights that are exercised by group members individually. Thus, for instance, the right of francophones in Canada to use French in federal courts constitutes a personal cultural right. In contrast, cultural rights that are exercised by the group as a collective body are best termed corporate cultural rights. For example, exemptions covering Jewish ritual slaughter apply to the Jewish community as a whole, which authorises officers to handle ritual slaughter. In a similar vein, special hunting, fishing and land rights granted to indigenous people are usually exercised by the tribe or band. It tends to be the tribal or band council which determines when hunting and fishing can occur and how land is to be used or disposed of.

To gain a clearer understanding of the challenges that demands for personal and corporate cultural rights pose for liberal conceptions of citizenship, it is important to draw a number of distinctions.

Minorities currently campaigning for recognition can be categorised in terms of the nature and origins of particular groups and the character of the specific rights they demand. In terms of the former it is helpful to differentiate between national minorities and ethnic groups, while with regard to the latter Kymlicka[52] aptly distinguishes between rights to self-determination, polyethnic rights and special representation rights.

Multination and polyethnic states

Many liberal democracies, including the UK, Spain, Canada and the United States, contain more than one nation and are therefore best described not as one nation states, but as multination states. In some instances multination states are the product of a voluntary agreement among two or more nations to form a federation for mutual benefit, whereas in other cases they arise due to involuntary processes, such as conquest, invasion, the settlement of homelands by colonisers or the secession of territory from one imperial power to another.[53] National minorities tend to occupy a particular territory, which usually has been their homeland for many centuries. As Kymlicka notes, at the point of incorporation each national minority constituted an ongoing society with 'a full range of social, educational, economic and political institutions, encompassing both public and private life'.[54] National minorities have tended to fight to retain the integrity of their distinctive culture and society. First nations, including native North Americans, the Maori in New Zealand and the Aboriginals in Australia, as well as groups such as the Quebecois in Canada, the Scots and Welsh in the UK and the Basques and Catalans in Spain all constitute national minorities. However, national minorities are not the only source of cultural diversity within liberal democracies. In recent years many liberal democracies have experienced a notable influx of immigrants and refugees, who have brought with them their own distinct culture and heritage, giving rise to a range of distinct ethnic groups. Whereas multinational states are the product of incorporating complete societies, *polyethnic states* arise as a consequence of the decisions of individuals and families to leave their own national community and enter another society. Consequently, in contrast to national minorities, ethnic minorities tend not to be territorially based, although they may establish recognisable communities and neighbourhoods.

Self-government rights

These differences in the character and origin of minority groups are also reflected in the types of rights various groups have demanded. Self-government rights are usually associated with the desire on the part of a national minority for a degree of political autonomy or in some instances secession. For example, whereas the Catalans in Spain and the Scots in the UK have secured a degree of regional autonomy, the Quebecois in Canada are campaigning for outright secession. Such groups regard self-government as vital to the maintenance of their distinct culture and the protection of the interests of their members. The right to self-government is by definition exercised by the collective as a whole and thus constitutes a clear case of a corporate cultural right. Not only is the right to national self-determination recognised in international law, it can arguably be seen as an extension of liberal principles. For example, according to James Tully[55], the demand for self-determination should be seen as an extension of the principles of anti-imperialism and constitutionalism. These principles can be viewed as an expression of the liberal belief in the value of individual autonomy or self-expression. Indeed recently a number of liberal writers have argued that national self-determination should be regarded as an instance of the liberal principle of individual autonomy. As Joseph Raz notes, if people's membership of cultural groups is accepted as an important aspect of the identity of the individual and if the individual's well-being depends upon giving full expression to this identity, it may be vital for individuals also to express their group membership in the political sphere. Consequently a number of contemporary liberal thinkers – including Will Kymlicka and Joseph Raz – have expressed sympathy with the demands of national minorities for self-determination. In this context Kymlicka explicitly distinguishes between the rights of national minorities and the recent demands by some ethnic minorities for self-determination in terms of the recognition of their mother tongue and state support for separate ethnic institutions.[56] For Kymlicka the claims of immigrant groups to self-determination are considerably weaker than those of national minorities, because not only have immigrants voluntarily chosen to leave their own national community, but, unlike long-standing and indigenous groups, they lack viable cultural structures which they can claim a right to preserve. Hence, in order to succeed, immigrants ought to be encouraged to integrate into the wider society. However, as Parekh notes,[57] these objections are open to question. Immigration occurs for a wide variety of reasons and the decision to leave one's country does not necessarily 'signify a decision to leave one's culture'.[58] Furthermore, while immigrant cultural life may lack 'the cohesion and continuity characteristic of indigenous and long-established groups' it is not 'devoid of a cohesive cultural structure'.[59] On the contrary, immigrant groups often form their own distinct communities and neighbourhoods and, even where these are absent, 'they tend to form nationwide and communal institutions to sustain their way of life'.[60] Parekh's objections suggest that in principle the demands for self-determination on the part of ethnic minorities may at least in some instances be on par with those of national minorities and hence should be given serious consideration.

However, although the concept of self-determination is widely respected among liberal theorists, the specific demands voiced by minorities have frequently been problematic for liberal democracies, since these demands often are incompatible with the liberal commitment to formal equality. As Halstead observes:

The danger to a minority culture might arise not from a failure on the part of the state to treat the members of the minority group on equal terms with all other citizens, but precisely as a result of such equal treatment. If all the citizens of a state are equally free to work and settle in any part of the state, then over time a territory associated with a particular cultural minority may be settled by other citizens and the territory's distinct cultural identity may not survive.[61]

Just as the distinct cultural identity of territorially based national minorities may not survive unless special restrictions are placed upon immigration into their territory, so the identity of immigrant communities may be threatened if the state is not prepared to grant additional support and protection. In this context the objections voiced by many minority groups mirror the fears expressed by feminists with regard to the liberal conception of formal equality. Just as many feminists argue that an emphasis upon formal equality gives rise to a discourse which privileges male perspectives and experiences, so many minority groups maintain that the principle of formal equality favours dominant groups. Consequently, many minorities have sought measures which place restrictions on the rights and freedoms of the majority. Thus, for instance, the Quebecois have sought to limit the use of English in public places, whereas some indigenous peoples have attempted to secure special rights to control settlements in their homelands.

Polyethnic rights

The second set of rights currently claimed by minorities is, following Kymlicka, best described as polyethnic rights. While self-determination rights are based upon the assertion that there is more than one political community, minorities demanding polytechnic rights recognise the integrity of the existing political community but demand that the cultural diversity of society be recognised in its public and political institutions. Such demands are most closely associated with religious and ethnic minorities. Just as many feminists have challenged the alleged neutrality of the norms and standards governing public life, numerous ethnic minorities regard existing cultural norms and practices as merely a reflection of the cultural heritage of the dominant group or groups and as such an obstacle to genuine equality. In the eyes of many minorities such a bias encourages 'an overt or hidden sense of cultural superiority on the part of [dominant] social groups leading to various forms of prejudice, racism, discrimination, social avoidance and inferior treatment.'[62] In response to these difficulties many minorities have sought measures such as anti-racist legislation to protect them from discrimination and prejudice and have demanded that the public institutions of the dominant culture be reformed so as to provide some recognition and accommodation of their cultures. Such reforms may imply public funding for cultural practices, such as ethnic associations, magazines and festivals or, more controversially, the granting of exemptions from laws and regulations which, in the eyes of the minority, disadvantage them.[63] The latter has been particularly prevalent with regard to religious practices. As this list of demands suggests, polyethnic rights can imply both personal and corporate cultural rights. For instance, while exemptions to dress codes imply rights that are typically exercised by group members individually, exemptions which allow for the ritual slaughter of animals in accordance with religious practices are usually exercised by the collective as a whole. Although demands for polyethnic rights can be seen as attempts by minorities to obtain genuine equality, and therefore have been viewed sympathetically by some contemporary liberals (see Chapter 5), calls for polytechnic rights have nonetheless frequently proven to be controversial, since the specific aspirations of minority groups often are in conflict with core liberal values and norms. For example, in France the campaign by Muslim girls to be permitted to wear traditional headscarfs in schools, has tended to be perceived as a threat to the firm separation between state and church, which by many is regarded as a cornerstone of French liberal democracy.[64] According to many liberal defenders of the French civic tradition, an 'ostentatious' display of religious allegiance is incompatible with an expressly secular, culturally and religiously neutral education, which seeks to socialise children into the civil values and norms of French citizenship.

Special representation rights

The third set of minority demands identified by Kymlicka focuses upon special representation rights. In the overwhelming majority of liberal democracies the legislative processes tend to be dominated by white, middle-class males, while historically disadvantaged groups such as women, ethnic and racial minorities, the poor and the disabled are usually under-represented. Just as feminists like Anne Phillips[65] have sought to remedy such under-representation via a 'politics of presence' which guarantees women greater representation through measures such as quotas, some minority groups have campaigned for the extension and/or maintenance of special representation rights. For example, in New Zealand, Maori have fought to retain and extend the number of parliamentary seats set aside for Maori, so as to ensure that the representation of Maori in parliament reflects the proportion of Maori in the overall population.[66] As Kymlicka notes, such measures are frequently regarded as temporary steps to overcome specific historical disadvantages and as such are best viewed as an aspect of a wider agenda for affirmative action. However, some writers have advanced a more principled defence of group rights, arguing that such rights should be seen as an important aspect of the wider right to self-government. While the question of affirmative action has given rise to a lively debate among liberals,[67] demands for temporary measures are potentially less controversial than proposals for permanent group-specific representation, such as Iris Marion Young's[68] model of 'differentiated citizenship', which grants traditionally disadvantaged groups the right to veto specific proposals which directly affect the group. The difficulties here spring in part from the corporate nature of such demands. In the eyes of many liberals such proposals for group-specific representation undermine the commitment to the common good central to democratic citizenship. For many liberals group-specific voting rights merely encourage the promotion of group-specific interests, and as such may undermine the sense of social cohesion and allegiance so valued by liberals such as J. S. Mill and T. H. Green.

Campaigns for self-government, polytechnic and representational rights have in many liberal democracies given rise to intricate and multilayered sets of demands and aspirations, which are subject to

numerous tensions and conflicts. The complexities potentially inherent in such demands for recognition are aptly illustrated by the
debates which accompanied attempts to 'affirm a unifying Canadian
constitutional identity in the Canadian Charter of Rights and Freedoms'.[69] As James Tully observes, not only did the Quebecois demand
recognition of their distinctive language and culture, the English
speaking minority within Quebec sought to assert their rights vis-à-vis
the Quebec provincial government. In a similar vein, demands for the
constitutional recognition of indigenous cultures were complicated by
differences between indigenous 'people who lived on reserves as
opposed to those who lived off reserves'.[70] Finally, while women
argued that the Charter needed to be amended to secure substantive
equality for women, the women in English speaking Canada voiced
their demands in a slightly different manner than that adopted by the
women in Quebec, whereas indigenous women who objected to 'the
way in which Aboriginal men articulated the identity of Aboriginal
cultures'[71] disagreed among themselves as to whether to demand
representation through group-specific levels of government or to seek
protection by having the Charter applied directly to such indigenous
governments. As this example highlights, the groups currently
campaigning for specific group rights should not be thought of as
internally undifferentiated, enclosed or self-contained entities. On the
contrary, as the earlier discussion of contemporary feminist thought
indicated, group identities overlap, are interactive and internally
differentiated. Not only do group identities overlap geographically,
with minority groups spanning across national boundaries or con-
taining within them further recognisable subgroups, individuals find
themselves members of a variety of different groups which place at
times incompatible demands upon them. Furthermore, groups inevitably interact and group differences are frequently defined
relationally in an attempt to clearly distinguish an 'us' and 'them'.
Finally, as the various strands of feminist thought so ably illustrate,
groups tend to be subject to internal disagreements and tensions.
Group identities are internally negotiated and as such are fluid and
subject to change. As the Canadian experience illustrates, these
complexities of group identities are reflected in the demands for
recognition within many liberal democracies.

Thick and thin multiculturalism

Despite these complexities, it is possible to identify common themes
which unite these campaigns. Just like feminist critics, minorities
campaigning for cultural recognition maintain that the existing laws

and institutions of contemporary liberal democracies fail to give
sufficient recognition to diversity and hence are unjust. Consequently
the demand for cultural recognition rests upon 'the assumption that
culture is an irreducible and constitutive aspect of politics'.[72] Indeed
demands for self-government, polyethnic and representational rights
are frequently referred to as aspects of a wider movement for a
multicultural politics. While the concept of multiculturalism is widely
used both in political and academic discourses, multiculturalism has
been taken to stand for a wide variety of different ideas and policies.
Thus the term has been used to assert 'the rights of immigrants to
express their own culture without fear of prejudice and discrimination',[73] to describe processes which allow for powersharing between
different national communities or as a label for policies which aim to
promote the position of traditionally marginalised groups such as
women or racial minorities. In the broadest sense multiculturalism can
be defined as a commitment to the equal standing and treatment of all
stable and viable cultural or social groups within a particular political
society.[74] Here 'equality of standing and treatment' refers to equality in
substantive terms rather than a mere formal equality of universal
political and legal rights. However to gain a clearer picture of
multiculturalism it is important to distinguish between 'thin' and
'thick' versions of multicultural politics.[75]

Thin multiculturalism refers to instances of diversity where the
various protagonists continue to subscribe to a shared set of liberal
values. While the advocates of thin multiculturalism stress the
political significance of group membership and as such reject the
notion that difference and particularity should be relegated to the
private sphere, they nonetheless endorse the liberal vision of
individual rights and freedoms, including core liberal values such as
individual autonomy and the equality of moral worth of all persons.
Advocates of thin multiculturalism tend to see group membership as a
key aspect of individual identity and, consequently, regard the
recognition of cultural and social differences as vital if all individuals
are to be guaranteed a secure environment in which they can flourish.
Thus, for example, the debate between French and English speaking
Canadians or the demands by feminists for the recognition of women's
distinctive experiences and perspective are best seen as instances of
thin multiculturalism.

These debates need to be carefully distinguished from the demands
of minorities whose values and aspirations are in conflict with the
wider liberal framework. For instance, while some religious minorities, such as 'born again' Christians in America or some members of
the Muslim community in the UK, have attempted to ensure that in
the course of their schooling their children are not exposed to views

and values which challenge their religious commitments, many liberals view such demands as a threat to the aims of a liberal education, which seeks to encourage critical rationality and independence in an attempt to foster the development of an autonomous life-style. While most liberals regard personal autonomy as an integral aspect of human dignity and as such take it to be of paramount importance, some religious minorities fear that an autonomy-valuing education will undermine their children's faith commitments. After all, whereas autonomy requires critical rationality, faith implies a readiness to suspend disbelief.[76] Debates which are characterised by such a fundamental conflict of values are best described as 'thick multiculturalism'. As this example illustrates, thick multiculturalism is frequently distinguished by a genuine difficulty on the part of the various protagonists truly to understand and appreciate each others values, culture and perspective. Hence, whereas thin multiculturalism entails a shared commitment to core liberal values such as autonomy and individual freedom, the protagonists in instances of thick multiculturalism lack such common ground. Not surprisingly it is the demands associated with thick multiculturalism which have proved particularly problematic for liberals.

The Challenge of Diversity

Clearly the 'politics of difference' poses a complex and diverse set of challenges for contemporary liberals. If liberals are to meet the aspirations of the modern advocates of cultural pluralism and diversity, they must seek to accommodate instances of both thin and thick multiculturalism. Yet, while both types of multiculturalism entail a recognition of the political significance of particularity and differences, the demands and challenges inherent in these two strands differ notable. Whereas thin multiculturalism demands that liberals redefine the scope and nature of individual rights and freedoms in the light of the claims of difference and diversity, thick multiculturalism challenges the validity of the very values liberals and thin multiculturalists share. Liberals have responded to these challenges in a variety of ways, ranging from restatements of the traditional liberal emphasis upon impartiality to attempts to develop a distinctly liberal theory of group rights. Parts II, III and IV will assess these various strategies with the aim of identifying the potentially most promising avenue for liberals who wish to engage with the 'politics of difference'.

Notes and References

1. E. V. Spelman, *Inessential Woman* (Boston: Beacon Press, 1988); A. Harris, 'Race and Essentialism in Feminist Legal Theory', *Stanford Law Review*, 1990, Vol. 42, pp. 581–616; bell hooks, *Ain't I A Woman* (London: Pluto Press, 1981); J. Flax, 'Race, Gender and the Ethics of Difference', *Political Theory*, Vol. 23, No. 3, August 1995, pp. 500–10.
2. I. M. Young, *Justice and the Politics of Difference* (Princeton: Princeton University Press, 1990).
3. R. Evans, *The Feminists* (London: Croom Helm, 1977) p. 17.
4. For Maculay: 'those vices and imperfections which have generally been regarded as inseparable from the female character, do not in any manner proceed from sexual causes, but are entirely the effects of situation and education.' C. Maculay, cited in M. Ferguson, *First Feminists British Women Writers 1578–1799* (Bloomington: Indiana U. P., 1985) p. 402.
5. M. Wollstonecraft, *A Vindication of the Rights of Woman* (London: Everyman, 1995).
6. A. Phillips, *Democracy and Difference* (Cambridge: Polity Press, 1993) p. 43.
7. S. Mendus, 'Loosing the Faith' in J. Dunn (ed.), *Democracy the Unfinished Journey* (Oxford: Oxford University Press, 1992) pp. 207–19.
8. C. Pateman, 'The Theoretical Subversiveness of Feminism', in C. Pateman and E. Gross (eds), *Feminist Challenges* (Sydney: Allen & Unwin, 1988) pp. 1–10.
9. Ibid. p. 8.
10. Ibid. p. 7.
11. E. Frazer, 'Feminism and liberalism', in J. Meadowcroft (ed.), *The Liberal Political Tradition* (Cheltenham: Edward Elgar, 1996) pp. 115–37.
12. I. M. Young, *Justice and the Politics of Difference*.
13. I. M. Young, 'Polity and Group Difference: A Critique of the Ideal of Universal Citizenship', *Ethics*, Vol. 99, January 1989, pp. 251–74, p. 259.
14. J. B. Elshtain, *Public Man, Private Woman* (Princeton, New Jersey: Princeton University Press, 1981); D. Dinnerstein, *The Mermaid and the Minotaur: Sexual Arrangements and Human Malaise* (New York: Haper Colophon, 1976); S. Ruddick, *Maternal Thinking: Towards a Politics of Peace* (London: Women's Press, 1989).
15. Many of these early attempts to formulate a 'politics of maternal thinking' were influenced by Carol Gilligan's work on moral development (C. Gilligan, *In A Different Voice*, Cambridge, MA: Harvard University Press, 1982). For Gilligan not only the self but also the other person towards whom one is acting has to be viewed as radically situated and particularised. Thus, the generalised other of liberal theory is replaced by the notion of the concrete other. Whereas liberalism invites us to view the individual abstractly in terms of a rational being entitled to the same rights and duties, the standpoint of the concrete other asks us to consider the specific needs, interests and welfare of the other person. In this way the liberal preoccupation with formal equality is replaced by consider-

ations of equity and complementary reciprocity. From such a perspective, moral reasoning cannot be reduced to the level of formal rationality alone. To recognise the other's concrete being and specific needs requires care, love, empathy, compassion and emotional sensitivity. This is not to suggest that the standpoint of the concrete other implies a rejection of rationality. After all, such a standpoint is not without principle. However, while liberalism's preoccupation with abstract reason leads to an emphasis on universally applicable rules, the emphasis on contextuality required by the standpoint of the concrete other gives rise to the notion of 'appropriate response'. Here what is considered to be 'appropriate' is established by reference to notions of care and responsibility. From the standpoint of the concrete other individuals are therefore unquestionably particular. In place of the independent, autonomous individual of liberalism, we are offered a picture of the self as encumbered by the specific relationships one has formed with concrete persons. For discussions of Gilligan's work see: L. Blum, 'Gilligan and Kohlberg: Implications for Moral Theory', *Ethics*, Vol. 98, April 1988, pp. 472–91; S. Benhabib, 'The Generalized and the Concrete Other: The Kohlberg-Gilligan Controversy and Feminist Theory', in S. Benhabib and D. Cornell (eds), *Feminism as Critique* (Cambridge: Polity Press, 1987) pp. 77–95.

16. Sara Ruddick, for example, argues that the traditionally female role of nurturing gives rise to a way of thinking which prioritises the preservation and growth of vulnerable life and which emphasises humility, resilient good humour and attentiveness to others. According to Ruddick, such a way of thinking will, in the context of public life, lead to an anti-militaristic stance and promote a politics of peace. In a similar vein Dorothy Dinnerstein asserts that, if public life was informed by a nurturing and conserving attitude towards life and nature, we would be able to counteract the male fascination with technology and domination. Here Elshtain places particular emphasis on women's experience as mothers. Elshtain argues that maternal thinking, based upon responsibility, attentiveness to others, empathy and love, could transform public values, creating an ethical polity informed by a politics of compassion and citizen involvement. For Elshtain this implies that we must protect the private realm from public encroachment.

17. E. V. Spelman, *Inessential Woman*; A. Harris, 'Race and Essentialism in Feminist Legal Theory'; bell hooks, *Ain't I A Woman*; J. Flax, 'Race, Gender and the Ethics of Difference'.

18. Harris, p. 603.

19. The qualitative differences between black and white women are vividly illustrated by Angela Harris' analysis of the different manner in which black and white women in the US experience rape. Not only have black women been historically uniquely vulnerable to rape, since during slavery the rape of black women was not regarded as a legal offense, black women have also been keenly aware that rape has played a significant role in the oppression of black men. Black men have tended to be treated more harshly than their white counterparts, especially in cases where the

victim is white. Hence 'the experience of rape for black women includes a unique ambivalence. Black women have simultaneously acknowledged their own victimization and the victimization of black men by a system that has consistently ignored violence against women while perpetrating it against men' (Harris, 'Race and Essentialism in Feminist Legal Theory', p. 601).

20. C. Mouffe, 'Citizenship and Political Identity', *October*, Vol. 61, 1992, pp. 28–32, p. 28.

21. I.M. Young, 'Gender as seriality: thinking about women as a social collective', in L. Nicholson and S. Seidman, *Social Postmodernism: Beyond identity politics* (Cambridge: University Press, 1995) pp. 187–215. As Young notes, it is, for example, simply misleading to assume that a working class woman's gendered experiences can only be properly identified by comparing her situation to that of working class men. After all, gendered experiences, such as sexual harassment, cut across class lines.

22. Ibid. p. 195.

23. See, S. Mendus, 'Time and Chance: Kantian Ethics and Feminist Philosophy', *Morrell Discussion Paper* (York: Department of Politics, University of York, 1990).

24. A. Phillips, *Democracy and Difference* (Cambridge: Polity Press, 1993).

25. S. Moller Okin, 'Inequalities between the Sexes in Different Cultural Contexts', in M. C. Nussbaum and J. Glover (ed.), *Women, Culture and Development* (Oxford: Clarendon Press 1995) pp. 275–97; M. C. Nussbaum, 'Human Capabilities, Female Human Beings', in M. C. Nussbaum and J. Glover (ed.), *Women, Culture and Development*, pp. 61–104.

26. For Nussbaum the commitment to the 'radical otherness' of different cultures has led some theorists to defend or at least condone many traditional cultural practices which systematically discriminate against women. Here Nussbaum cites two vivid examples of the approaches she objects to: the first one refers to an American economist who cites the extension of the idea that menstruating women pollute the kitchen to the workplace as an instance of the integration of the values that prevail in the workplace with those that shape home life; an integration which he regards as lacking in Western countries. The second one refers to a French Anthropologist who 'expresses regret that the introduction of small pox vaccination in India by the British eradicated the cult of Sittala Devi, the goddess to whom one used to pray in order to prevent small pox.' (M. C. Nussbaum, 'Human Capabilities, Female Human Beings', p. 65.)

27. I. M. Young, *Justice and the Politics of Difference*. For other influential feminist attempts to reconceptualise citizenship see C. Mouffe, *The Return of the Political* (London: Verso, 1993) and S. Benhabib, *Situating the Self* (Cambridge: Polity Press, 1992).

28. I. M. Young, *Justice and the Politics of Difference*, p. 105.

29. For the distinction between universal and consociational incorporation

see W. Kymlicka, *Liberalism, Community and Culture* (Oxford: Clarendon Press, 1989).

30. For a good discussion of the liberal preoccupation with the relationship between individual and state see V. Van Dyke, 'The Individual, the State, and Ethnic Communities in Political Theory', in W. Kymlicka (ed.), *The Rights of Minority Cultures* (Oxford: University Press, 1995) pp. 31–56.

31. J. Locke, *Two Treatises of Government*, edited by P. Laslett (Cambridge: University Press, 1993) pp. 330–1.

32. J. S. Mill, *On Liberty* (London: Penguin Books, 1985).

33. J. Rawls, *A Theory of Justice* (Oxford: Oxford University Press, 1986).

34. J. J. Rousseau, 'The Social Contract' in D. Wootton, *Modern Political Thought: Readings from Machiavelli to Nietzsche* (Cambridge: Hackett, 1996) p. 477.

35. J. Madison, *The Federalist No. 10*, in A. Hamliton, J. Jay and J. Madison, *The Federalist*, edited by Max Beloff (Oxford: Basil Blackwell, 1948).

36. See W. Kymlicka, *Multicultural Citizenship* (Oxford: Clarendon Press, 1995) pp. 52ff.

37. W. Kymlicka, *Liberalism, Community and Culture*, p. 140.

38. J. J. Rousseau, *The Social Contract* (London: Penguin Books, 1968) p. 75.

39. J. Rawls, *A Theory of Justice*; R. Dworkin, 'Liberalism', in M. Sandel, *Liberalism and its Critics* (Oxford: Blackwell, 1984) pp. 60–79.

40. For a discussion of Quebecois language laws see C. Taylor, *Multiculturalism and 'The Politics of Recognition'* (Princeton: Princeton University Press, 1992).

41. For a collection of papers exploring the demands of Maori see M. Wilson and A. Yeatman (eds), *Justice & Identity* (Wellington: Bridget Williams Books, 1995).

42. In 'Justice, Biculturalism and the Politics of Law' (in M. Wilson and A. Yeatman (eds), *Justice & Identity*, pp. 33–44). E. T. Durie summarises the case as follows: Eddie Mabo, an Australian Torres Strait Islander, 'sought recognition of a legal right to certain property inherited from his ancestors. In 1992, seven judges of the High Court of Australia declared in his favour', thereby granting legal recognition to Mabo's ancestoral entitlement.

43. See the Delgamukw Case in British Columbia, Canada. For a discussion of this case see E. T. Durie, 'Justice, Biculturalism and the Politics of Law'.

44. For a full discussion of these demands see Chapter 3.

45. See N. M. Moruzzi, 'A Problem With Headscrafs', *Political Theory*, Vol. 22, No. 4, November 1994, pp. 653–72 and A. E. Galeotti, 'A Problem With Theory: A Rejoinder to Moruzzi', *Political Theory*, Vol. 22, No. 4, November 1994, pp. 673–7.

46. For a discussion of this case see W. A. Galstone, 'Two Concepts of Liberalism', *Ethics*, Vol. 105, April 1995, pp. 516–34.

47. For a discussion of the case see N. M. Stolzenberg, '"He Drew a Circle That Shut Me Out": Assimilation, Indoctrination, and the Paradox of a Liberal Education', *Harvard Law Review*, Vol. 106, No. 3, January 1993, pp. 582–

667; S. Macedo, 'Liberal Civil Education and Religious Fundamentalism: The Case of God v. John Rawls, *Ethics*, 105, April 1995, pp. 468–96.

48. A. Margalit and J. Raz, 'National Self-Determination', in W. Kymlicka (ed.), *The Rights of Minority Cultures*, pp. 79–92.

49. V. Van Dyke, 'The Individual, the State and Ethnic Communities in Political Theory', in W. Kymlicka (ed.), *The Rights of Minority Cultures*.

50. D. Bell, *Communitarianism and its Critics* (Oxford: Clarendon, 1993).

51. For this distinction see G. B. Levey, 'Equality, Autonomy, and Cultural Rights', *Political Theory*, Vol. 25, No. 2, April 1997, pp. 215–48.

52. W. Kymlicka, *Multicultural Citizenship* (Oxford: Clarendon Press, 1995).

53. This description draws upon Will Kymlicka's account of national minorities in *Multicultural Citizenship*, p. 11.

54. Ibid. p. 78.

55. J. Tully, *Strange Multiplicity* (Cambridge: Cambridge University Press, 1997).

56. W. Kymlicka, *Multicultural Citizenship*.

57. B. Parekh, 'Cultural Pluralism and the Limits of Diversity', *Morrell Conference on Toleration, Identity and Difference*, 18–20 Sept. 1995, University of York, York, UK.

58. Ibid. p. 2.

59. Ibid. p. 3.

60. Ibid. p. 3.

61. M. Halstead, 'Voluntary Apartheid? Problems of Schooling for Religious and Other Minorities in Democratic Societies', *Journal of Philosophy of Education*, Vol. 29, No. 2, 1995, pp. 252–72.

62. Ibid. p. 261.

63. W. Kymlicka, *Multicultural Citizenship*.

64. For a discussion of this case see N. M. Moruzzi, 'A Problem With Headscrafs', and A. E. Galeotti, 'A Problem With Theory: A Rejoinder to Moruzzi'.

65. Anne Phillips, *The Politics of Presence* (Oxford: Clarendon Press, 1995).

66. Margaret Wilson, 'Constitutional Recognition and the Treaty of Waitangi: Myth or Reality', in M. Wilson and A. Yeatman (ed.), *Justice & Identity*, pp. 1–17.

67. While some liberals, such as Ronald Dworkin, have defended affirmative action measures as a means to ensuring genuine equality, affirmative action programmes have remained problematic since granting special rights to minorities frequently involves restricting the rights of other members of society (see R. Dworkin, *Taking Rights Seriously*, London: Duckworth, 1978; and M. Cohen et al. (ed.), *Equality and Preferential Treatment*, Princeton: Princeton University Press, 1977). The difficulties here are well illustrated by the controversy surrounding the use of women only shortlists by the British Labour Party. On 8 January 1996 an industrial tribunal in Leeds ruled that Labour's policy of women only shortlists amounted to sex discrimination and therefore was contrary to the Sex Discrimination Act. The case had been brought, with the support of the Equal Opportunities Commission, by two potential male candidates

who had been rejected by Labour constituency parties which had adopted women only shortlists.

68. I. M. Young, *Justice and the Politics of Difference*.
69. J. Tully, *Strange Multiplicity*, p. 12.
70. Ibid.
71. Ibid.
72. Ibid. p. 5.
73. W. Kymlicka, *Multicultural Citizenship*, p. 198.
74. This definition draws upon and extends the definition of multicultural-ism offered by J. Raz, who argues that 'multiculturalism requires a political society to recognise the equal standing of all the stable and viable cultural communities in that society' (J. Raz, 'Multiculturalism: A Liberal Perspective', in *Ethics in the Public Domain* (Oxford: Clarendon Press, 1996) p. 174).
75. For this distinction see Y. Tamir, 'Two Concepts of Mutliculturalism', *Journal of Philosophy of Education*, Vol. 29, No. 2, 1995, pp. 161–72.
76. For a full discussion of these tensions see Chapter 3.

Part II: The Quest for Impartiality

The Quest for Impartiality

In response to the demands voiced by the advocates of a 'politics of difference' a number of liberals have sought to re-emphasise the traditional liberal commitment to neutrality and impartiality. The works of John Rawls and Jürgen Habermas constitute probably the two most prominent examples of this approach. Both Rawls and Habermas maintain that if the state is to be perceived as legitimate, it must secure the free and willing assent of those it governs. In a culturally and ethically diverse society such assent can only be assured if the state can be shown to respect the different moral, religious and philosophical beliefs of its citizens. In their quest for such an impartial point of view Rawls and Habermas are inspired by Kant's deontological approach, which gives priority to questions of moral rightness over considerations of the good life for the individual. Therefore, while the liberal state should seek to protect individual rights and uphold general principles of justice, it is not the function of the state to promote a particular conception of the good life. On the contrary, individual citizens should be free to decide which lifestyle they wish to pursue. For Rawls and Habermas this distinction between moral and ethical questions ensures that the liberal state remains neutral vis-à-vis competing conceptions of the good, and therefore guarantees that the state can potentially win the assent of most, if not all, citizens in modern liberal democratic societies. Thus both writers seek to bridge difference and particularity by generating a new consensus based upon liberal principles. According to this school of liberal thought, such a consensus is vital if social cohesion is to be maintained in the face of the disagreements and tensions which characterise culturally and ethically diverse societies. However, despite their common goals and shared background Rawls and Habermas develop two very distinct approaches to the question of impartiality. While Chapter 3 focuses upon Rawls's conception of political liberalism, which seeks to establish an impartial point of view by removing all controversial questions from the political sphere, Chapter 4 explores Habermas's context responsive conception of impartiality.

Chapter 3: John Rawls:
Privatising Diversity

The question of justice has been central to most of Rawls's work. However, in his most recent writings Rawls has stressed that in developing his vision of political liberalism he does not aim to provide a conception of justice for all conceivable societies, but merely seeks to establish which forms of social institutions can secure justice within the context of a modern democratic society. According to Rawls, modern democratic societies are not only characterised by a fundamental commitment to liberty and equality but also display a marked diversity of opposing and irreconcilable, yet perfectly reasonable, religious, philosophical and moral doctrines. Rawls argues that within the context of modern democracies such reasonable pluralism is both inevitable and desirable, since such diversity follows directly from the exercise of human reason under conditions of liberty. Thus reasonable pluralism should be seen as the product of the profound commitment of modern democratic societies to the principle of liberty. Consequently, the central question that preoccupies Rawls is how we can, in the face of such reasonable pluralism, build a just and stable society of free and equal citizens. Rawls attempts to answer this question through his two most important works: *A Theory of Justice* and *Political Liberalism*.[1]

The first step of his argument is outlined in *A Theory of Justice*, in which Rawls seeks to establish 'the most appropriate conception of justice for specifying the fair terms of social co-operation between citizens regarded as free and equal'.[2] For Rawls a society can only be just if the terms of co-operation embodied in the basic rules governing society have the free and willing support of at least the substantial majority of its politically active citizens. In *Political Liberalism* Rawls attempts to show that, provided the scope of the principles of 'justice as fairness' is properly defined, his conception of justice is capable of gaining the support of citizens who subscribe to a wide variety of conflicting, yet reasonable conceptions of the good. Rawls's case here rests on two distinctive features of political liberalism: firstly, political liberalism is 'free standing', and secondly, it is the focus of an overlapping consensus among reasonable comprehensive doctrines. The former centres upon the reasonableness of persons, while the latter is concerned with the reasonableness of doctrines. As the discussion in this chapter will show, on Rawls's account both instances of reasonableness imply a sharp distinction between the political and the non-political. Because the principles of political liberalism only apply to the political sphere and are based not upon a comprehensive conception of the good, but merely reflect certain fundamental ideas latent in the public political culture of a democratic regime, it can secure the support of all reasonable persons and generate an overlapping consensus among reasonable conceptions of the good. In the face of diversity, Rawls therefore aims to build a just and stable society by excluding contentious moral, ethical and philosophical questions from the public sphere. Hence on his account, the political sphere is grounded in principles all citizens can agree upon and thus is raised above the 'fray of rival views'.[3]

However, Rawls's claims have attracted considerable critical attention. Here critics have particularly focused upon the sharp distinction Rawls draws between the political and the non-political. From the perspective of both thin and thick multiculturalism[4] this distinction fails to recognise the complex interdependence between the private and the public. Yet proponents of thin and thick multiculturalism oppose the public/non-public distinction for rather different reasons. Thus while some feminists have been critical of Rawls's failure to extend the principles of justice to institutions such as the family, which predominantly operate in the private sphere, non-liberal minorities have expressed fears about the extent to which supposedly strictly political principles will inevitably encroach upon the non-political sphere. Such encroachment is seen by at least some non-liberal minorities as a potential threat to the long-term viability of their conception of the good. Here some critics have been particularly concerned about the demands Rawls's political liberalism makes with regard to the education of future citizens. These fears highlight the difficulties that ultimately surround Rawls's conception of reasonableness. On his account only those conceptions of the good which can accept the precepts of political liberalism are to count as reasonable. Yet if his critics are correct, many non-liberal conceptions of the good may well decide that political liberalism makes unacceptable demands upon them. In the face of such concerns, to declare all conceptions of the good which do not endorse the principles of political liberalism as unreasonable not only seriously undermines the pluralist credentials of political liberalism, but also puts into question political liberalism's ability to generate political stability. Given these difficulties this chapter will conclude that the basic strategy that governs Rawls's response to diversity is flawed. In the face of the fundamental diversity of values which characterises modern democratic societies and the complex interrelationship between the political and the non-political, any attempt to generate agreement by excluding controversial issues from the public arena is liable to fail. Thus, in the final analysis, Rawls does not provide an adequate answer to the question of justice in a genuinely diverse society.

Political Liberalism

The original position

Like many theorists Rawls regards a commitment to liberty and equality as definitive of modern democratic societies. Therefore, a conception of justice that is to be acceptable to the citizens of modern democratic societies must respect their status as free and equal persons. In *A Theory of Justice* Rawls adopts the tools of liberal contract theory in order to determine which principles of justice would be acceptable to a group of free and rational persons who find themselves in an initial position of equality and who are mutually disinterested. The aim here is to determine principles of justice for the basic structure of society, that is a society's basic political, social and economic institutions. As his emphasis upon self-interest suggests, Rawls views society as essentially a form of social co-operation for mutual advantage. The terms of social co-operation are fair, if they can secure the assent of citizens conceived as free and equal.

In order to generate the conditions under which a fair agreement on the principles of justice can be reached, Rawls employs the idea of the original position. The original position aims to place the parties to the agreement in an initial position of equality by eliminating 'the bargaining advantages that inevitably arise within the background institutions of any society from cumulative social, historical and natural tendencies'.[5] Thus Rawls constructs a hypothetical situation in which the parties are placed behind a 'veil of ignorance', which denies them all knowledge of their particular position in society, their conception of the good, their race, ethnic group, sex and gender as well as 'various native endowments such as strength and intelligence'.[6] This 'veil of ignorance' ensures that the condition of equality is met.

Rawls addresses the question of freedom in the original position via his conception of the person. He maintains that the persons in the original position should be conceived of as characterised by two moral powers and by two corresponding higher order interests. The first of these moral powers refers to the capacity for an effective sense of justice, while the second relates to 'the capacity to form, to revise and rationally to pursue a conception of the good'.[7] The parties in the original position therefore regard themselves as autonomous agents and do not 'view themselves as inevitably tied to the pursuit of the particular conception of the good that they affirm at any given time'.[8] The persons in the original position are assumed to have a corresponding higher order interest in pursuing and exercising these two powers. Hence the parties do not only have the capacity to formulate their own conception of the good, they have an inalienable interest in doing so. In addition Rawls's conception of the moral powers implies that the parties have the powers of reason and the related capacities of judgement, thought and inference. Thus by virtue of their two moral powers and their capacity to reason the persons in the original position are free.

This emphasis upon freedom and autonomy is further reinforced by Rawls's insistence that in a just society 'deep and pervasive differences of religion, philosophical and moral doctrine remain'.[9] On his account human beings are essentially diverse and will therefore choose to adopt a wide variety of different life-plans.[10] This commitment to diversity is reflected in Rawls's assumption that the parties in the original position are mutually disinterested. Thus each person is assumed to have a distinctive life-plan and is merely concerned with advancing her own conception of the good.

Since the conditions of the original position ensure that the parties are free and equal, the conception of justice adopted by the parties in the original position can provide the basis of fair terms of social co-operation. Given these suppositions together with additional assumptions he makes regarding the psychology of the parties in the original position, the circumstances of justice, the formal constraints on the concept of right and the preferred strategy of choice,[11] Rawls maintains that the parties in the original position would adopt his two principles of 'justice as fairness'. The first of these two principles guarantees each citizen the most extensive system of basic equal liberties (Principle of Greatest Equal Liberty). The first part of the second principle ensures equality of opportunity (Principle of Equal Opportunity), while the second part stipulates that social and economic inequalities are to be arranged so as to benefit the least advantaged (Difference Principle).[12]

Reasonable persons and reasonable doctrines

In *Political Liberalism* Rawls attempts to show that, provided the scope of these principles is properly defined, his conception of justice is capable of securing the support of citizens who subscribe to a wide variety of conflicting, yet reasonable, conceptions of the good. It is in this context that he develops his distinctive vision of *political liberalism*. Rawls argues that in contrast to traditional models of liberalism, his conception of political liberalism can guarantee justice and stability in the face of diversity. His case here rests on two distinctive features of political liberalism: firstly political liberalism is 'free-standing', and secondly, it is the focus of an overlapping consensus among reasonable comprehensive doctrines. The former centres on the reasonableness of persons, while the latter is concerned with the reasonableness of doctrines.

Political liberalism is free-standing in so far as it is not based upon a particular comprehensive doctrine. While the citizens of modern liberal democracies subscribe to a range of comprehensive conceptions, political liberalism is 'expanded apart from or without reference to' the wider background culture of a citizen's comprehensive doctrines. Political liberalism differs from traditional liberal conceptions of justice in terms of its scope. In contrast to the comprehensive liberalism of, for example, Kant and Mill, Rawls's political liberalism does not aim to provide a moral conception for a person's life in general. Rather, it is a moral conception that applies only to the basic structure of a constitutional democratic regime. Consequently, political liberalism merely aims to determine the principles that should apply to the basic political, social and economic institutions. However, these principles do not govern the non-public sphere,[13] nor do they stipulate the specific policies to be adopted with regard to issues beyond the basic structure.[14] Although political liberalism invokes certain moral ideas, these ideas are distinctly political ones. Thus, while for Rawls justice is the first virtue of social institutions, he maintains that the principles of justice as fairness merely reflect certain fundamental ideas implicit in the public political culture of democratic regimes.

Rawls believes that reasonable and rational people would acknowledge the two principles of justice as fairness as the basis of a 'free-standing' political conception of justice. Rationality here refers to empirical practical reason. Therefore people are rational in as far as the principles they adopt serve both their short-term interests and their overall plan of life. They are reasonable in as far as 'they are ready to propose principles and standards as fair terms of co-operation and abide by them willingly, given the assurance that others will likewise do so'.[15] Thus reasonable people desire 'a social world in which they, as free and equal, can co-operate with others on terms all can accept.'[16] Furthermore, those who are reasonable will recognise the 'burdens of judgement', which explain why even reasonable people might arrive at different and conflicting judgements. Given the many difficulties which surround the correct and conscientious exercise of our powers of reason and judgement – including contradictory scientific and empirical evidence, the need to weigh up different claims, the indeterminacy of concepts etc.[17] – even reasonable people are liable to disagree. Reasonableness therefore implies an acceptance of the facts of pluralism. This clearly has important consequences for the legitimate exercise of political power. Since the burdens of proof indicate that there is a wide variety of reasonable comprehensive doctrines, reasonable people will not seek to use political power to impose their comprehensive doctrine upon others or to suppress competing doctrines.[18] Reasonable people will therefore endorse a free-standing conception of justice.

As long as everyone accepts the fact of pluralism and 'refrains from pressing for their "comprehensive view" to be given a privileged position where "constitutional essentials" and the "basic structure of society" are concerned',[19] a society based upon the principles of political liberalism will be stable. Yet, these criteria of reasonableness may in practice prove contentious. Even if reasonable people accept the 'burdens of judgement', they may not necessarily acknowledge the normative claim that it is wrong to force people to act contrary to their reasonable conception of how to live. According to Attractra Ingram,[20] as democrats, even people who accept the 'burdens of judgement' may nonetheless argue that in cases where they constitute the overwhelming majority the law of the state should support their claim. Furthermore, the assumption of 'reasonable disagreement' central to Rawls's idea of the 'burdens of judgement' is highly problematic. As Brian Barry claims,[21] only those comprehensive doctrines which subscribe to a degree of scepticism at the epistemological level will readily accept the facts of pluralism. After all the facts of pluralism stem from the idea of reasonable disagreement which implies that all truth claims about how people should live are at some level questionable. On these criteria potentially a wide variety of views would be disqualified as unreasonable. For example, many of the adherents to the three major monotheistic religions do not endorse such an epistemological position. On the contrary, many believers regard the central tenets of their religion as revealed truth to be accepted and cherished. From such a perspective scepticism constitutes a crisis of faith. Rawls himself appears to be keenly aware of the difficulties here and he explicitly insists that in the final analysis his political conception does not depend upon a particular epistemological doctrine. Therefore, if political stability is to be guaranteed, other mechanisms must be available to strengthen the commitment of citizens to a Rawlsian political conception of justice. Here Rawls switches his focus from the reasonableness of persons to the reasonableness of comprehensive doctrines.

If we reject scepticism at the epistemological level, then stability can only be guaranteed if the content of the various comprehensive doctrines is compatible with the tenets of political liberalism. Rawls maintains that his conception of political liberalism will gain the endorsement of, or at least will be compatible with, all reasonable comprehensive doctrines. Political liberalism is therefore capable of generating a partial agreement, or, in his terms, an overlapping consensus, among reasonable comprehensive doctrines. Here Rawls stresses that this partial agreement should not be seen as a mere modus vivendi. Rather than secure a purely strategic and temporary agreement, political liberalism seeks a stable consensus on a conception of justice, which is endorsed by participants for moral reasons of one sort or another.[22] According to Rawls, such agreement will be forthcoming, because political liberalism is formulated 'in terms of certain fundamental ideas viewed as latent in the public political culture of a democratic regime.'[23] In *Political Liberalism* Rawls not only suggests that these ideas are distinctly liberal ones, but argues that the original position provides us with a device for representing these fundamental ideas. Thus the original position mirrors the fundamental ideas inherent in the public political culture of liberal democratic societies: the idea that citizens are free and equal, and the notion that the basic rules of society have to be justified to all who are forced to recognise them. Rawls therefore concludes that reasonable comprehensive doctrines will, with regard to the political sphere, endorse or at least accept the liberal values inherent in his conception of justice as fairness. Thus, for example, reasonable comprehensive doctrines will accede to the protection of certain basic rights and liberties. But, can such a consensus really be expected in contemporary liberal societies? To determine whether Rawls's vision of political liberalism can deliver such a consensus, its principles must be assessed in the light of the aims and aspirations associated with both thin and thick multiculturalism.

Political versus Non-political: the Feminist Critique

At first glance Rawls's emphasis upon an overlapping consensus based upon liberal values appears to be well placed to accommodate the concerns central to thin multiculturalism. After all, as the discussion in the previous chapter indicated, thin multiculturalism endorses the liberal vision of individual rights and freedoms, including core liberal values such as individual autonomy and the equality of moral worth of all persons. Thus in instances of thin multiculturalism the debate among the various protagonists takes place within the context of a shared set of liberal values. However, because of the emphasis thin multiculturalism places upon the political significance of group membership, proponents of this position have tended to view attempts to draw a sharp distinction between the public and the private sphere with suspicion. Feminists, for example, have been keen to highlight the extent to which women's disadvantaged position in the private sphere undermines their ability to act effectively in the public arena. It is therefore not surprising that feminists have expressed concern about the implications of Rawls's sharp distinction between the political and the non-political. While critics such as Susan Moller Okin[24] are sympathetic to many of the values of political liberalism, they fear that Rawls's failure to extend the principles of political liberalism to institutions such as the family, which operate primarily in the non-political sphere, will ultimately undermine his commitment to liberty and equality in the political sphere.

Rawls contrasts the political with the non-political sphere of the ethical, the moral and the personal (i.e. the 'familial', the 'domestic', 'associational, or 'communal').[25] However, his own discussion of the family in *Political Liberalism* serves to highlight some of the difficulties inherent in this political/non-political dichotomy. In Okin's opinion, Rawls himself struggles to locate the family along the political/non-political distinction. On the one hand he maintains that the family is part of the basic structure of society, while on the other hand he stresses that as part of 'the personal and the familial' the family is non-political.[26] Yet if the family is part of the non-political sphere, it falls outside the scope of the principles of political liberalism. The basic problem confronting Rawls is that the family does not fit the political/non-political dichotomy. While the family fulfils a vital role within society – not least in terms of the socialisation and education of future citizens – and thus is clearly part of the basic structure of society, the relationships within the family are primarily private and based upon bonds of affection. Nonetheless these private, non-political relations can have a profound impact upon our ability to fulfil our role as citizens. Since the family plays an important role in the processes of socialisation and education, the beliefs and values that are taught within the family will shape children's self-image. For example, children raised in fundamentalist or orthodox religious households and educated within a religious school, church, temple or mosque may be raised to believe that there is a '[g]od-given hierarchy of the sexes, each with its own proper sphere – the female's being narrow, circumscribed, and without authority, and the male's the opposite'.[27] As Okin notes, if the relationships within the family are clearly unequal and/or children are taught that males are superior to females, children may not be able to develop the kind of self-image that will enable them as adults to see themselves and others as free and equal citizens.

According to Frazer and Lacy,[28] Rawls's failure to consider the degree to which relationships in the non-political sphere may undermine our ability to effectively fulfil our role in the political arena highlights the extent to which Rawls neglects structural aspects of injustice based on factors such as gender, ethnicity or class. In this context Frazer and Lacy highlight the absence in *Political Liberalism* of any clear criteria to determine under which circumstances the state may intervene within non-political institutions. Rawls suggests that the state may step in to protect the basic structure, provided such actions respect the integrity of reasonable comprehensive doctrines. However, not only does this constitute a rather vague criterion, Rawls's application of this criterion remains problematic. For instance, while he recognises the extent to which economic inequality may constitute a barrier to equal citizenship, and therefore permits the state to intervene within non-political institutions in order to redistribute wealth and income through taxation, he does not appear to recognise that the sexual division of labour in the domestic sphere raises similar questions.

Here Okin suggests that Rawls's reluctance to intervene in institutions such as the family may simply reflect his desire to accommodate the widest possible range of comprehensive conceptions of the good. However, for feminists such as Okin, Rawls's 'emphasis on toleration of a wide range of comprehensive philosophical, religious, and moral doctrines comes into conflict with some important means by which greater equality between the sexes might be promoted.'[29] In the light of well established feminist arguments (see Chapter 2) about 'the spillage of "non-public" disadvantages into the "public" world',[30] Rawls's failure to promote equality between the sexes in the non-political sphere is clearly worrying, since it threatens to undermine his commitment to equal citizenship in the political arena. If this failure is to be seen as a 'by-product' of Rawls's attempt to accommodate non-liberal conceptions of the good, the potential appeal of political liberalism will in part depend on the extent to which it captures the concerns and aspirations associated with thick multiculturalism.

'Deep Diversity' and Liberal Values

Political liberalism and thick multiculturalism

While debates surrounding thin multiculturalism can be described as intra-liberal disputes, thick multiculturalism focuses on the demands of religious, ethnic and cultural groups whose values and beliefs are in conflict with those of liberalism. Thick multiculturalism is usually associated with orthodox religious minorities or traditional indigenous cultures, which reject the liberal emphasis on personal autonomy in favour of conceptions of the good that emphasise tradition and are based upon the acceptance of established hierarchies. Yet Rawls nonetheless believes that even such non-liberal minorities would accept the precepts of political liberalism. Here he places particular emphasis upon the limited scope of political liberalism. Rawls argues that his appeal to liberal values differs qualitatively from that of comprehensive liberals, since political liberalism only requires individuals to pursue liberal values with regard to their role as citizens, leaving them, in their capacity as private individuals, free to subscribe to any lifestyle compatible with the basic conditions of justice. For example, while he views personal autonomy as one of the fundamental moral powers of citizens and, thus, believes that citizens have a fundamental interest in protecting their capacity to 'form, revise and rationally to pursue a conception of the good',[31] this commitment to autonomy only applies to the political sphere. Therefore in the non-political sphere citizens will be able to pursue non-liberal lifestyles which do not value the pursuit of personal autonomy. For Rawls, this distinction between our political and our private, comprehensive conception is vital, if we are to establish unity and stability in a society characterised by reasonable pluralism. Although reasonable disagreement regarding comprehensive conceptions of the good is inevitable, our shared political conception provides us with the necessary common framework.

While political liberalism is based upon the acceptance of liberal values in the political sphere, Rawls maintains that it would not discriminate against or undermine non-liberal comprehensive conceptions of the good. Clearly, political liberalism will not enable all lifestyles that are potentially of value to flourish to an equal degree and some comprehensive doctrines which are compatible with the principles of justice may fail to gain adherents under the political and social conditions associated with political liberalism. But, for Rawls, political liberalism could only be said to discriminate against certain comprehensive conceptions 'if, say, individualistic ones alone can endure in a liberal society, or they so predominate that associations affirming values of religion or community cannot flourish'.[32]

The role of education

Yet how realistic is Rawls's assessment of political liberalism's ability to accommodate the fundamental diversity of beliefs and values so typical of contemporary democratic societies? Clearly the degree to which political liberalism will be acceptable to proponents of non-liberal conceptions of the good will to a considerable extent depend upon the viability of Rawls's distinction between citizens' political and private comprehensive conception of the good. Here one of the potentially most difficult issues is that of education. Although the values and virtues of political liberalism only apply to the political sphere, these practices and attitudes will nonetheless have to be learned. If children, once they reach adulthood, are to be capable of full citizenship, then clearly they will have to be educated to understand and appreciate the role of the individual (including the conception of personal autonomy) and the ideal of society which underpins the notion of citizenship in a Rawlsian society. Education therefore plays a vital role. That such an education implies more than merely making children aware of the institutions and the constitutional framework is underlined by Rawls's positive, strong, neo-republican conception of citizenship. This demands that citizens 'have to a sufficient degree the "political virtues" . . . and be willing to take part in public life'.[33] Thus children will need to be educated to make an active commitment to the values and beliefs which underpin the political framework. In his brief discussion of education Rawls maintains that children can be made aware of their constitutional and civil rights and be socialised into the political virtues within the context of a quite specific, narrowly defined civic education and that, in line with the principles of overlapping consensus, such an education could gain the support of all reasonable comprehensive doctrines. While Rawls admits that this type of civic education may, to some extent, predispose children to adopt personal autonomy-valuing lifestyles in their capacity as private individuals, he maintains that this would in practice not constitute a serious threat to the viability of non-autonomy-valuing lifestyles. In this context he stresses the limited scope and objectives of political liberalism. Rawls therefore assumes that the type of education required by political liberalism will not conflict with the values and aspirations of reasonable comprehensive doctrines, including reasonable non-liberal conceptions of the good.

However, while this claim is quite plausible with regard to the narrower aim of raising children's awareness of constitutional and civic rights, the work of liberal educationalists suggests that such a picture may be rather misleading if education is also to encourage the political virtues. Here Rawls's inclusion of autonomy among the political virtues is particularly troubling. Liberal educationalists tend to stress that autonomy is primarily concerned with a particular attitude of mind. For example, the liberal philosopher of education R. M. Hare maintains that, as an educational ideal, autonomy is best regarded as a 'disposition to think in a certain way'.[34] Unlike mathematics and geography, autonomy cannot be taught as a separate, distinct subject. The main concern of an autonomy-valuing education will be with the overall ethos of education. This suggests that it will be difficult to restrict personal autonomy to certain aspects of the curriculum in the manner which Rawls appears to imply. Nor will it be easy to exclude certain areas of the curriculum, such as, for example, religious education. If we wish to avoid serious discontinuities or conflicts and contradictions in the way we educate children, we have to accept that the beliefs and values that inform personal autonomy will have to apply to the curriculum as a whole. Therefore, in the educational arena Rawls's distinction between autonomy-valuing as an aspect of citizenship and autonomy-valuing as a comprehensive ideal will be difficult to maintain. Consequently, the impact of an autonomy-valuing education will depend upon the types of skills and dispositions which will be fostered by such an educational ethos.

The arguments presented by liberal philosophers of education indicate that such an education will be highly sensitive to the dangers of indoctrination, and emphasise the attainment of critical reflective abilities, intellectual independence and open-mindedness. Implicit here is the notion that children should be invited to examine critically the justification for beliefs. Pupils will therefore be encouraged to distance themselves from their beliefs and to entertain the possibility of doubt. This indicates that they will be asked to regard their beliefs as provisional and subject to revision. The aim of such an education will be to ensure that students become free, rational choosers, whose life-choices are not determined by the circumstances of their birth or the pressures of socialisation.[35] In the light of the cultural diversity so characteristic of most contemporary liberal societies, many liberal philosophers and educationalists contend that these educational goals are best attained through a 'multicultural' education. In the eyes of advocates such as Bhikhu Parekh,[36] a multicultural education which presents a student with a variety of cultural perspective and practices will foster the powers of self-criticism, self-reflection and independent thought by providing 'a cluster of mini Archimedean standpoints in the shape of other perspectives from which to reflect on and explore the strength and limitations of one's own'.[37] Furthermore, an awareness of a plurality of perspectives is seen as encouraging curiosity, imagination and a broadened range of sympathies, while avoiding the dangers of superficial judgements and sweeping generalisations. For Parekh the aim of a multicultural education is to free students from inherited prejudices and to enable them, through the exploration of other cultures and points of view, to develop their own perspective.

If a Rawlsian society is to ensure that children are socialised into the political virtues, it will have to adopt an educational ethos akin to Parekh's vision of multicultural education. However, the responses of non-liberal minorities to such educational initiatives suggest that this type of educational ethos will not be acceptable to many proponents of religious or community based conceptions of the good. The potential difficulties here are clearly illustrated by the debates that have surrounded the education of ethnic minority children in Britain.

Political Liberalism and the Dilemma of Education

Multicultural education

Probably the most far reaching and influential attempt to implement the principles of a liberal, multicultural education within the context of English educational policy is contained in the recommendations of the 'Committee of Inquiry into the Education of Children from Ethnic Minority Groups'. In its report *Education for All* the Committee maintains that in a multiracial and culturally diverse society such as contemporary Britain, the educational needs of children from both ethnic minorities and the dominant cultural majority are best met via a culturally enriched curriculum, which presents elements of minority cultures, such as religion, history and language, within the context of a shared framework of values.[38] Thus, in the eyes of the Swann Report, education should promote 'diversity within unity'. Here the parallels between the conception of multicultural education advocated by the Swann Report and Rawls's political liberalism are rather instructive.

Just like Rawls's political liberalism, the Committee's conception of multicultural education is premised on the belief that in contemporary democratic societies cultural diversity is both inevitable and desirable. Consequently, the Swann Report stresses that, if all children are to regard their education as relevant to their own experience and as a source of a positive self-image, the cultural pluralism characteristic of society in general has to be reflected in the school curriculum. This is seen as the basis for enabling all groups to feel accepted by society and to participate fully in shaping society. Multicultural education therefore regards a policy of active cultural pluralism as essential if minority groups are not to feel alienated from society. This approach is reminiscent of Rawls's claim that in a society characterised by reasonable pluralism political stability can only be assured by gaining the reasoned support of citizens who are committed to reasonable, yet conflicting, doctrines.

However, as the Report's emphasis on the notion of 'diversity within unity' suggests, the Swann Committee's conception of multicultural education rests on the belief that pluralism has to take place within the framework of a common culture, which provides the basis for cultural continuity and social cohesion. Here the Committee's conception of a common framework is similar to Rawls's notion of reasonable pluralism within the context of an overlapping consensus. Furthermore, just as Rawls acknowledges that political liberalism will not be able to accommodate all potentially valuable forms of life, the Report accepts that the common cultural framework sets limits to the extent to which minorities can preserve their culture and lifestyle.

The common framework of values therefore fulfils a function similar to that performed by the shared political conception in political liberalism. Consequently, it is not surprising to find that it is within the framework of common values that the Swann Report's liberal, autonomy-valuing perspective is most evident. Thus, the Committee stresses, for example, that the shared framework should be based upon universally acceptable rational principles, that education should 'be more than the reinforcement of beliefs, values and identities which the child brings to school'[39] and that it should provide children with a range of options and alternatives. These recommendations reflect the Report's typically autonomy-valuing preoccupation with rationality, critical ability, intellectual independence, choice and self-determination.

The Muslim critique

Given that multicultural education as advocated by the Swann Report reflects both Rawls's approach to pluralism and his commitment to autonomy as an aspect of a shared set of values, it provides a good basis for assessing Rawls's claim that in principle political liberalism does not discriminate against non-liberal lifestyles, such as religious perspectives or communitarian lifestyles. In this context the response to the Swann Report by the British Muslim community is of particular interest. The Muslim community constitutes one of the largest and most vocal ethno-religious minorities in Britain[40] and has a well-established perspective on, and long-standing interest in, education. Furthermore, Islam combines a belief in revealed truth with a commitment to community in the form of the umma or community of believers,[41] which plays an important role in the construction and interpretation of beliefs. The views of elements of the Muslim community therefore provide a useful focal point for an assessment of the concerns of those perspectives that are liable to regard a liberal education as problematic.

Research[42] suggests that the educational goals of the British Muslim community are essentially twofold: on the one hand Muslim parents want to ensure that their children have access to the opportunities offered by the general education system, while on the other they wish to preserve, maintain and transmit their distinctive beliefs and values, 'both through direct teaching and through a school ethos informed by these values'.[43] While some Muslim parents give priority to the former and are prepared to see the latter dealt with in the home and the mosque, others seek an education that integrates these two goals. Indeed, many of the submissions by the Muslim community to the Swann Committee reflect the desire for such an integrated approach. Not only do many of the representations made by the Muslim community stress the need to address factors such as racism within and outside the school, which may undermine the performance of ethnic minority pupils, they also express fears about the extent to which 'existing schools can provide an educational environment which parents will find acceptable in terms of their beliefs'.[44] With regard to this second set of concerns, many Muslim submissions to the inquiry and responses to the Report's conclusions express particular concern about the nature and content of religious education. The discrepancies between the Report's conclusions and the views of Muslim parents regarding religious education highlight the extent to which a liberal, autonomy-valuing education may conflict with the educational aspirations of non-liberal minorities.

In line with its overall emphasis on autonomy the Swann Report favours a phenomenological approach to religious education. As it is not the function of schools to reinforce children's existing beliefs, schools should refrain from religious instruction. Instead, they should assist children to understand the nature of religion as such and help them to appreciate the diversity of beliefs and their significance for individuals and the community.[45] For the Swann Committee the aim of religious education should be to enable pupils to determine their own religious position.[46] In their reply to these recommendations, Muslim organisations such as the Council of Mosques[47] and the Islamic Academy[48] have been particularly critical of the autonomy-valuing ethos which underpins such an approach to religious education. Here the objections of these Muslim organisations focus on 1. the manner in which such an education prioritises critical rationality and 2. the extent to which it concentrates on the individual at the expense of notions of community.

With regard to the prioritisation of critical rationality many Muslims have expressed serious reservations about the non-prescriptive attitude which underpins a phenomenological approach to education. According to the Report's Muslim critics, to present Islam as one of a variety of equally valid perspectives is to fail to recognise the special significance for Muslims of the Qur'an as the revealed word of God and 'will create doubt in the minds of children about faith in divine revelation'.[49] From this perspective, to be a Muslim is to accept the truth of the Qur'an and to recognise it as qualitatively different from other ideologies and worldviews. Thus, the critical examination of the central tenets of Islam would be for many devout Muslims synonymous with a denial of faith.[50] Although Muslims acknowledge that individual believers may suffer crises of faith, such doubt is viewed as a temporary weakness to be overcome, rather than a permanent state of mind to be cherished. Hence in the eyes of many Muslims, education should aim to promote a clear and secure religious commitment. Muslims are not alone in regarding the Swann Report's approach as alien to their conception of the status of revelation. The Report itself cites the then Archbishop of Canterbury, who feared that to simply set Christianity alongside other religions is 'selling Christianity short by carrying our anti-confessionals too far'.[51]

Furthermore, numerous Muslim critics have questioned whether the Swann Report's emphasis on critical rationality can convey the actual meaning of faith. In line with its commitment to personal autonomy, the Swann Report construes faith as a question of individual choice based upon rational deliberation. However, most Muslims, like many believers in general, regard faith as a gift from God, requiring not so much rational deliberation, but emotional involvement and a readiness to suspend disbelief. Subsequently, Muslim organisations such as the Council of Mosques have questioned the Report's rejection of religious instruction, since, in their opinion, 'education without an appreciation of one's faith commitment is even at best an incomplete education'.[52] These fears are again echoed by non-Muslims. John McIntyre, for example, notes that the descriptive presentation of religion advantages non-religious, agnostic positions. After all, 'one standard attack on religions is to show their variety and to add that it is a matter of indifference which you choose'.[53]

In relation to the Committee's preoccupation with the individual, Muslim critics have argued that the Report's individualistic conception of faith robs religion of its social and political significance. Unlike most interpretations of Christianity, Islam does not recognise a secular sphere. The Shari'a, or divine law, integrates political, social and economic life and regulates both private and public life.[54] Furthermore, Islam does not share Christianity's other-worldliness, but is characterised by a commitment to action in this world and a belief that it is possible to build a prosperous and just social order in this world. These values, together with piety on both the social and the individual level, indicate the extent to which the socio-political dimension is an integral part of Islam's self-image.[55] Thus, the Council of Mosques accuses the Swann Report of failing to 'grasp . . . that we cannot see Islam as anything other than our way of life . . . and therefore regard it as essential that our children understand what it means to be a Muslim.'[56] According to the Council of Mosques, children will only be able to gain such an understanding if they are raised firmly within the Islamic tradition.

In this context the Muslim critique of multicultural education reflects the wider concerns of communitarian critics of personal autonomy, who have expressed serious reservations regarding the manner in which advocates of personal autonomy construe the 'self'. For proponents of personal autonomy our beliefs are mere possessions of the 'self'. Consequently, we are able to distinguish between our 'self' and our beliefs. Because of this conception of belief and believer as distanced, advocates of personal autonomy tend to view beliefs as chosen and propose an open-ended, critical attitude vis-à-vis beliefs. However, for numerous communitarian critics of personal autonomy,[57] this conception of the 'self' fails to appreciate the extent to which the 'self' is constituted by the beliefs we hold and the communities we live in. From a communitarian perspective, membership of a community is not something which we choose but an attachment which we discover. This process of discovery requires a firm sense of rootedness. Therefore, an education which encourages children to distance themselves from their most fundamental beliefs is likely to be regarded as a threat to the attainment of a secure identity. The emphasis Muslim critics of the Swann Report have placed on the need to instruct children in Islam and raise them as members of the Muslim community can therefore be seen as a challenge to the conception of the 'self' which underpins multicultural education.

As these objections to the Swann Report's conception of religious education indicate, the educational goals of a liberal autonomy-valuing education are liable to be seriously at odds with the educational aspirations of at least some parents who subscribe to non-liberal lifestyles. Given that the multicultural education advocated by the Swann Report reflects both Rawls's conception of pluralism and his commitment to personal autonomy as an aspect of a shared framework of political values, the problems encountered by the Swann Report can be seen as indicative of the difficulties a Rawlsian education system is likely to face. Here the Muslim critique of the Swann Report highlights the extent to which the emphasis an autonomy-valuing education places on individuality and rationality is at odds with the ethos of both revelation-based and communitarian perspectives. This suggests that the kind of autonomy-valuing education fundamental to citizenship in a Rawlsian society may well threaten the long-term viability of communitarian and revelation-based lifestyles, since it systematically socialises children of parents committed to such lifestyles into values and beliefs alien to those lifestyles. As Stephen Macedo bluntly admits:

promoting core liberal political virtues – such as the importance of a critical attitude toward contending political claims – seems certain to have the effect of promoting critical thinking in general . . . Even a suitably circumscribed political liberalism is not really all that circumscribed: it will in various ways promote a way of life as a whole.[58]

Rawls and the dilemma of education

Faced with such difficulties Rawls might respond by treating comprehensive doctrines such as Islam as unreasonable. After all, the overlapping consensus essential to political liberalism can only be generated if all doctrines are prepared to acknowledge the reasonableness of rival positions. Subsequently, Rawls regards a commitment to the political framework based upon the precepts of political liberalism as an important criterion of reasonableness. He could therefore argue that to count as reasonable the content of a doctrine must be compatible with the precepts of political liberalism. Such a response may be welcomed by feminist critics such as Okin, who have urged Rawls to intervene in the non-political sphere to ensure that children are brought up to view themselves as free and equal citizens. Although the imposition of the values of political liberalism in the educational sphere would still fall short of feminist demands regarding justice in the non-political arena, it would nonetheless ensure that children are exposed to ideas such as free and equal personhood. This may be sufficient for children to learn to view themselves and others as free and equal citizens (yet it would make Rawls's reluctance to ensure justice within the family all the more puzzling). However, since the reservations expressed by Muslim critics of the Swann Report reflect in general terms the kind of concerns shared by many communitarian and revelation-based life-styles, such a move is likely to have far-reaching consequences. Not only would this run counter to Rawls's claim that political liberalism does not discriminate against religious or communitarian conceptions of the good, thereby undermining the pluralist credentials of political liberalism, it would also put into question political liberalism's ability to generate political stability. As Rawls himself is keenly aware, a liberal democratic regime cannot be successfully maintained unless it has the active support of the overwhelming majority of the population. However a Rawlsian education is liable to meet with the opposition of at least some parents on the grounds that such an education threatens their ability to socialise their children in accordance with their values. The persistent concerns expressed by sections of the Muslim community in Britain suggests that such opposition would be probable.[59] Furthermore, if children are educated contrary to their parent's values and beliefs, there is a real danger of alienating children from their parents.[60] Not only is such alienation likely to generate intergenerational conflict, it could also have a detrimental effect on the children's development.

In the light of these problems, Rawls may choose to abandon the notion of an overlapping consensus in favour of an emphasis on the need to ensure that children are taught to hold doctrines in a reasonable manner. Therefore, instead of emphasising the reasonable-ness of doctrines, the stress would now be on ensuring that children are educated in a manner which leads them to develop the qualities associated with Rawls's notion of a reasonable person.[61] Thus, rather than demand that all reasonable comprehensive doctrines acknow-ledge the values of political liberalism, he could argue that his principles merely demand that children be taught that while their beliefs may well be true it is unreasonable to seek to use political power to impose these beliefs upon others. Although this would remove the burden upon comprehensive doctrines to ensure that their teachings are compatible with the tenets of political liberalism, the overall impact of such a shift would be marginal.[62] As noted earlier, according to Rawls, reasonable persons accept the 'burdens of judgement' and therefore acknowledge that even reasonable people might arrive at different and conflicting judgements. Such a position implies a degree of scepticism at the epistemological level. Thus to educate children to be reasonable persons requires not only that they be introduced to a wide variety of possible world views, including a range of religious views, but also implies that children must be made aware that their own beliefs and convictions are merely one among a variety of reasonable views and as such do not have a privileged status. This would do little to placate the fears of those Muslims critical of the provisions recommended in the Swann Report. Furthermore, the criteria Rawls stipulates with regard to reasonableness on the part of persons are so stringent that some of the measures he himself proposes fail this test. If these criteria are to be met, then the principles which govern the basic structure of society must not be based on values which are contested. However, as Caney notes,[63] on such a strict interpretation Rawls's own difference principle would not be able to meet the criteria of reasonableness. After all, the difference principle rests upon the contentious assumption that the distribution of talents is arbitrary, an assumption denied by desert theorists and libertarians.

Privatising Diversity

The problems inherent in Rawls's response to the dilemma of education can be seen as indicative of the general difficulties which surround his definition of reasonableness and his conception of an overlapping consensus. Rawls's concern for stability and his emphasis on the historical contingency of political liberalism may at times suggest that he is merely elucidating the assumptions underpinning an actual overlapping consensus in society on important questions regarding liberty and justice. However, the care Rawls takes to distinguish the overlapping consensus from a mere modus vivendi, and the conclusivity and determinacy of the principles of political liberalism, indicate that his overlapping consensus constitutes much more than a mere practical political agreement. For example, whereas the role of the state with regard to abortion is subject to substantial disagreement among comprehensive conceptions of the good, Rawls maintains that the issue of abortion can be resolved by an appeal to the equality of women as equal citizens and that any comprehensive conception of the good which denies women 'a duly qualified right to abortion in the first trimester is to that extent unreasonable'.[64] Such a conclusion indicates that Rawls employs a rather substantive conception of 'reasonableness'. This suggests that Rawls may indeed wish to regard comprehensive doctrines such as Islam, which challenge the principles of a Rawlsian education, as unreasonable. After all on such a substantive account, all conceptions of the good which challenge political liberalism's prescription of the basic liberties or which question the manner in which it distinguishes between the public and private realm will be regarded as unreasonable and, therefore, are to be excluded.

Whereas Rawls portrays the acceptance of the principles of political liberalism as a moral requirement, for critics such as Chantal Mouffe[65] the exclusion of conceptions of the good which cannot be confined to the private, and which fail to satisfy liberal principles, is clearly a political decision aimed at safeguarding the dominance of liberal principles in the public sphere. Rawls aims to secure this dominance by embedding the liberal values of freedom and equality in the basic institutions, thereby ensuring that they become immune from the contingencies of political life. Hence, according to John Gray 'the key move in Rawlsian political liberalism . . . is the removal from political life of the principles specifying the basic liberties and justice in distribution.'[66] But by thus entrenching liberal principles, the diversity which can be accommodated within the precepts of political liberalism is rather limited. After all, liberalism constitutes only one of a wide variety of possible ideological perspectives. Different belief systems may well favour alternative political and economic practices and patterns of organisation. For instance, Muslim critics of liberalism, such as S. Akhtar,[67] have highlighted the degree to which Islam aims to integrate political, social and economic life. As noted earlier, in contrast to Christianity's 'other-worldliness', Islam is characterised by a commitment to action in this world and a belief that it is possible to build a prosperous and just society here and now. This belief, together with Islam's concern with piety on both the social and the individual level, indicate the extent to which this political dimension is an integral part of Islam's self-image. Thus, for instance, the Shari'a or divine law regulates both private and public life. This vision of an integrated political, social and economic life clearly challenges the political/non-political distinction central to Rawls's conception of political liberalism. Consequently, in a society characterised by genuine value pluralism, the principles of political liberalism are unlikely to provide the basis for a universally acceptable overlapping consensus. On the contrary, rather than offering a mechanism for social integration, these principles may well give rise to tensions.

In the final analysis Rawls fails to provide an adequate answer to the question of justice in a genuinely diverse society. His strategy of establishing an impartial point of view by removing all controversial questions from the political sphere rests upon a distinction between the political and the non-political that ultimately cannot be sustained. Not only does such a distinction ignore the complex interrelationship between the political and the non-political, and thus fails to take into account the concerns raised by well-established feminist critiques of traditional liberal conceptions of justice, it also disregards the profound diversity of values within contemporary liberal societies.

Notes and References

1. Rawls, *A Theory of Justice* (Oxford: University Press, 1986) and *Political Liberalism* (New York: Columbia Press, 1993).
2. Rawls, *Political Liberalism*, p. 3.
3. A. Ingram, 'Rawlsians, Pluralists and Cosmopolitans', in D. Archard (ed.), *Philosophy and Pluralism* (Cambridge: University Press, 1996) pp. 147–61.
4. For a definition of thin and thick multiculturalism see Chapter 2.
5. Rawls, *Political Liberalism*, p. 23.
6. Ibid. p. 25.
7. Rawls, 'Kantian Constructivism in Moral Theory', *Journal of Philosophy*, Vol. 77, No. 9, 1980, pp. 515–77, p. 525.
8. Rawls, *Political Liberalism*, p. 30.
9. Rawls, 'Kantian Constructivism', p. 539.
10. Rawls's position here should be seen in the light of his discussion of the burdens of judgement in *Political Liberalism*. In this context Rawls sets out to show that even well-intentioned reasonable persons may arrive at different and conflicting judgements.
11. In *A Theory of Justice* Rawls makes a number of assumptions to shape the original position: 1. Veil of Ignorance; 2. Psychological Assumptions (the parties are rational and do not suffer from envy); 3. Circumstances of Justice (moderate scarcity and mutual disinterest); 4. The formal constraints of the Concept of Right (the principles of justice must be universal, general, publicly known, able to order conflicting claims and be final); 5. In choosing between rival conceptions of justice the parties will adopt a maximin strategy, that is they will attempt to maximise the minimum.
12. The principles of justice as fairness stipulate that: First Principle: 'Each person is to have an equal right to the most extensive total system of equal basic liberties compatible with a similar system of liberty for all.' (Greatest Equal Liberty Principle, *A Theory of Justice*, p. 250). Second Principle: 'Social and economic inequalities are to be arranged so that they are both (a) to the greatest benefit of the least advantaged (Difference Principle) and (b) attached to offices and positions open to all under conditions of fair equality of opportunity.' (Principle of Equal Opportunity, *A Theory of Justice*, p. 83.) These principles are ranked so that the first principle is

prior to the second and the second part of the second principle is prior to the first part of the second principle.

13. For a discussion of Rawls's conception of the non-public sphere see E. Frazer and N. Lacy, 'Politics and the Public in Rawls's Political Liberalism', *Political Studies*, Vol. 43, No. 2, June 1995, pp. 233–47.

14. As R. Fullinwider notes, the principles adopted in the original position only define 'a range of possible constitutional and legislative institutions, which in turn define a range of permissible policies' (R. K. Fullinwider, 'Citizenship, Individualism and Democratic Politics', *Ethics*, Vol. 105, April 1995, pp. 497–515, p. 504).

15. Rawls, *Political Liberalism*, p. 49.

16. Ibid. p. 50.

17. For Rawls's list of potential difficulties see *Political Liberalism*, p. 56–7.

18. See P. Jones, 'Two Conceptions of Liberalism, Two Conceptions of Justice', *British Journal of Political Science*, Vol. 25, 1995, pp. 515–50.

19. B. Barry, 'John Rawls and the Search for Stability', *Ethics*, Vol. 105, July 1995, pp. 874–915, p. 902.

20. Ingram, 'Rawlsians, Pluralists and Cosmopolitans'.

21. Barry, 'John Rawls and the Search for Stability'.

22. According to Rawls the participants affirm the overlapping consesus on moral grounds since: 'All those who affirm the political conception start from within their own comprehensive view and draw on the religious, philosophical and moral grounds it provides. The fact that people affirm the same political conception on those grounds does not make their affirming it any less religious, philosophical or moral, as the case may be, since the grounds sincerely held determine the nature of their affirmation.' (J. Rawls, *Political Liberalism*, pp. 147–8). For a discussion of the distinction between overlapping consensus and modus vivendi see S. Scheffler, 'The Appeal of Political Liberalism', *Ethics*, Vol. 105, October 1994, pp. 4–22.

23. Rawls, *Political Liberalism*, p. 197.

24. S. Moller Okin, 'Political Liberalism, Justice and Gender', *Ethics*, Vol. 105 (October 1994) pp. 23–43.

25. Frazer and Lacy, 'Politics and the Public in Rawls's Political Liberalism'.

26. J. Rawls, cited in Okin, 'Political Liberalism, Justice and Gender', p. 26.

27. S. Moller Okin, 'Political Liberalism, Justice and Gender', p. 29.

28. Frazer and Lacy, 'Politics and the Public in Rawls's Political Liberalism'.

29. S. Moller Okin, 'Political Liberalism, Justice and Gender', p. 28.

30. Frazer and Lacy, 'Politics and the Public in Rawls's Political Liberalism', p. 245.

31. Rawls, *Political Liberalism*, p. 90.

32. Ibid. p. 199.

33. Ibid. p. 205.

34. R. M. Hare, 'Autonomy As An Educational Ideal–Chairman's Remarks', in S. C. Brown (ed.), *Philosophers Discuss Education* (London: Macmillan, 1975), pp. 36–42, p. 36.

35. See, for example, C. Bailey, *Beyond The Present And The Particular*

(London: Routledge, 1984) or J. White, *The Aims of Education Restated* (London: Routledge, Keagan and Paul, 1982).

36. B. Parekh, 'The Concept of Multi-Cultural Education', in S. Modgil et al. (ed.), *Multicultural Education – The Interminable Debate* (London: Falmer Press, 1986) and B. Parekh, 'Education for a Multicultural Society' (*Papers for the Philosophy of Education Society of Great Britain*, 31 March–2 April 1995) pp. 1–10.

37. B. Parekh, 'Education for a Multicultural Society', p. 6.

38. The Committee was charged to 'review in relation to schools the educational needs and attainment of children from ethnic minority groups taking account, as necessary, of factors outside the formal education system relevant to school performance, including influences in early childhood and prospects for school leavers'. (Swann, *Education for All*, HMSO, February 1985, p. vii.)

39. Ibid. p. 10.

40. According to Halstead, Muslims make up about 2% of the total population of Britain. See J. M. Halstead, 'Should Schools Reinforce Children's Religious Identity?', *Religious Education*, Vol. 30, No. 3–4, 1995, pp. 360–77.

41. It is within the umma that the public structure of beliefs is objectified, legitimised and given internal coherence. Reflection upon and interpretation of beliefs takes place within the umma and the individual is encouraged to trust and accept the knowledge established in the process of debate within the umma. Every Muslim is automatically a member of the umma and of the five injunctions of Islam three, prayer, fasting and haj, relate to group activity.

42. J. M. Halstead, 'Voluntary Apartheid? Problems of Schooling for Religious and Other Minorities in Democratic Societies', *Journal of Philosophy of Education*, Vol. 29, No. 2, 1995, pp. 57–72.

43. Halstead, 'Voluntary Apartheid?', p. 265.

44. Swann, *Education for All*, p. 202.

45. Here the Report's recommendations are at odds with current practice. At present the law requires that the RE syllabus places the main weight on Christianity.

46. Here there is clearly a tension between the Swann Committee's recommendations and existing statutory requirements regrading religious worship in schools.

47. The Council of Mosques, *The Muslims and Swann* (Bradford: Council of Mosques, 1984).

48. The Islamic Academy, *Swann Committee Report* (Cambridge: The Islamic Academy, 1985).

49. Ibid. p. 5.

50. According to Sharifi, the aim of an Islamic education is to produce the insan-al-kamil (the perfect man) who fully subscribes to the Islamic code of life, who never doubts the existence of God and who never loses sight of his relationship with God. (see H. Sharifi, 'The Islamic as opposed to the Modern Philosophy of Education', in S. M. al-Naquib al-Attas (ed.),

Aims and Objectives of Islamic Education (Jedda: Hodder and Stoughton, 1979).

51. Archbishop of Canterbury, cited in Swann, *Education for All*, p. 473.
52. Council of Mosques, *The Muslims and Swann*, p. 15.
53. J. McIntyre, 'Multi-Cultural and Multi-Faith Societies: Some Examinable Assumptions', in E. Hulmes (ed.), *Occasional Papers 3* (Oxford: The Farrington Institute for Christian Studies, 1981).
54. See J. R. Muir, 'The Isocratic Idea of Education and Islamic Education', *Papers of the Philosophy of Education Society* (31 March–2 April, 1995) pp. 28–36.
55. S. Akhtar, *The Final Imperative*, (London: Bellew Publishing, 1991).
56. Council of Mosques, *The Muslims and Swann*, p. 10.
57. See, for example, A. MacIntyre, *After Virtue* (London: Duckworth, 1985) or M. Sandel, *Liberalism and The Limits of Justice* (Cambridge: University Press, 1982).
58. S. Macedo, 'Liberal Civic Education and Religious Fundamentalism: The Case of God v. John Rawls?', *Ethics*, Vol. 105, April 1995, pp. 468–96, p. 477.
59. The British experience is by no means unique here. In The US, for example, Christian fundamentalists have taken legal action in an attempt to secure the right to withdraw their children from aspects of the public school curriculum which they regard as detrimental to their ability to teach their children their particular religious views (for a discussion of these issues see Macado, Liberal Civic Education and Religious Fundamentalism: The Case of God v. John Rawls?).
60. In the eyes of some commentators the riots which took place in Bradford in June 1995 can be attributed in part to underlying cultural and generational tensions. Halstead, for example, argues that while public schools have educated young Muslims into values different from those of their home, these young Muslims are not able to integrate into the wider society due to racial and religious prejudice. For Halstead a tension between the values of the home and those transmitted in the school may well lead to social dislocation (Halstead, 'Should Schools Reinforce Children's Religious Identity?).
61. Both Jones ('Two Conceptions of Liberalism, Two Conceptions of Justice') and Barry ('John Rawls and the Search for Stability') suggest that Rawls would be well-advised to make such a move. While Barry maintains that the overlapping consensus is essentially superfluous to Rawls's argument, Jones stresses the difficulties which surround any attempt to generate an actual agreement among a wide variety of comprehensive doctrines.
62. For a discussion of this issue see G. Parry, 'Political Liberalism and Education', in I. Hampshire-Monk and J. Stanyer (eds), *Contemporary Political Studies 1996*, Vol. 3, Short Run Press Ltd., Exeter, pp. 1697–1708.
63. S. Caney, 'Anti-perfectionism and Rawlsian Liberalism', *Political Studies*, Vol. 43, No. 2, June 1995, pp. 248–64.
64. Rawls, *Political Liberalism*, p. 243.

65. C. Mouffe, *The Return of the Political* (London: Verso, 1993).
66. J. Gray, 'Agnositic Liberalism', *Social Philosophy and Policy*, Vol. 12, Sept. 1995, pp. 110–35, p. 124.
67. S. Akhtar, *The Final Imperative*.

Chapter 4: Jürgen Habermas: Discourse in a Multicultural Society

Habermas's long-standing concern with questions of social cohesion and legitimacy has recently led him to address the challenges the 'politics of difference' pose to traditional liberal conceptions of citizenship. Habermas insists that social and political institutions cannot be maintained solely by strategic manipulation and force. On the contrary, mass loyalty and stability can only be guaranteed if all members of society recognise and accept that there are good grounds for holding a particular norm. Yet how is such general agreement to be reached in a modern society in which citizens subscribe to a wide variety of moral, religious and philosophical beliefs? It is this concern which drives Habermas's preoccupation with the legitimacy of social orders and the regulation of social conflicts. Here Habermas's approach shares important features with Rawls's vision of political liberalism. Just like Rawls's theory of justice, Habermas's response to the diversity of lifestyles and socio-cultural groups so typical of modern liberal societies is inspired by a commitment to Kant's deontological approach. Thus not only do both writers give priority to questions of moral rightness over considerations of the good life for the individual, both seek to accommodate difference and diversity by establishing an impartial point of view. Yet, despite this common framework, Habermas's vision of impartiality differs notably from Rawls's model of political liberalism.

In contrast to Rawls, Habermas insists that the impartial standpoint can only be identified in the process of an actual discussion or discourse among real participants. Here he bases his approach upon the analysis of communicative action; that is, everyday social interaction aimed at reaching an understanding. According to Habermas, communicative action plays a vital role in the development of individual identity, the formation of solidarity and the process of social integration. Since communicative action depends upon a set of shared background assumptions, the participants must seek to restore this background consensus should it be disrupted. To do so they must engage in what Habermas terms practical discourse. Habermas derives his principle of discourse ethics from the unavoidable and hence universal presuppositions inherent in such practical discourse. To ensure that the rules of practical discourse are observed, these rules are institutionalised in the form of legal norms, which stipulate the formal rights of all citizens. The rule of law therefore provides the context for public debate among citizens regarding the status of controversial norms. Since the principle of discourse ethics stipulates that norms are only valid if they meet with the approval of all participants, such debate will aim to establish an impartial set of norms, which will be acceptable to all citizens.

According to Habermas, his vision of discourse ethics can be reconciled with the struggle for recognition on the part of many groups traditionally marginalised in liberal democracies. Here Habermas has placed particular emphasis upon three distinctive features of his approach: the equiprimordiality of private and civic autonomy, the distinction between the formulation and the application of norms, and the ethical patterning of the constitutional state. As the discussion in this chapter will show, these features ensure that Habermas's discourse ethics is indeed sensitive to many of the demands associated with thin multiculturalism. Here the attractions of his approach are quite apparent if discourse ethics is viewed in the light of two of the pivotal concerns of thin multiculturalism: the protection of minority cultures and effective political participation.

Yet, despite these apparent strengths, the response by proponents of a 'politics of difference' to Habermas's discourse ethics has at best been ambivalent. This ambivalence reflects serious reservations regarding Habermas's model of communication and his preoccupation with consensus and the general point of view. In the eyes of critics such as Young, Benhabib and Warnke,[1] Habermas's emphasis upon critical, rational argumentation excludes or devalues the speech patterns of many traditionally marginalised groups, whereas his preoccupation with universality and the general point of view gives rise to an unsustainably narrow conception of the moral domain.

These worries become particularly troublesome if Habermas's model is viewed from the perspective of thick multiculturalism. While the promotion of both personal and civil autonomy constitutes a key feature of discourse ethics, this preoccupation with autonomy leads Habermas to conceive of rights to cultural membership in a manner which is problematic in instances of thick multiculturalism on at least four counts: it misconceives the value of cultural membership, fails to recognise corporate rights, equates autonomy and reasonableness and views toleration exclusively in terms of the liberal principle of individual freedom of conscience. These difficulties suggest that Habermas underestimates the degree of diversity associated with thick multiculturalism. Ultimately, the consensus Habermas seeks can only be secured if he excludes conceptions of the good, that do not share the liberal commitment to autonomy, from practical discourse in the constitutional state. Thus while Habermas's discourse ethics may be better placed than Rawls's political liberalism to accommodate many of the demands associated with thin multiculturalism, Habermas, like Rawls, fails to appreciate the role fundamental value conflict plays in the political sphere.

Discourse Ethics

Communicative action

One of the distinctive features of Habermas's vision of discourse ethics is his strong cognitive stance. For Habermas moral norms or principles of justice are not merely statements of 'preference', but are open to rational evaluation. From such a cognitivist perspective claims to moral rightness are analogous to truth claims and can therefore be justified 'independent of the prejudices or biases of any particular tradition or culture'.[2] Habermas bases his defence of universal, rationally justified moral norms upon his analysis of everyday communicative action. 'Communicative action' refers to social inter-action which is solely oriented towards reaching an understanding between two or more actors. An understanding is reached if all participants accept a particular claim as valid. Habermas contrasts this focus upon validity claims characteristic of communicative action with strategic action which is oriented just to the successful attainment of our private goals. While in the case of strategic action we treat others we interact with merely as instruments or means towards the success of our personal goals, communicative action requires that we respect those we communicate with as ends in themselves. Thus communicative action requires that we recognise others as 'autonomous agents whose capacity for rational judgement must be respected'.[3] When we engage in communicative action we try to 'justify, convince, defend, criticise, explain, argue, express our inner feelings and desires, while interpreting those of others'.[4] Habermas maintains that whenever we engage in communicative action we must make certain unavoidable and hence universal presuppositions. For instance, if the sole aim of two actors is to reach an understanding they have to presuppose that both are motivated to accept the validity of claims raised on the basis of nothing but the force of reason. However, before examining these unavoidable presuppositions, it is important to grasp why Habermas attaches such significance to communicative action.

The lifeworld

According to Habermas, all processes of reaching an understanding take place within the context of a shared set of 'unquestioned cultural givens' and 'agreed upon patterns of interpretation'.[5] Habermas refers to this shared background knowledge as the lifeworld. Communicative action and the lifeworld are complementary. While the shared background assumptions make successful interaction possible, communicative actions perpetuate and reproduce the symbolic structures of the lifeworld. This reproduction of the symbolic structures of the lifeworld takes place through three processes: cultural tradition, social integration and socialisation. Each of these three processes can operate only 'in the medium of action oriented towards reaching an understanding'.[6] Thus communicative action aids the transmission and renewal of cultural knowledge, supports social integration and the establishment of solidarity, and provides the foundations for the formation of personal identities.

This complex relationship between communicative action and the lifeworld is central to Habermas's conception of individual identity. Given that for Habermas 'persons are individualized only by way of socialization',[7] individual identity is intersubjective. Consequently, since '[i]ndividuals acquire and sustain their identity by approximating traditions, belonging to social groups, and taking part in socialising interactions',[8] individuals cannot in the long-run abstain from engaging in communicative action.

In addition to its role in individual identity formation, communicative action also plays an important part at the political and social level. Political and social institutions are rooted in the lifeworld and play an important role in the processes of social integration and solidarity formation. Since social integration and solidarity can only be facilitated through action orientated towards reaching an understanding, communicative action is central to the political and social realm. As O'Neill notes, although 'strategic action may well play an inelliminable role in political and social life', the symbolic structure of the lifeworld can only survive 'the atomising effects of pervasive strategic action and its instrumental rationality' if communicative action also has 'priority in the realm of politics'.[9] Due to its role in the formulation of individual identity and the perpetuation of political and social institutions, Habermas maintains that communicative action should be regarded as the original mode of language use and as such has priority over strategic action.

Practical discourse

Since successful communicative action depends upon a set of shared background assumptions, a breach in the background consensus that constitutes the lifeworld calls into question the validity claims negotiated via communicative action. Given the importance of successful communicative action, participants in communication must seek to restore the consensus that has been disrupted. To achieve this, participants 'continue their communicative action in a reflexive attitude'.[10] Habermas refers to this reflexive continuation of communicative action as practical discourse. The task that Habermas sets himself in developing his discourse ethics is to clarify and formalise the unavoidable presuppositions actors engaged in practical discourse must make, if they wish to resolve normative disputes to the satisfaction of all participants. By making explicit the rules and assumptions of communicative action, Habermas arrives at three sets of rules:[11] firstly, all participants must speak the same language according to the same general conventions. Habermas is here concerned with logical and semantic rules. Thus, for instance, no speaker may contradict himself, speakers must use predicates consistently, and different speakers may not use the same expression with different meanings. Secondly, certain procedural rules must be observed. Given that the participants desire to reach agreement, they may only state what they actually believe to be the case. Thirdly, given that practical discourse seeks to persuade and convince participants so as to gain their free assent,

the structure of their communication rules out all external or internal coercion other than the force of the better argument and thereby also neutralises all motives other than that of the cooperative search for truth.[12]

To ensure that practical discourse is 'immunised against' coercion, a set of rules relating to the processes of communication must be observed. The aim of these rules is to ensure discursive equality, freedom and fair play. Thus every subject with the competence to speak and act is allowed to take part in discourse; everyone is allowed to question or introduce any assertion; everyone is allowed to express his/her attitudes, desires and needs; and no one may be prevented by internal or external coercion from exercising these rights. This clearly constitutes a very demanding set of conditions and as such may never be fully met. However, if we are to engage in genuine practical discourse we must assume that the conditions under which we engage in argumentation at least approximate to a sufficient degree these rules of argumentation.

Habermas uses these unavoidable presuppositions to derive his principle of universalisation (U), which stipulates that a contested norm cannot meet with the consent of all participants in practical discourse:

'Unless all affected can freely accept the consequences and side effects that the *general* observance of the controversial norm can be expected to have for the satisfaction of the interests of *each individual*.'[13]

According to Habermas, anyone who seriously engages in practical discourse implicitly acknowledges this principle of universalisation. To prove that any attempt to deny the universal validity of (U) is incoherent, Habermas employs a cautious version of Karl Otto Apel's idea of a transcendental justification of ethics.[14] Central to Apel's argument is the notion of performative contradictions. A performative contradiction occurs when the propositional content of a speech act contradicts the propositional content of certain presuppositions implicit in the speech act itself. According to Habermas, the position of a moral sceptic who denies the existence of universal norms involves a performative contradiction and is therefore self-contradictory. The sceptic must assume that there are good grounds for holding his position. If the sceptic does not want merely to cajole, manipulate or coerce others to agree to his claim, he must attempt to convince them of the validity of his claim via the force of reason alone. Yet any attempt to convince others via the force of argument alone implies the acceptance of the logical-semantic, procedural and process rules of practical discourse. Given that these rules imply the principle of universalisation (U), the sceptic appears to presuppose the validity of the very principle he is determined to refute. He is therefore caught in a performative contradiction. Having thus established proof for the universal validity of (U), Habermas is now in a position to formulate the principle of discourse ethics (D) which stipulates that:

Only those norms can claim to be valid that meet (or could meet) with the approval of all affected in their capacity as participants in a practical discourse.[15]

Practical discourse therefore aims to establish common or generalisable interests.[16] Discourse ethics demands that we critically evaluate and assess our individual interests and needs in an attempt to generate an agreement on those norms that satisfy a common interest. Since we perceive and come to understand our needs and interests in the light of cultural values, such an agreement can only be achieved in the course of a genuine public dialogue. Actual discourse therefore helps us to clarify what our true interests and needs are. This activity of understanding and interpreting needs involves a process of 'ideal role taking' whereby 'everyone is required to take the perspective of everyone else'.[17] The process of coming to understand the self and the world of others allows for the development of an 'extended we-perspective from which all can test in common whether they wish to make a controversial norm the basis of their shared practice.'[18] Actual discourse therefore fosters a sense of solidarity around common norms and thus re-creates a sense of community.

Legal norms

Given that practical discourse fulfils important social functions, not least in the justification of principles of social and political justice, it is important that the rules which regulate such discourses are institutionalised to ensure that the ideal conditions of discourse are observed as closely as possible. This is done in the form of legal norms, which institutionalise the rules of practical discourse as the formal rights of all citizens. The rule of law therefore provides the context for public debate among citizens regarding the status of controversial norms. The aim of such debate is to establish a set of norms acceptable to all citizens. In this context it is important to bear in mind the distinction Habermas draws between moral and ethical questions. While the moral standpoint focuses upon what is in the interest of everyone, and as such is concerned with issues that are in principle universalisable, ethical questions focus on 'issues which are related to conceptions of the good life or of a life not mis-spent'.[19] For Habermas ethical questions are open to rational debate only within the context of a particular, concrete way of life or conception of the good and hence are not universalisable. As the emphasis discourse ethics places upon universalisablity suggests, practical discourse gives primacy to moral questions. This focus upon questions which can, in principle, be agreed upon by all, is particularly significant in the face of the diversity of socio-cultural groups and lifestyles typical of contemporary liberal democracies. Clearly the greater the diversity of lifestyles and socio-cultural groups within a particular society, the more likely it is that the background consensus which enables communicative action breaks down and that norms will have to be justified via practical discourse. Here the emphasis Habermas places upon engagement with the specific understanding of the self and lifeworld of particular others suggests that Habermas's vision of discourse ethics is potentially well placed to respond to the concerns expressed by the advocates of a 'politics of difference'. Indeed in his recent work he aims to show that his vision of discourse ethics can be reconciled with the struggle for recognition on the part of many groups traditionally marginalised in liberal democracies and that, properly understood, a liberal theory of rights is not blind to cultural differences.

Discourse Ethics and Cultural Diversity

According to Habermas, his vision of discourse ethics can be reconciled with the struggle for recognition on the part of many groups traditionally marginalised in liberal democracies. Here three distinctive features of Habermas's approach are particularly significant: the equiprimordiality of private and civic autonomy, the distinction between the formulation and application of norms, and the ethical patterning of the constitutional state.

The equiprimordiality of private and civic autonomy

On Habermas's account the equiprimordiality of private and civic autonomy refers to the complex interrelationship between the private and the public sphere. Given that legal persons, just like natural ones, are individuated through the processes of socialisation, personal autonomy can only be effectively safeguarded if the life context within which an individual's identity is formulated is also protected. This can only be achieved if all citizens participate in the formulation and interpretation of the rights and norms that safeguard individual autonomy. Therefore the democratic process must protect both private and civic autonomy. Citizens are only autonomous if they can regard themselves as the authors of the law they are subject to, and if they feel assured that the procedures by which the law has been established at least approximate the demands of practical discourse. At the same time the idea of popular sovereignty implies the protection of basic rights and liberties so as to ensure that citizens are sufficiently independent. Consequently, the individual rights protected by law and democracy presuppose one another. Human rights are therefore not to be regarded as prior to popular sovereignty. On the contrary, 'the private autonomy of citizens must neither be set above, nor made subordinate to their political autonomy'.[20] Thus discourse ethics aims to strike a balance between the traditional liberal emphasis upon individual rights and limited government, and the classical republican preoccupation with the formulation of a political will aimed at the common good. In line with republicanism, discourse ethics gives 'centre stage to the process of political opinion- and will-formation',[21] but without regarding the individual rights protected within the constitution as secondary. Quite the reverse: these rights are seen as the institutionalised expression of the rules of practical discourse. Therefore, while the democratic process seeks to secure the common good, such an understanding can only be reached if the rules of practical discourse are respected. Hence for Habermas securing the common good and protecting individual rights imply one another.

This recognition of the equiprimordiality of private and civic autonomy leads Habermas to emphasise the need for political participation. While a system of rights may grant citizens formal equality, equal rights and liberties can be used differently and may impact upon citizens differentially depending upon their circumstances. Hence, if the autonomy of all citizens is to be protected equally, it is vital that all citizens participate in the political process. After all, unless all citizens participate in public debate and express their specific needs, there is a real danger that the needs of socially disadvantaged groups will be misunderstood, which in turn may undermine the capacity of such groups to pursue effectively their own conception of the good life.

Formulation and application of norms

This emphasis upon the political significance of particularity and difference is reinforced by Habermas's distinction between the formulation and application of norms. While norms are justified impartially by reference to generalisable interests, the impartial application of a norm asks us to consider whether, in the light of all the relevant facts, a specific norm is the most appropriate one in these circumstances. The impartial application of norms therefore requires attention to the particular needs of actual persons and socio-cultural groups. Such attention can only be assured if 'the political culture of a democratic regime reflects the different perspectives of all the collective identities that exist within the state'.[22] Hence it is important that social groups organise themselves politically so as to articulate their differences and their political needs. Yet such participation and organisation may only be possible if groups are granted special cultural and social rights. As Habermas notes:

multicultural societies can be held together by a political culture, however much it has proven itself, only if democratic citizenship pays off not only in terms of liberal individual rights and rights of political participation but also in the enjoyment of social and cultural rights. The citizen must be able to experience *the fair value of their rights* in the form of social security and the reciprocal recognition of different forms of cultural life. Democratic citizenship can only realise its integrative potential – that is it can only found solidarity among strangers – if it proves itself to be a mechanism that actually realises the material conditions of preferred forms of life.[23]

Not only must cultural and social rights be recognised, the specific application of universally valid norms will differ among democratic states in accordance with the constellation of social groups which make up the state and the particular historical context in which the state operates.

The ethical patterning of the constitutional state

This recognition of the unique character of particular democratic states is further underlined by Habermas's readiness to accept that all constitutional states are ethically patterned. While it is the primary aim of the rule of law in a constitutional state to uphold universally valid norms, such as basic human rights, 'every legal system is *also* the expression of a particular lifeform and not merely a reflection of the universal features of basic rights'.[24] Hence every state will interpret constitutional principles in the light of its particular historical experiences. Consequently every state is ethically patterned.[25] However, Habermas stresses that the distinctive political identity of a particular state is only legitimate if it does not violate the demands of moral discourse. Thus, for instance, every constitutional state must ensure that human rights are effectively guaranteed for all citizens. Furthermore, while states are ethically patterned, this does not imply that the constitutional state should not aim to be neutral between the various conceptions of the good and the different socio-cultural subgroups within the state. Here Habermas distinguishes between the common civic identity of a group of citizens and the particular ethical discourses of specific subcultures. While the ethical discourses of specific subcultures provide the basis for and feed into the collective identity of a particular nation, Habermas stresses the importance of decoupling the majority culture from the wider political culture.[26] The political culture must, therefore, reflect the ethical commitments of all citizens and must not favour or discriminate against any specific subculture. Hence, while '[f]or historic reasons, in many countries the majority culture is fused with the general culture that claims to be recognised by *all citizens* . . .', '[th]is fusion must be dissolved if it is to be possible for different cultural, ethnic and religious forms of life to coexist and interact on equal terms within *the same* political community'.[27] According to Habermas, battles for recognition arise whenever a state fails in this task. If minorities perceive the existing arrangements as discriminatory, they will demand that these arrangements be changed so as to take into account their interests and needs.

Two Conceptions of Impartiality

Taken together Habermas's account of the equiprimordiality of personal and civic autonomy, the formulation/application distinction and the ethical patterning of the state provide a complex and sophisticated account of the distinction between public and private and the relationship between the right and the good. Here Habermas's position differs notably from Rawls's vision of political liberalism. While Rawls attempts to establish the impartial point of view by abstracting the individual from her particular background, values and commitments, Habermas's intersubjective account of human identity leads him to recognise the significance of the particular life context within which a given individual's identity has been formed. Thus whereas Rawls aims to formulate the fundamental principles of justice by placing the parties in the original position behind a veil of ignorance which denies them all knowledge of their particular selves, Habermas maintains that genuine equality and impartiality can only be achieved if the interdependence of private and public autonomy is recognised, and if the particular needs and aspirations of actual persons and socio-cultural groups are taken into account in the public-political sphere.

Secondly, in contrast to Rawls, whose vision of impartiality is based upon a sharp public/private distinction, which seeks to 'privatise' difference by removing all controversial matters from the political sphere, Habermas sets no specific limits on the subject matter which can be discussed by participants in a practical discourse. As Habermas recognises, what is to be regarded as an appropriate topic for public discussion and legislation is liable to vary from society to society. For Habermas any attempt to draw an a priori boundary between the public and the private not only 'contradicts the republican intuition that popular sovereignty and human rights are nourished by the same root',[28] but also runs counter to historical experience, which shows that the boundary between the public and the private has been subject to a considerable amount of flux. Consequently Habermas leaves 'the task of finding common ground to the political participants themselves'.[29] From Habermas's perspective Rawls's attempt to fix a priori what is to constitute the common ground, reflects a failure to recognise the complexity of ongoing processes of public-political communication.

Finally, according to Habermas, the desire to establish substantive principles of justice leads Rawls to move beyond the realm of what can be settled in advance by political theory. Common ground cannot be found or 'discovered' theoretically, but can only emerge in the course of actual, ongoing debate. Political theory can only establish which rules need to be observed if such debate is to be conducted fairly and equally. Consequently, in contrast to Rawls, Habermas favours a purely procedural approach to the question of justice.

Discourse Ethics, Diversity and Representation

These distinctive features of Habermas's discourse ethics make his vision of liberalism potentially rather more attractive to advocates of a 'politics of difference' than Rawls's account of political liberalism. Indeed Habermas's perspective appears to be particularly well placed to reflect the concerns central to thin multiculturalism. As the discussion in Chapter 2 indicated, thin multiculturalism seeks to combine a commitment to key liberal values such as autonomy and equality of moral worth with the recognition of difference at the political level. Thus, for example, while the Francophone minority in Canada has sought to protect their particular culture and language, both French and English speaking Canadians share a common set of liberal democratic beliefs. In a similar vein many feminists critical of traditional liberal accounts of impartiality, equality and the public/private distinction have nonetheless continued to endorse liberal values such as individual freedom and equal moral worth. Given the demands and preoccupations characteristic of thin multiculturalism, Habermas's context responsive conception of impartiality avoids many of the pitfalls traditionally associated with the liberal perspective. Here the attractions of this approach are quite apparent if discourse ethics is viewed in the light of two of the pivotal concerns of thin multiculturalism: the protection of minority cultures and effective political participation.

Discourse ethics and the protection of linguistic and cultural minorities

Habermas's intersubjective account of individual identity suggests that in the application of legal norms the state must be sensitive to the needs of linguistic and cultural minoritities. Indeed:

the integrity of the individual legal person cannot . . . be guaranteed without at the same time protecting those intersubjective shared complexes of experiences and contexts of life in which he or she was socialised and in which they formed their identity.[30]

A person's native language and the culture associated with this language clearly constitute a vital part of a person's identity and as such deserve protection. Consequently, in applying legal norms the state must be sensitive to the needs of linguistic and cultural minorities. This may imply specific minority rights, akin to the provisions demanded by minorities such as the Quebecois, so as to ensure that the minority language and culture is not 'swamped' by that of the majority and thus effectively marginalised. After all, the particular ethical horizons which shape political and social debate in a given constitutional state should not be merely based upon the concerns of the majority, but should reflect the ethical perspective of all citizens. Hence in a multilingual or multicultural state the language and culture of the minority must be given official recognition. Here Habermas stresses that rights to cultural recognition do not only apply to national minorities but also extend to ethnic minorities such as immigrant groups. While immigrants must accept the constitutional principles anchored in the political culture of a given constitutional state, they should not be expected to take on board 'the basic ethical orientations of a particular cultural lifeform prevailing in the country'.[31] On the contrary, given that the particular ethical patterning of a given constitutional state should reflect the concerns of the various social and cultural groups within its boundaries, the arrival of new ethnic groups should, in the long-run, lead to changes in the political identity of a constitutional state.

Discourse ethics and representation

Not only is Habermas sympathetic to the needs of linguistic and cultural minorities, his recognition of the equiprimodiality of private and civic autonomy makes him also sensitive to the demands for greater political representation on the part of traditionally marginal-ised or socially disadvantaged groups. Since personal autonomy can only be safeguarded effectively if the life context in which an individual's identity is formulated is also protected, it is important that the specific needs and aspirations associated with a particular lifestyle or social position are clearly perceived and understood. Given that the needs of socially disadvantaged groups are liable to differ notably from those of the majority, and taking into account that even the most benevolent majority is liable to misunderstand the needs of minority groups, it is vital that members of minority groups participate in public debate so as to ensure that the needs and interests of minorities are clearly articulated. Thus Habermas stresses, for example, that genuine equality between men and women cannot be achieved unless women take part in the formulation of the criteria which determine what kind of treatment is to count as equal. In this context Habermas supports the demands of traditionally marginalised groups such as women for de facto rather than mere de jure equality. Given that rights and liberties may impact upon citizens differentially, a state which seeks to protect the autonomy of all citizens equally must seek to ensure de facto rather then mere de jure equality. Just as Habermas recognises the need for greater representation for women, his vision of discourse ethics is liable to be sympathetic to the demands of aboriginal groups to be a given greater say in the formulation of public policies which affect their lives.[32]

The case for greater representation of traditionally marginalised groups is further strengthened by Habermas's sophisticated account of the relationship between the public and the private. Thus for instance, his fluid account of the public/private boundary is well placed to overcome the worries expressed by feminists who fear that the traditional liberal public/private distinction has prevented women from participating effectively in the political sphere. As Seyla Benhabib notes, second wave feminists have not only demanded the protection of women's position in the public sphere as citizens and wage earners, but have also thought to redraw the line between public and private so as to ensure that 'domestic violence, child abuse and the sexual division of labour in the family become matters of public concern'.[33] Habermas's refusal to draw an a priori boundary between the public and the private allows participants in the public realm to argue for the inclusion of previously excluded issues. Thus discourses ethics remains sensitive to shifts in public debate.

Discourse Rationality and the Generalised Other

Despite these apparent strengths the response by advocates of a 'politics of difference' to Habermas's discourse ethics has at best been ambivalent. While proponents of difference and diversity have expressed interest in and made use of key concepts of discourse ethics, such as communicative action, dialogical ethics and discourse, many have been critical of Habermas's model of communication and his preoccupation with consensus and the general point of view. In the eyes of these critics Habermas's emphasis upon critical, rational argumentation excludes or devalues the speech patterns of many traditionally marginalised groups, whereas his preoccupation with universality and the general point of view gives rise to an unsustainably narrow conception of the moral domain.

Discourse and social power

Although Habermas is sensitive to the impact of political and economic power, critics such as Young[34] have focused upon his failure to recognise the extent to which differences in social power may undermine the ability of participants in practical discourse to take part in debate on equal terms. Differences in social power and cultural background are frequently reflected in people's style of speech and the manner in which these speech patterns are evaluated by others. Yet, although Habermas's model of discourse ethics emphasises the need for actual discussion among real participants, he fails to consider the impact of actual speech patterns upon practical discourse. As his emphasis upon 'the force of the better argument' suggests, Habermas believes that communicative action requires critical, rational argumentation. Here Habermas explicitly contrasts his emphasis upon the purely cognitive aspects of discourse with conceptions of dialogue which see communication predominately in terms of empathy and the strengthening of social ties.[35]

This regard for critical, rational argumentation leads Habermas to adopt an adversarial model of communication. Participants try to arrive at a resolution by contesting each other's arguments with the view of establishing the strengths and weaknesses of particular lines of reasoning. Such a model of communication relies upon assertive and confrontational speech patterns and consequently tends to devalue speech which is tentative, exploratory or conciliatory. Furthermore, the idea of rational deliberation privileges speech that is 'formal and general' and 'proceeds from premises to conclusions in an orderly manner'.[36] While Habermas equates critical, rational argumentation with impartiality, critics have argued that such a model of communication favours the speech patterns of socially privileged and powerful groups. Thus, for instance, feminists have pointed towards the differences in the speech patterns of men and women. In a review of reseach into male and female speech patterns, Nancy Love[37] concludes that men and women employ different 'frames' of conversation and forms of expression. While men seek to differentiate themselves as individuals in a social hierarchy, and view conversation as powerplay, women tend to position themselves in a communal network and employ conversations to create connections and reach consensus. Consequently men are more likely to employ assertive and confrontational speech patterns, whereas women are liable to be conciliatory and supportive. These differences are reflected in the forms of expressions men and women use. While men tend to employ 'neutral', scholarly, objective and unemotional language, women's language is tentative, polite and characterised by a desire to seek approval. For Nancy Love such different speech patterns reflect men and women's different social roles and power. Indeed male speech patterns tend to be taken as the standard whereby all speech is evaluated. As Love notes, this tends to place women in a double bind: if they follow female speech patterns their speech is liable to carry less weight than that of men. If, on the other hand, they choose to follow male speech patterns they are in danger of being perceived as unfeminine, cold, harsh, tough and threatening. Research indicates that members of lower or socially marginalised groups experience similar difficulties. This suggests that in the context of actual discussion among real participants traditionally marginalised groups such as women will find it difficult to make their voices heard. In the eyes of critics these difficulties clearly undermine the democratic potential of Habermas's model of discourse ethics.

Discourse and the generalised other

For many critics this preoccupation with formal, rational speech is indicative of more deep-rooted difficulties inherent in Habermas's approach. Here Seyla Benhabib[38] has drawn particular attention to the role the ideas of universality and the general point of view play in Habermas's theory. For Habermas moral judgements must be universalisable and acceptable to all participants in practical discourse. The moral domain is therefore concerned with common or generalisable interests.[39] As Habermas notes, this emphasis upon universal or generalisable interests requires a sharp distinction between moral and evaluative questions. While moral questions can 'in principle be decided rationally in terms of criteria of justice or the universalisability of interests', evaluative questions focus on issues relating to the good life and 'are accessible to rational discussion only within the horizons of a concrete historical form of life or an individual life style.'[40] Habermas therefore restricts the moral domain to questions of justice. However, for critics such as Benhabib, this constitutes an unsustainably narrow conception of the moral sphere. Here Benhabib takes her cue from Carol Gilligan's influential critique of a so-called 'ethics of justice'. For Gilligan a preoccupation with questions of justice overlooks important elements of the moral domain. Whereas Habermas equates the moral point of view with the perspective of the generalised other, Gilligan highlights the moral significance of our particular obligations and commitments to specific others. For Gilligan morality cannot simply be reduced to universal principles, but also requires that we take into account the standpoint of the concrete other and consider the specific needs, interests, desires and welfare of the other. Such an attitude is driven by the recognition of human vulnerability and requires care, compassion, empathy and emotional sensitivity. In his recent work Habermas[41] acknowledges that Gilligan does draw attention to an important moral problem by highlighting the manner in which moral agents behave in concrete life-situations. Yet, in Habermas's opinion, Gilligan's failure clearly to distinguish between the justification of moral norms on the one hand and their application on the other leads her to misidentify the significance of her findings. While the justification of norms demands that we adopt the perspective of the generalised other, the impartial application of a norm requires careful attention to the specific circumstances of concrete others. Thus while Gilligan's work sheds light on the manner in which moral agents apply norms, it does not impact upon the justification of norms.

However in the eyes of some critics such an attempt to defuse Gilligan's critique remains highly problematic. Georgia Warnke,[42] for instance, has questioned the viability of Habermas's distinction between the justification and the application of norms. According to Warnke, justification and application cannot be separated neatly. On the contrary, our very understanding of a norm depends upon how it is applied. To illustrate this point Warnke considers the current controversy surrounding surrogate motherhood. Proponents of enforceable surrogacy contracts maintain that, as human beings, women should be free to use their bodies as they choose. Therefore, to deny women the right voluntarily to enter into enforceable surrogacy contracts would undermine women's equality. However, opponents of enforceable surrogacy contracts argue that to allow the sale of babies is to violate the dignity of human beings and the sanctity of the infant-mother bond. On Habermas's account this controversy does not impact upon the justification of fundamental principles of freedom and equality, but merely reflects difficulties with regard to the application of these principles. However, for Warnke the controversy about enforceable surrogacy contracts cannot be easily limited to questions of application. After all at the heart of this dispute lie two very different views of what principles of equality, liberty and responsibility are justified. Whereas the proponents of enforceable surrogacy contracts view freedom, equality and responsibility predominately in contractual terms, the position of their opponents rests on the 'protection and promotion of non-contractual relationships and responsibilities'.[43]

For Warnke these difficulties suggest that our understanding of a norm cannot be separated from our understanding of how to apply it. This has far reaching implications for Habermas's attempt to draw a clear distinction between moral and evaluative questions. Since the application of a norm requires careful attention to the particular situation, values and sensitivities of specific others, the application of a norm involves evaluative questions. This suggests that if the distinction between the application and the justification of norms cannot be maintained, we will not be able to separate firmly our normative judgements from our evaluative assessments. Yet, if our normative judgements are inevitably tainted by our evaluative assessments, it is unlikely that we will always be able to resolve our normative differences via 'the force of the better argument'. After all, what counts for us as the better argument always involves our values, sensibilities, cultural traditions and conceptions of the good. Consequently Warnke concludes that Habermas's emphasis upon consensus and universal agreement is misplaced. In a genuinely pluralist society people are liable to disagree frequently about what constitutes the better argument. To appeal, in the face of such profound diversity, to the common good and a shared consensus is merely to perpetuate privilege. As Young notes, if, in the search for the 'common good' participants are invited to leave behind their particular experience and interests, the 'perspectives of the privileged are likely to dominate the definition of the common good.'[44] Given differences in social power, members of the dominant group are liable to 'assert their experiences and perspectives on social events as impartial and objective'.[45] This clearly marginalises groups which lack the social power to frame the terms in which debate is conducted.

The fears expressed by critics in relation to Habermas's conception of communication and his preoccupation with the general point of view and consensus suggest that, despite his sensitivity to some of the concerns expressed by advocates of a 'politics of difference', his account of discourse ethics neglects the fundamental conflict of values associated with diversity and hence underestimates the potential for conflict. These worries become particularly troublesome if Habermas's approach is viewed in the context of thick multiculturalism.

The Dilemma of 'Deep Diversity'

The dilemma thick multiculturalism poses for Habermas becomes clearly apparent in the light of the limits he sets to the claims of difference and diversity. Here Habermas's considerations focus upon the question of autonomy. Clearly the promotion of both personal and civil autonomy constitutes a key feature of discourse ethics. After all, practical discourse implies questioning established norms and perspectives. It is therefore not surprising that for Habermas it is autonomy which limits the claims of diversity. Therefore, while Habermas supports rights to cultural membership, he stresses that this does not imply that we should seek to preserve cultures in the same manner in which we may attempt to preserve endangered species. For Habermas 'cultural rights are legitimate only when exercised as individual liberties'.[46] Hence on Habermas's account cultural rights do not constitute group rights exercised by the collective as a whole, but are merely special rights held by certain individuals. While the constitutional state should ensure that the reproduction of particular lifeworlds remains possible, it is up to the members of a particular society or cultural group to decide whether they want to preserve their cultural heritage. For Habermas cultures and traditions only deserve protection in so far as they promote the well-being and freedom of individuals. Therefore individual autonomy provides the rationale for, and sets the limits to, rights to cultural recognition. However, this emphasis upon autonomy is liable to prove problematic in instances of thick multiculturalism on at least four counts: it misconceives the value of cultural membership, fails to recognise corporate rights, equates autonomy and reasonableness, and views toleration exclusively in terms of the liberal principle of individual freedom of conscience.

The value of cultural membership

From the perspective of groups whose conception of the good is at odds with the liberal vision of individual freedom and autonomy, Habermas's justification of rights to cultural recognition in terms of autonomy misconstrues the value of cultural membership and and may threaten the long-term viability of their way of life. The difficulties here are probably most readily apparent in relation to the objections raised by various religious minorities to a broadly liberal education. As the discussion of mutlicultural education in Chapter 3 indicated, various religious minorities regard an emphasis upon critical rationality and individual autonomy as incompatible with a secure and settled faith commitment. For these religious communities faith is best regarded as a gift from God and does not require individual rational choice but emotional involvement and a readiness to suspend disbelief. Consequently some religious groups have attempted to ensure that in the course of their schooling their children are not exposed to views which challenge their religious commitments. While in the United States Christian families living in Tennessee attempted to withdraw their children from a reading programme which exposed children to a diversity of perspectives,[47] in Britain Muslim organisations such as the Council of Mosques and the Islamic Academy[48] have been critical of multicultural approaches to religious education which emphasise open-mindedness and individual choice. Thus, the Islamic Academy maintains that an emphasis on open-mindedness in the religious education of Muslim children fails to recognise the special significance of the Qur'an as the revealed word of God and 'will create doubt in the minds of children about faith in divine revelation.'[49] As these worries indicate, for these groups the value of cultural membership is not grounded in autonomy, but in the attainment of a secure identity.

Corporate rights

In addition to the difficulties which surround Habermas's account of the value of cultural membership, his vision of cultural and social rights as individual rights fails to account for important aspects of the demands for greater self-government. For instance, religious minorities, such as the Amish, Mennonites or Hasidic Jews, have sought special rights and protections to maintain their distinctive way of life. Such demands frequently imply group or corporate rights, that is to say rights that are exercised not by individual members of the community, but by the collective as a whole. Thus the demand for special legal exemptions to allow for the ritual slaughter of animals implies rights that are not held and exercised by individuals but by the group. In a similar vein policies such as the Quebec language laws, which seek to systematically socialise future citizens into the language, values and norms definitive of a particular culture, extend well beyond what could be justified as 'just providing . . . a facility to already existing people'.[50] Thus while demands for cultural rights are typically driven by a desire to preserve and perpetuate a particular cultural community, Habermas conceives such rights as individual liberties, which protect the freedom and well-being of existing citizens. Yet such a conception of cultural rights cannot accommodate demands for genuine group or corporate rights.

Autonomy and the burdens of reason

From the perspective of non-liberal minorities the worries regarding Habermas's account of the value of cultural membership and the nature of cultural rights are reinforced by the manner in which Habermas equates autonomy and reasonableness. For Habermas all worldviews which 'lack an awareness of the fallibility of their validity claim'[51] and do not to respect what John Rawls refers to as 'the burdens of reason', are incompatible with practical discourse in a constitutional state. For Habermas such worldviews are liable to lead to intolerance and dogmatism since, 'they have no space for reflection on their relationship to those other worldviews with which they share *the same* universe of discourse and against whose competing validity claims they can assert themselves only with reason'.[52] Hence multicultural societies can only recognise doctrines which are not unreasonable, because 'equally protected coexistence requires the mutual recognition of the various cultural memberships'.[53] However, this emphasis upon fallibility and critical rationality leaves Habermas's discourse ethics open to objections akin to those raised by Brian Barry with regard to Rawls's conception of reasonableness.[54] Like Rawls's conception, Habermas's fallibility criterion implies a degree of scepticism at the epistemological level. After all to regard your commitments, values and beliefs as potentially fallible requires a critical distance vis-à-vis your present conception of the good life. Yet, as the discussion in the previous chapter suggested, a variety of conceptions of the good life, including the three main monotheistic religions, do not subscribe to such an epistemological position.[55]

The difficulties inherent in Habermas's approach here are further underlined by his insistence that ethical questions are open to rational debate only within the context of a particular, concrete way of life or conception of the good. Thus, according to Habermas, participants in ethical discourse seek recognition of their ethical validity claims only from those who share their particular conception of the good. However, while individuals committed to the ideal of autonomy may well recognise that their ethical validity claims are only shared by those who have also chosen to follow their specific way of life, many ethical discourses, including those which centre around religious beliefs, do not regard their validity claims as only applicable to those who share their conception of the good. From the perspective of at least some conceptions of the good, if a claim is ethically valid, it is valid for everyone and not just those who share this particular conception of the good.[56]

Autonomy and toleration

Finally, Habermas's preoccupation with autonomy leads him to equate toleration with the liberal principle of individual freedom of conscience. While Habermas fears that conceptions of the good that fail to meet his fallibility criterion are liable to be intolerant, historical experience suggests that this is not necessarily the case. Although the liberal model of toleration centres upon the idea of individual freedom, alternative conceptions of toleration have emphasised group rights, with each subgroup being permitted to govern itself in accordance with its own conception of the good.[57] Thus, for example, under the 'millet system' of the Ottoman Empire Muslims, Christians and Jews were all viewed as self-governing units. While the Ottomans exercised tolerance by allowing minority religions to exist alongside the dominant one, they did not accept the principle of individual freedom. Although the millets tolerated each other, internally they enforced orthodoxy to varying degrees. In a similar vein the American Bill of Rights grants self-government rights to the tribal governments of Native Americans. This has enabled some tribes to establish non-liberal forms of government, which seek to restrict the liberty of members in order to preserve traditional religious practices. As these examples indicate, non-liberal societies can potentially accommodate diversity in a tolerant and peaceful manner. Hence Habermas's rejection of non-liberal conceptions of the good as inevitably intolerant is unwarranted.

Discourse Ethics and the 'Politics of Difference'

While Habermas's conception of discourse ethics does respond positively to many of the concerns of advocates of thin multiculturalism and thus proves to be more sensitive to the claims of difference and diversity than Rawls's model of political liberalism, in the final analysis, Habermas fails to take radical difference seriously.[58] Ultimately Habermas believes that difference can be overcome in the course of rational discourse and that a neutral and impartial view can be established. This, however, appears to underestimate the diversity of values and the fundamental nature of value conflict. The agreement Habermas seeks is only possible if those conceptions of the good which do not share the liberal commitment to autonomy are excluded from practical discourse in the constitutional state. It is difficult to see how the liberal state can win the loyalty and gain the support of all citizens, if the concerns of those members of society whose conception of the good does not accord with the liberal commitment to autonomy are excluded from public debate. Yet in the absence of such loyalty and support the liberal state may well prove unstable. The liberal quest for impartiality therefore appears to be misplaced.

Notes and References

1. I. M. Young, 'Communication and the Other: Beyond Deliberative Democracy', in M. Wilson and A. Yeatman, *Justice and Identity* (Wellington: Bridget Willimans Books, 1995) pp. 134–52; S. Benhabib, 'The Debate over Women and Moral Theory Revisted', in J. Meehan, *Feminists Read Habermas: Gendering the Subject of Discourse* (London: Routledge, 1995) pp. 182–203; G. Warnke, 'Discourse Ethics and Feminist Dilemmas of Difference', in J. Meehan, *Feminists Read Habermas: Gendering the Subject of Discourse*, pp. 247–61.

2. S. O'Neill, *Impartiality in Context: Grounding Justice in a Pluralist World* (Albany: State University of New York Press, 1997) p. 131.

3. S. Chambers, *Reasonable Democracy, Jürgen Habermas and the Politics of Discourse* (Ithaca and London: Cornell University Press, 1996) p. 100.

4. Ibid. p. 97.

5. J. Habermas, *Moral Consciousness and Communicative Action*, translated by C. Lenhardt and S. Weber Nicholsen (Cambridge: Polity Press, 1992) p. 135.

6. Ibid. p. 102.

7. J. Habermas, 'Struggles for Recognition in Constitutional States', *European Journal of Philosophy*, Vol. 1, No. 2, pp. 128–55, p. 132.

8. J. Habermas, *Moral Consciousness and Communicative Action*, p. 102.

9. S. O'Neill, *Impartiality in Context*, p. 125.

10. J. Habermas, *Moral Consciousness and Communicative Action*, p. 67.

11. See J. Habermas, *Moral Consciousness and Communicative Action*, pp. 86–9. This summary of these presuppositions draws upon S. Chambers, *Reasonable Democracy*, pp. 98–100.

12. J. Habermas, *Moral Consciousness and Communicative Action*, pp. 88–9.

13. Ibid. p. 93.

14. To meet the charge of ethnocentrism, Habermas modifies Apel's transcendental-pragmatic justification of ethics. In *Moral Consciousness and Communicative Action* he gives up any claim to 'ultimate justification'. As Habermas notes '[i]t is by no means self-evident that rules that are unavoidable *within* discourse can also claim to be valid *outside* discourse.' Therefore, 'a separate justification is required to explain why the normative content discovered in the pragmatic presuppositions of *argumentation* should have the power to regulate action. . . . Nevertheless, in . . . practical discourse we always already make use of substantive normative rules of argumentation. It is *these rules* alone that transcendental pragmatics is in a position to derive' (pp. 86–7).

15. Ibid. p. 93.

16. As S. Chambers (*Reasonable Democracy*, p. 103) notes, generalisable

interests need not rest on identical particular interests nor are they to be understood exclusively in materialistic terms. Interests may refer to attaining a particular ideal rather than securing a specific personal benefit. Finally, 'the appeal to generalisable interests does not presuppose a set of universally true human needs which we attempt to discover in discourse. Except for the most basic physical needs, such as food and shelter, interests and needs are understood to be socially and culturally constituted'. Consequently, given that generalisable interests are the product of collective will interpretation, they are open to revision.

17. J. Habermas, 'Reconciliation through public use of reason: remarks on John Rawls's Political Liberalism', *The Journal of Philosophy*, Vol. XCI, No. 3, March 1995, pp. 109–31, p. 117.
18. Ibid. p. 117.
19. J. Habermas, 'Struggles for Recognition in Constitutional States', p. 137.
20. J. Habermas, *Between Facts and Norms* (Cambridge, MA: MIT Press, 1996) p. 104.
21. J. Habermas, 'Three Normative Models of Democracy', in S. Benhabib (ed.), *Democracy and Difference: Contesting the Boundaries of the Political* (Princeton: Princeton University Press, 1996) pp. 21–30.
22. S. O'Neill, *Impartiality in Context*, p. 170.
23. J. Habermas, 'The European Nation State: On the Past and Future of Sovereignty and Citizenship', *Public Culture*, Vol. 10, No. 2, pp. 397–416, p. 409.
24. J. Habermas, 'Struggles for Recognition in Constitutional States', p. 138.
25. Thus for Habermas, 'legal norms do not norm possible interactions between competent subjects *in general* but the interaction context of a concrete society. . . . Legal norms stem from the decisions of a historical legislature; they refer to geographically delimited legal territory and to a socially delimitable collectivity of legal consociates, and consequently to particular jurisdictional boundaries.' (J. Habermas, *Between Facts and Norms*, p. 124.)
26. J. Habermas, 'Multiculturalism and the Liberal State', *Stanford Law Review*, Vol. 47, No. 5, 1995, pp. 849–53.
27. J. Habermas, 'The European Nation State: On the Past and Future of Sovereignty and Citizenship', p. 408.
28. J. Habermas, 'Reconciliation through public use of reason: remarks on John Rawls's Political Liberalism', p. 129.
29. T. McCarthy, 'Kantian Constructivism and Reconstructivism: Rawls and Habermas in Dialogue', *Ethics*, Vol. 105, October 1994, pp. 44–65, p. 61.
30. J. Habermas, 'Struggles for Recognition in Constitutional States', p. 141.
31. Ibid. p. 147.
32. See for example the James Bay and Northern Quebec Treaty of 1975 which gives the indigenous people of northern Quebec the right to participate, along with local government, in the formulation of policies and regulations concerning the development of the region.
33. S. Benhabib, 'Liberal Dialogue Versus a Critical Theory of Discursive

Legitimation', in N. Rosenblum, *Liberalism and the Moral Life* (Cambridge, MA: Harvard University Press, 1991) pp. 143–58.

34. I. M. Young, 'Communication and the Other: Beyond Deliberative Democracy', in M. Wilson and A. Yeatman, *Justice and Identity*.

35. J. Habermas, 'Justice and Solidarity: On the Discussion Concerning "Stage 6"', *Philosophical Forum*, Vol. 21, Nos 1–2, Fall-Winter, 1989–90, pp. 32–52.

36. I. M. Young, 'Communication and the Other: Beyond Deliberative Democracy', p. 139.

37. N. Love, 'Disembodying Democracy: Habermas's Legalistic Turn', *1998 Annual Meeting of the American Political Science Association*, Boston 3–6 September 1998. Love here draws upon research by Deborah Tanner (*You Just Don't Understand: Women and Men in Conversation*, New York: Ballantine Books, 1990) and Robin Lakoff (*Langauage and Women's Place*, New York: Harper and Row, 1975).

38. S. Benhabib, 'The Debate over Women and Moral Theory Revisted', in J. Meehan, *Feminists Read Habermas: Gendering the Subject of Discourse*.

39. To clarify and support this perception of the moral sphere, Habermas invokes Lawrence Kohlberg's well-known theory of moral development. According to Kohlberg moral development culminates in a postconventional approach to moral questions. Rather than simply endorse existing social mores and conventions, moral agents at the postconventional stage seek to evaluate existing social norms in the light of universal moral principles. Actions and norms are regarded as valid in as far as they respect these principles. The principles adopted here are 'the principles of universal justice: the equality of human rights and respect for the dignity of human beings as individuals' (L. Kohlberg, cited in J. Habermas, *Moral Consciousness and Communicative Action*, p. 125). Moral agents accept these principles, because as rational persons they have come to recognise their validity.

40. Ibid. p. 178.

41. Ibid. pp. 175–82.

42. G. Warnke, 'Discourse Ethics and Feminist Dilemmas of Difference', in J. Meehan, *Feminists Read Habermas: Gendering the Subject of Discourse*.

43. Ibid. p. 254.

44. I. M. Young, 'Communication and the Other: Beyond Deliberative Democracy', p. 141.

45. I. M. Young, 'Polity and Group Difference: A Critique of the Ideal of Universal Citizenship', *Ethics*, January 1989, pp. 251–74, p. 259.

46. G. B. Levey, 'Equality, Autonomy and Cultural Rights', *Political Theory*, Vol. 25, No. 2, April 1997, pp. 215–48, p. 232.

47. See S. Macedo, 'Liberal Civic Education and Religious Fundamentalism: The Case of God v. John Rawls?', *Ethics*, Vol. 105, April 1995, pp. 468–96.

48. Council of Mosques, *The Muslims and Swann* (Bradford: 1986); Islamic Academy, *Swann Committee Report* (Cambridge: 1985).

49. Ibid. p. 5.

50. J. Habermas, 'Struggles for Recognition in Constitutional States', p. 131.

51. Ibid. p. 143.
52. Ibid. pp. 143–4.
53. Ibid. p. 144.
54. See Chapter 3, p. 54.
55. On this point also see M. Cooke, 'Authenticity and Autonomy: Taylor, Habermas, and the Politics of Recognition', *Political Theory*, Vol. 25, No. 2, April 1997, pp. 258–88, pp. 278–9.
56. For example, Catholics who strongly oppose abortion on moral grounds are unlikely to support legislation which views abortion as a question of individual choice.
57. W. Kymlicka, 'Two Models of Pluralism and Tolerance', *Analyse und Kritik*, Vol. 13, 1992, pp. 33–56. For a discussion of the millet system and other examples see pp. 35–40.
58. For a discussion of this point see N. O'Sullivan, 'Difference and the Concept of the Political in Contemporary Political Philosophy', *Political Studies*, Vol. 45, No. 4, September 1997, pp. 739–54.

Part III: Liberalism and Group Rights

Liberalism and Group Rights

In the light of the significance advocates of a 'politics of difference' attach to the recognition of particular identities, it is not surprising that demands for group-differentiated cultural and social rights have played a prominent role in debates regarding cultural and social diversity. Group-differentiated rights can take the form of either personal or corporate cultural rights.[1] Whereas personal cultural rights apply to group members individually, corporate group rights are exercised by the collectivity as a whole. For example, while the campaign by French Muslim girls to be permitted to wear traditional headscarfs in schools is best seen as a demand for a personal cultural right, the desire of many indigenous people for special rights to control the use of ancestral lands constitutes a call for corporate cultural rights. After all, control here is usually not exercised by individual members of the group, but by the governing bodies and authorities who act for and are recognised by the group as a whole. Given the traditional liberal emphasis upon individual rights, many liberals view demands for corporate cultural rights with suspicion. Thus, although Habermas acknowledges that *individuals* may be entitled to special cultural and social rights, his approach does not readily allow for the recognition of rights that are to be exercised by the community as a whole.

Yet, while liberals such as Habermas reassert the traditional liberal conception of rights as entitlements of individuals, others have acknowledged the special status of collectivities and, consequently, have sought to develop a distinctly liberal account of group rights, which can accommodate the desire for both personal and corporate group rights. These liberals typically recognise the importance to individual identity and well-being of collective activity, such as the participation in cultural festivities and rituals, and the significance of goods that are only collectively available, such as the right of a community to self-determination. Here it is helpful to distinguish between theories which ground group rights in traditional liberal commitments to equality of respect, individual freedom and state neutrality, and accounts which maintain that a liberal state can actively pursue particular collective goals and support specific conceptions of the good, provided it respects 'the basic rights of citizens who have different commitments'.[2] While advocates of the first position maintain that the state should not pursue any collective goals, proponents of the second position believe that a liberal state can legitimately abandon the principle of neutrality in order to secure the survival of a particular culture. Whereas Chapter 5 will focus on the work of three prominent liberal writers – Will Kymlicka, Chandran Kukathas and Joseph Raz – whose approaches to the question of group rights are informed by a commitment to the traditional liberal values of individual liberty and equality of respect, Chapter 6 considers the idea – developed by Charles Taylor and Michael Walzer – that the liberal state can promote a distinctive conception of the good, provided it respects the basic rights of citizens who wish to pursue a different conception of the good.

Notes and Reference

1. For this distinction see G. B. Levey, 'Equality, Autonomy, and Cultural Rights', *Political Theory*, Vol. 25, No. 2, April 1997, pp. 215–48.
2. M. Walzer, 'Comment', in C. Taylor and A. Gutmann (eds), *Multiculturalism and the "Politics of Recognition"* (Princeton: Princeton University Press, 1992) pp. 99–103, p. 99.

Chapter 5: Liberty, Equality and Group Rights

In recent years many minority groups and cultural communities have demanded the right to control their own affairs. Indeed, demands for 'self-government' have been a key element of the 'politics of difference'. Thus, for instance, national minorities, such as the Basques and Catalans in Spain, have sought greater regional autonomy. In a similar vein, many indigenous people, like, for instance the North American Pueblo Indians, have demanded not only the right to maintain their traditional tribal structures, but have also called for greater control over government policies that affect their way of life. Finally, religious minorities, such as the Hutterites and the Amish, have tried to maintain their distinctive way of life. These claims have proved particularly problematic for liberals, since demands for 'self-government' frequently imply corporate cultural rights, that is to say rights that are exercised not by individual members of a particular community, but by the collective as a whole. At first glance, such demands for corporate cultural rights appear to run counter to the traditional liberal vision of the state as protector and promoter of individual rights and interests. As the discussion in Chapter 2 indicated, this emphasis upon the individual is widely regarded as a direct consequence of the values and commitments definitive of the liberal position. Since all individuals are 'ends in themselves' and therefore have equal moral status, all deserve to be treated with equal concern and respect by government. Consequently liberals have maintained that all individuals should have the same fundamental rights and entitlements. This ensures that 'individual citizens stand in the same direct relationship to the state' and, thus, are incorporated 'universally'.[1]

This emphasis upon the individual has continued to inform many liberal responses to the 'politics of difference'. Thus, while liberals such as Habermas accept that a commitment to genuine equality may entail special cultural and social rights, they stress that such rights should be conceptualised as individual rights. Yet many of the claims made by minority groups not only entail demands for individual rights but also appear to imply corporate cultural rights. For example, a number of indigenous groups want traditional tribal homelands to be owned and administered collectively. Thus, whereas liberalism has typically emphasised the idea of universal incorporation, many minorities seek to be incorporated into the state not as individuals but consociationally that is as members of a particular cultural community.

These demands have led to a lively debate among liberals, provoking a wide variety of responses. While some liberals attempt to reassert the liberal commitment to individual rights, others acknowledge the special status of collectivities and, consequently, seek to develop a distinctly liberal account of group rights. One of the most influential arguments in favour of a liberal theory of group rights is closely associated with the work of Will Kymlicka. In *Liberalism, Community and Culture* and *Multicultural Citizenship*,[2] Kymlicka seeks to establish that, contrary to the widely held view that group rights are incompatible with the liberal emphasis upon individual freedom, autonomy and equality, these liberal ideas actually entail certain group-differentiated rights so as to protect minorities from external pressures. For Kymlicka, secure cultural membership is vital to individual well-being and provides the basis for the effective exercise of individual autonomy. Members of minority groups, however, frequently find themselves disadvantaged in relation to the good of cultural membership. Given that a liberal state committed to equality of respect should not favour any particular conception of the good, the liberal state should grant special cultural and social rights to minority groups, so as to compensate them for the disadvantages they incur.

While Kymlicka's conception of multicultural citizenship offers an innovative response to the question of group rights, it is questionable whether his approach can adequately account for the concerns of liberals or advocates of diversity. Not only are liberals liable to doubt whether group rights constitute the most appropriate form of compensation for the disadvantages Kymlicka identifies, they may also fear that group rights will undermine individual autonomy. In the final analysis Kymlicka's vision of a culturally-embedded identity is only compatible with autonomy if the distinction he draws between the structure of a culture and its character can be maintained. Yet, in the eyes of critics, this distinction simply cannot be sustained. Furthermore, while Kymlicka stresses the link between secure cultural membership and self-respect, feminist critics such as Okin have been quick to point out that the degree to which a culture supports an individual's self-respect depends to a considerable extent upon the role the individual occupies within that culture. This may constitute a particularly acute problem for women who in many traditional cultures have not been highly valued.

However, while liberals will be critical of the impact of group rights upon individual autonomy, advocates of diversity have questioned whether Kymlicka's commitment to autonomy is compatible with genuine diversity. For Kymlicka, the promotion of individual autonomy at once provides the rationale for and sets limits to cultural rights. Consequently, on liberal grounds cultural groups can only legitimately expect support in their attempts to maintain themselves, if these supportive measures do not undermine individual freedom and autonomy. In the face of thick multiculturalism, advocates of diversity fear that this emphasis upon liberal values will threaten the long-term viability of cultural groups who value autonomy and individual liberty much less than liberals. Thus, in the eyes of these critics, Kymlicka's belief in the overriding value of autonomy is ultimately incompatible with the aim of neutrality.

Given the difficulties which surround Kymlicka's attempt to reconcile a distinctly liberal theory of group-differentiated rights with a commitment to state neutrality, Joseph Raz's openly perfectionist approach to the question of group rights potentially provides a more convincing account of the nature and limitations of a liberal theory of group rights. However, while Raz's account allows him to offer a more realistic assessment of the limits and character of a liberal theory of group rights, he remains too optimistic about the possibility of generating a common culture grounded in liberal multiculturalism.

In the light of the failure by theorists such as Kymlicka and Raz to establish a viable liberal theory of group rights, libertarians such as Chandran Kukathas have questioned the very need for a theory of group rights. While Kukathas, like Kymlicka, endorses a version of liberal neutrality, he believes that all legitimate demands for self-government on the part of minority groups and cultural communities can be accommodated via a robust account of the individual right to freedom of association. However, it is questionable whether such an approach is compatible with either liberalism or genuine diversity. While liberals will fear that his approach grants too much power to the collective and fails to ensure that individuals are equipped to exercise their right of exit from the group, non-liberal minorities are likely to view Kukathas's conception of cultural groups as voluntary associations as a misconstrual of the value of cultural membership, and as a threat to the long-term survival of at least some minority groups.

The problems inherent in the approaches advocated by Kymlicka, Raz and Kukathas suggest that attempts to respond to demands for group rights via an appeal to the liberal values of freedom and equality of respect are liable to encounter objections from both liberals and advocates of diversity. In the light of their concerns about the impact of the demands and expectations of the collective upon individual autonomy and liberty, liberal critics will reject the link Kymlicka, Raz and Kukathas wish to establish between a commitment to liberal values and a right to self-government on the part of minority groups. On the other hand, non-liberal minorities will regard the emphasis on individual liberty and autonomy as a potential threat to the long-term viability of non-liberal minorities. However, if individual well-being is as intricately linked to secure cultural membership as Kymlicka and Raz propose, the continued viability of non-liberal minorities will be vital to the sense of self-respect of their members.

Will Kymlicka: Multicultural Citizenship

Contrary to the widely held view that group rights are incompatible with the liberal emphasis on individual freedom, autonomy and equality, Kymlicka argues that these liberal ideals actually imply certain group-differentiated rights. Here Kymlicka focuses on: 1. the relationship between individual freedom and group membership, and 2. the connection between group rights and the guarantee of equality for minorities.

For Kymlicka, individual freedom is in important ways tied to group membership, since a person's 'capacity to make meaningful choices depends on access to a societal culture.'[3] A societal culture encompasses the full range of public and private human activities, including social, educational, religious, recreational and economic life.[4] Therefore, to his mind a societal culture provides the individual with a framework of values, beliefs and institutions which enable her to render the choices open to her meaningful. It is through her culture's language and history that an individual becomes aware of the options available to her and their significance. Membership of a societal culture is therefore a 'precondition of making intelligent judgements about how to lead our lives.'[5] Given that a societal culture provides individuals with a set of choices and assigns value to these choices, it is important that the cultural context within which an individual is raised remains stable. If a societal culture decays or is discriminated against, the options available to its members will diminish and become less attractive. Furthermore, given that cultural membership plays an important role in people's self-identity, a person's self-respect is closely linked to the esteem in which their group is held. As individuals can only develop meaningful identities and life-plans within the context of shared cultural traditions, Kymlicka argues that liberals should seek to support societal cultures. Since people are bound via important ties such as language and socialisation to their own cultural community, and thus cannot readily be transplanted from one culture to another, liberals should not merely attempt to provide individuals with a cultural society, but should respect people's existing cultural membership.

Although Kymlicka regards a stable societal culture as vital to individual well-being, he stresses that members of a cultural community should be free to 'modify the character of the culture, should they find its traditional ways of life no longer worthwhile.'[6] Here Kymlicka invites us to distinguish between the underlying cultural structures and the specific cultural character of a community. The cultural structure of a community refers to the distinctive ordering of the roles within that culture, while the character of a culture is a reflection of a culture's 'norms, values and their attendant institutions (e.g. membership in churches, political parties etc.)'.[7] Most importantly, changes in a culture's character do not undermine the stability of its structure. Thus, the need for a stable cultural structure is compatible with the freedom of members to revise a culture's norms values and traditions.[8] If members of a cultural community choose from within their stable context of choice to alter the character of their culture, this does not signal the demise of this culture, but merely reflects the autonomy of its members. So for Kymlicka '[l]iberal values require both individual freedom and a secure cultural context from which to choose.'[9]

Kymlicka argues that, contrary to the claims of many contemporary liberals, historically liberalism has been sensitive to the aspirations of cultural communities. While contemporary liberals tend to emphasise the importance of equal, universal citizenship and, thus, are inclined to 'play down the importance of membership in a cultural community',[10] earlier liberals such as Mill, Green, Hobhouse and Dewey were keenly aware of the link between secure cultural membership and individual liberty. Not only did these writers acknowledge the importance of a sense of community, they also recognised that cultural minorities may require special protections. Kymlicka proposes that contemporary liberals have lost touch with the insights of this earlier liberal tradition due to their failure to appreciate the complex relationship between political and cultural community. While the political community constitutes the arena in which fellow citizens 'exercise the rights and responsibilities entailed by the framework of liberal justice',[11] the cultural community is the place 'within which individuals form and revise their aims and ambitions'.[12] To respect individuals as fellow members of the political community implies granting all individuals equal citizenship rights. However, to respect individuals as members of distinct cultural communities requires recognition of the importance of their specific cultural heritage and the legitimacy of their claims to have their culture protected. While, according to Kymlicka, contemporary liberals often implicitly assume that the boundaries of the political and the cultural community coincide, this is not necessarily the case. In culturally-diverse societies, the two types of respect owed to individuals may impose contradictory demands. Thus, in a culturally-diverse society, liberals committed to the idea of equality of respect will need to balance claims for cultural recognition vis-à-vis a commitment to equal rights.

Confronted with this dilemma, Kymlicka maintains that liberals committed to equality of respect must bear in mind the vulnerability of minority cultures. Since government decisions on languages, cultural identities, public holidays and state symbols inevitably promote certain cultural values and identities, minorities are at risk of being unfairly disadvantaged in the cultural marketplace. Minorities will frequently be in danger of being 'outbid or outvoted on resources and policies that are crucial to the survival of their societal cultures'.[13] Unlike the majority culture, minority cultures are vulnerable to the decisions of the majority. Consequently, members of a minority culture may need 'to spend their resources on securing the cultural membership which makes sense of their lives', while members of the majority culture effectively obtain the good of cultural membership for free. Members of minority cultures suffer this disadvantage regardless of the particular life choices they make. Given the liberal commitment to equality of respect, Kymlicka argues that minority cultures deserve to be compensated for this disadvantage by granting them special group-differentiated rights. After all, while from a liberal perspective people are responsible for differences in resources that arise due to their own choices, many liberals accept that individuals who are disadvantaged due to circumstances, such as social environment or natural endowment, deserve to be compensated. Since members of minority cultures are disadvantaged independently of the particular life-choices they make, Kymlicka maintains that cultural membership is best seen as an aspect of people's circumstances rather than their choices. From this perspective, granting minorities special group-differentiated rights promotes fairness between groups.

Here Kymlicka draws a distinction between internal restrictions and external protections. While the former deals with the relationship between the group and its own members, the latter involves the claims of a group against the larger society. Since liberals value cultural membership because it enables individuals effectively to exercise their autonomy, groups may not seek to place internal restrictions on their members. Such restrictions would undermine individual freedom and are therefore not compatible with liberal principles. Cultural groups can only legitimately expect support in their attempts to maintain themselves if such measures do not undermine individual freedom and autonomy. Thus, according to Kymlicka, all children have to be encouraged to learn about other ways of life, all individuals must be free to abandon their cultural groups, and cultural groups themselves ought to be open to change brought about by co-existence with other groups, rather than attempt to preserve their culture in some pure form. To Kymlicka this commitment to individual freedom and autonomy implies not only that individuals have a right to re-assess moral values and traditional ways of life, but also that provisions, such as a liberal education, should be made to enhance these capacities. Hence, on this account, attempts by minorities, such as those of some North American Pueblo Indian communities, to ensure the survival of their way of life by denying their members the right to freedom of religion are not legitimate.[14] Theocratic groups such as the Pueblo Indians have at times discriminated against members who profess religious beliefs that deviate from the official religion of the band. For Kymlicka, such measures constitute an unacceptable restriction of the freedom of group members to use and interpret their own cultural heritage. However, while groups may not place internal restrictions on their group members, they are entitled to seek external protection to shield their members from the economic and political power of larger society. He recognises that such rights to external protection may place restrictions on the rights of members of the majority. However, such restrictions must be weighed against the benefit of a secure societal culture for the members of the minority. For example, in order to maintain the societal culture of indigenous peoples it may be necessary to place restrictions upon the rights of non-indigenous people to settle, own property and vote in aboriginal territories. Although this clearly restricts the citizenship rights of the majority, such measures are often vital to protect indigenous cultures and as such, according to Kymlicka, are justified.

    Kymlicka's conception of multicultural citizenship clearly offers an innovative attempt to formulate a distinctly liberal theory of group rights. However, it is questionable whether his approach can account adequately for the concerns of either liberals or advocates of diversity. Apart from liberal worries regarding the idea of compensation, the main difficulties inherent in Kymlicka's account of multicultural citizenship relate to the idea of autonomy. However, although his conceptualisation of autonomy is potentially problematic from the perspective of both liberalism and thick multiculturalism, proponents of these two perspectives are liable to find Kymlicka's notion of group rights objectionable for rather different reasons. While liberals will be critical of the impact of group rights upon individual autonomy, advocates of diversity will question whether, in the light of thick multiculturalism, Kymlicka's commitment to autonomy is compatible with genuine diversity.

The liberal critique

Although Kymlicka rests his defence of group-differentiated rights upon the liberal principles of equality and autonomy, it is doubtful whether these principles are compatible with the idea of group rights. For Kymlicka, the liberal idea of equality of respect implies group-differentiated rights, since such rights are vital to compensate members of minority groups for disadvantages in their circumstances. However, while liberals may well be ready to acknowledge the significance of cultural membership, it is questionable whether, from a liberal perspective, group-differentiated rights are the most appropriate form of compensation for individuals who are disadvantaged with regard to the good of cultural membership. As Kukathas notes, for liberals any deviation from the principle of equal basic rights can only be justified if additional 'derivative rights' are 'in principle, available to all individuals who share the similar circumstances that such rights are supposed to address'.[15] Whereas the liberal commitment to equality may well entail granting all blind people certain 'derivative rights', it is doubtful whether group-differentiated rights for ethnic and cultural minorities can be justified in this manner. Like all groups, minority groups are not internally homogeneous. Hence not all members of the minority group will be equally disadvantaged vis-à-vis all members of the majority group. Indeed some members of the minority may be 'better endowed with resources than some outsiders'.[16] After all in modern societies 'the sense of cultural precariousness is very widespread'.[17] Members of majority cultures also frequently experience intense disruptions of their culture involving profound institutional changes, which 'cut people off from crucial forms of cultural membership'.[18] Thus, for instance, for Walker,[19] the dislocation suffered by many traditional farming communities in North America is comparable with the pressures and sense of disruption experienced by cultural minorities. Given that individual circumstances vary widely, group rights may simply be too crude a measure to safeguard individual equality. However, even if compensation for specific groups could be justified, it is doubtful whether such measures could, on liberal grounds, be restricted to national minorities in the manner Kymlicka envisages. Not only are many ethnic minorities potentially capable of meeting Kymlicka's criteria of a societal culture (see Chapter 2) and thus on this account may legitimately seek compensation, many members of majority cultures may regard themselves as equally disadvantaged. Yet, if group-differentiated rights were to be extended to include groups such as, for instance, North American farming communities, any set of group-differentiated rights would be liable to be so complex that it would be difficult to administer. Furthermore, if group-differentiated rights are to be sensitive to the changing circumstances of various groups, the specific rights granted would need to be regularly re-assessed and revised. The question of which groups would qualify for compensation is further complicated by the amorphous and manifold character of cultural membership. While Kymlicka bases his case for group rights upon a comparison between socio-economic inequalities and cultural disadvantages, it is questionable whether these two forms of inequality can be treated in the same manner. While socio-economic status can be measured and compared, Kymlicka himself acknowledges that outsiders can judge neither the current state of a culture nor its potential. However, as Levey observes, '[i]f we cannot judge the condition of a culture . . . how is it that we can ascribe vulnerability at all?'[20]

One of the distinctly liberal features of Kymlicka's conception of multicultural citizenship is his depiction of cultural membership as the context that facilitates the effective exercise of autonomy. Thus, on Kymlicka's account, liberalism requires both secure cultural membership and freedom of choice. To attain both these goods it is vital that the distinction Kymlicka draws between the structure and the character of a culture can be maintained. Only if changes in the character of a culture can be shown not to undermine the good of secure cultural membership can individuals be said to be simultaneously autonomous and culturally embedded. However this distinction between the structure and the character of a culture is rather implausible. As Bricker notes:

the structure/character distinction is a distinction without a difference. 'Structure' allegedly consists of an 'ordering' of roles and their associated 'meanings'. 'Character' consists of a culture's 'norms, values and attendant institutions'. In truth Kymlicka is employing two ways of talking about the same thing. If 'attendant institutions' change then the order of the roles that comprise the institution must change because an institution is nothing more than an ordering of roles. If 'norms and values' change then 'meanings' change because norms and values are forms of meaning.[21]

Given the intricate links between the norms, values and institutions of a culture and the pattern of roles a culture provides for its members, it is not possible to draw a clear distinction between these two aspects of a culture.[22] Significant changes in one will inevitably give rise to changes in the other. Yet, if the structure/character distinction cannot be maintained, Kymlicka's account of the relationship between individual identity and cultural membership is no longer plausible. He assumes that although individuals are embedded in their culture's structure, they can nonetheless critically evaluate their culture's character. If, however, the structure/character distinction cannot be sustained, the link Kymlicka proposes between secure cultural membership and autonomy applies to the character of a culture as well as its structure. After all, if individual well-being requires a secure cultural structure, but the structure and character of a culture cannot be separated, any attempt to safe-guard cultural membership will extend to both structure and character. Yet, 'this makes normative reasoning relative to the norms and values of a culture',[23] and thus in liberal terms renders it heteronomous. Furthermore, if the structure/character distinction cannot be sustained, Kymlicka's emphasis upon the need for a stable societal culture implies that cultural groups may be able to make valid claims for group rights whenever the character of a community is threatened.[24] Such attempts to resist all change would leave little room for individuals to interpret and critically assess their cultural heritage, and threaten to undermine individual autonomy. As Beiner observes, Kymlicka 'does not fully face up to the fact that what he is advocating as an entailment of liberalism is assistance for a community to fend off liberalisation of its way of life.'[25]

These fears regarding individual autonomy also undermine the link Kymlicka makes between secure cultural membership and self-respect. While he regards secure cultural membership as vital to an individual's sense of self-respect, he does not consider the impact one's place within one's own culture may have upon the development of self-respect and self-esteem. Because of this oversight Kymlicka fails to consider the position of individuals who are held in low esteem by their cultural group. Here the position of women is particularly troubling. As Okin recognises:

There are many cultures that, though they may not impose their beliefs and practices on others and appear to respect the basic civil and political liberties of women and girls, do not, in practice, especially in the private sphere, treat them with anything like the same concern and respect as men and boys, or allow them to enjoy the same freedom.[26]

Subtle forms of sex-discrimination can be found in all cultures. These are usually exercised within the private sphere in the context of the family, and can range from the expectation that women and girls should perform most of the unpaid labour for the family to a failure to encourage girls to achieve academically. The comparatively low esteem in which women are held in most cultures, and the restrictions cultural expectations tend to place upon women's choices about the kind of lives they should lead, may well undermine women's ability to gain a secure sense of self-respect and thus threaten their ability effectively to exercise their autonomy. While Kymlicka's proposals for group rights offers traditionally disadvantaged groups such as women formal equality in terms of basic civil and political liberties, such formal equality cannot protect low-status groups from more subtle forms of discrimination. Consequently, although low status subgroups may well benefit from measures which protect and support their culture, discrimination ensures that they do not benefit from these measures to the same degree as privileged members of the group. Given that Kymlicka rests his case for group-differentiated rights upon an appeal to equality, he cannot easily ignore the impact of discriminatory practices upon vulnerable subgroups within minorities.

Kymlicka could allay many of the worries expressed by liberal critics by insisting that only those cultures which genuinely promote equality of respect and autonomy deserve to be protected via group rights. Such a move, however, would merely confirm the fears of non-liberal minorities. Whereas liberals are worried about the impact of group rights upon individual autonomy and equality of respect, adherents to non-liberal ways of life fear that a liberal theory of group rights will, in the final analysis, only protect those groups whose values and beliefs are compatible with liberal aspirations. Yet, if individual well-being is as intricately linked to secure cultural membership as Kymlicka proposes, such a failure to protect the viability of non-liberal minority cultures would undermine the self-esteem of their members and thus would violate Kymlicka's commitment to neutrality and equality of respect.

'Deep diversity' and group rights

Although Kymlicka believes that his conception of multicultural citizenship is sensitive to the demands of a wide variety of cultural and ethnic minorities, it is questionable whether his account can accommodate the profound diversity associated with thick multiculturalism. Whereas Kymlicka regards cultural membership as valuable because it enables people effectively to exercise their autonomy, his emphasis upon individual choice is alien to at least some of the groups currently campaigning for recognition. Indeed, groups whose conceptions of the good are at odds with the liberal vision of individual freedom and autonomy may well regard Kymlicka's conception of and limitations to group rights as a threat to their long-term viability. The difficulties here are probably most notable in relation to educational issues. If we regard autonomy as a fundamental human interest, we are, according to Kymlicka, inevitably 'led in the direction of a society which requires a broad liberal education of children'.[27] However the controversies that have surrounded educational initiatives that encourage liberal virtues such as critical rationality and individual choice suggest that non-liberal minorities may view such an education as deeply problematic. For example, within the context of the British multicultural education debate outlined in Chapter 3, Muslim organisations such as the Council of Mosques[28] and the Islamic Academy[29] have been critical of a typically liberal commitment to open-mindedness and individual choice in the context of religious education. Thus, the Islamic Academy maintains that an emphasis on open-mindedness in the religious education of Muslim children fails to recognise the special significance of the Qur'an as the revealed word of God and 'will create doubt in the minds of children about faith in divine revelation'.[30] Furthermore, in the opinion of the Council of Mosques, to portray faith as a question of individual choice is to misconstrue the meaning of faith. Muslims, like many believers, regard faith as a gift from God, requiring not so much rational individual choice, as emotional involvement and a readiness to suspend disbelief. Subsequently, the Council of Mosques has emphasised the significance of religious instruction aimed at generating a strong commitment to one's faith. As the worries expressed by the Council of Mosques and the Islamic Academy indicate, cultures that do not share liberalism's belief in the overriding value of autonomy therefore pose a dilemma for Kymlicka: while he regards secure cultural membership as vital to individual freedom and autonomy, a liberal education that seeks to develop the skills and virtues essential to the exercise of autonomy may well undermine the viability of certain cultures.

This clash between individual freedom and group values should not be seen as an isolated instance. In addition to the conflict of ultimate values outlined above, many of the measures regarded by minority groups as essential to the preservation of their culture and identity cannot be readily accommodated within Kymlicka's distinction between internal restrictions and external protections. Various measures demanded by minorities to protect them from external pressures also require significant restrictions on the individual freedom and autonomy of group members. For example, collective ownership of traditional homelands or restrictions on the sale of property held by group members may be essential in order to secure the long-term viability and integrity of a particular culture. Such provisions were integral to many of the native reserves established in the USA and Canada, and many native American tribes in these countries have campaigned to uphold these provisions or, where they perceive it necessary, to establish them. Indeed, Kymlicka acknowledges that historical evidence suggests that common ownership may well be the most effective way to protect indigenous communities from the greater economic and political power of the larger society. After all, as Kymlicka notes, 'one of the most common strategies that European settlers used for breaking open indigenous lands for settlement was to replace traditional communal ownership with individualised title'.[31] However, measures such as communal ownership may place significant limitations on the freedom of individual group members. For example, without the possibility of freely realising their assets, individuals may find it very difficult to leave the group. This not only restricts autonomy but may also undermine the self-respect of members of a group who wish to leave. For an individual to be denied control over resources, such as property, which enable her to make effective choices, will not enhance her self-esteem.[32] This sense of disrespect is liable to be felt particularly keenly, if the individual regards these resources as the product of her own labour.

The difficulties here are clearly illustrated by the problems encountered by religious communities such as the Hutterites, whose life-style is based upon common ownership. For example, in the mid 1960s several members of one Hutterite community, who had been expelled from both the Hutterite church and the colony for renouncing Hutterite religious beliefs and practices, demanded that they be given their share of the colony's assets. The case eventually reached the Supreme Court of Canada, which in 1970, in the case of Hofer vs Hofer, ruled in favour of the colony. In his ruling Justice Richie maintained that since the principle of communal property is fundamental to the Hutterite community, and since membership of the church is inseparable from membership of the colony, the members had been rightfully expelled from both church and colony and could not expect a share of the colony's assets.[33] Thus, according to the Supreme Court ruling, the principle of religious freedom must be respected even if this limits individual freedom and autonomy. For Kymlicka, however, such a stance is incompatible with the principle of individual freedom of conscience, which demands that individuals must be free rationally to revise their beliefs and commitments. To demand that apostates leave the community without taking a share of its assets is to place significant restrictions upon the freedom of members of the community. However, to impose such liberal principles upon communities such as the Hutterite would in the long-run destroy the communal nature of colony life. This conflict between cultural survival and individual autonomy is not limited to small religious communities or tribal societies. The language laws of Quebec, for instance, not only ensure that francophones are able to use French in public but actually limit the use of English in certain spheres. This restricts the freedom of francophones to freely choose to speak English. As the remainder of Canada is predominantly English-speaking, this may place significant restrictions on the mobility of French-speaking Quebecois.

These difficulties suggest that in the final analysis Kymlicka's emphasis upon individual freedom and autonomy is incompatible with the idea of state neutrality. To conceive of the good life in terms of self-determination implies that people must have access to the social conditions that enable them freely and rationally to question their commitments. However to pursue such a goal is to depart from the principle of neutrality. As Barry notes:

a conception of the good as autonomy does not imply that the pursuit of all substantive conceptions of the good is equally valuable. Only those conceptions that have the right origins – those that have come about in ways that meet the criteria for self-determined belief – can form a basis for activity that is valued.[34]

Kymlicka is therefore mistaken to assume that respect for people's self-determination implies neutrality on the part of the state. The limits to group rights inherent in the idea of autonomy ensure that Kymlicka's conception of cultural pluralism has a 'built in liberalising tendency'.[35] Indeed, for Chaplin, one of the most striking features of Kymlicka's discussion of group rights is that 'he fails to recognise . . . that liberalism is *itself* a distinctive cultural community'.[36] Liberalism does not constitute a neutral framework within which different cultural communities can live side by side, but is the expression of a distinctive set of values, beliefs and aspirations. Kymlicka's failure to recognise liberalism's specific character leads him to misconstrue the aims and aspirations of many of the groups demanding recognition. Frequently, such demands for recognition are not driven by the desire to safeguard individual freedom but by the wish to ensure the long-term survival of a particular way of life. However, on Kymlicka's account of group-differentiated rights this aim cannot be secured.[37]

In his more recent work[38] Kymlicka has attempted to respond to these fears by drawing a distinction between a defensible liberal theory of minority rights and imposing that theory upon non-liberal minorities. While practices that restrict individual freedom cannot be justified on the basis of a liberal theory of group rights, Kymlicka believes that, unless the minority commits gross and systematic violations of human rights, liberals should not impose liberal principles upon reluctant minorities. Since minorities may well perceive attempts to impose liberal principles as a form of aggression, such attempts are liable to backfire. Furthermore, 'liberal institutions can only really work if liberal beliefs have been internalised by the members of the self-governing society.'[39] Thus, by their very nature, liberal principles cannot be imposed externally. Also minorities are frequently protected by treaties or agreements that stipulate the terms under which the minority was incorporated into the state. According to Kymlicka, liberals have a duty to honour such agreements. However, this is not to suggest that liberals do not have a right or a responsibility to speak out if a minority conducts its affairs in an illiberal manner. Thus liberals can offer various incentives for liberal reforms and can give support to reformers inside the culture who wish to liberalise the culture from within. Finally, liberals can promote liberal principles by developing and strengthening international mechanisms for protecting human rights. After all, minorities which resist state interference may nonetheless be willing to be bound by international agreements.

However, it is questionable whether this distinction between a liberal theory of group rights and its imposition can allay the fears of either liberals or advocates of diversity. Given liberalism's fundamental commitment to the interests and well-being of individuals, liberals have typically sought to protect individuals from harm. Here the worries expressed by Kymlicka's liberal critics, such as Okin, suggest that many liberals will view such a reluctance to interfere with illiberal practices as incompatible with a commitment to the principles of equality and autonomy. After all, many liberals feel that the state is justified in interfering in the private sphere to stop seriously illiberal practices which discriminate against comparatively powerless groups such as children.[40] However, while liberals may feel that Kymlicka is unduly reluctant to interfere in non-liberal practices, proponents of genuine diversity will object that his long-term aim of liberalising illiberal cultures is incompatible with genuine diversity. To liberalise an illiberal culture implies profound changes in the culture's norms, values and institutions. Given the intricate links between a culture's norms, values and institutions and the pattern of roles a culture provides for its members, such profound changes in a culture's character would also transform its structure. Thus, it is simply implausible to claim, as Kymlicka does, that it is possible gradually to liberalise illiberal cultures without substantially altering their very essence. Therefore, in the final analysis, Kymlicka's conception of multicultural citizenship remains problematic from the perspective of both liberals and advocates of diversity.

Joseph Raz: Liberal Perfectionism and Group Rights

Given Kymlicka's failure to ground a distinctly liberal theory of group rights in a commitment to state neutrality, Joseph Raz's openly perfectionist approach to the question of group rights potentially provides a more convincing account of the nature and limitations of a liberal theory of group rights. Like Kymlicka, Raz believes that the liberal commitment to autonomy implies group rights. However, his acknowledgement of liberalism's perfectionist streak leads Raz to adopt a more cautious approach to the idea of multiculturalism. Raz refers to multiculturalism as a political and ethical problem and maintains that in a society characterised by genuine value pluralism conflict is inevitable. This leads him to reject the idea that liberalism can offer an ideal resolution to such conflicts. The key to Raz's pessimism lies in his acknowledgement of the significance and pervasiveness of cultural membership. The common character and common culture of cultural groups (including some religious groups) 'encompass many, varied and important aspects of life' and define 'styles of life, types of activities, occupation, pursuit and relation-ship'.[41] Given that different cultures are informed by and give expression to different values and beliefs, conflict is inevitable. Thus, even if we appreciate in the abstract the value of other ways of life 'this acknowledgement coexists with, and cannot replace, the feeling of rejection and dismissiveness. Tension is an inevitable concomitant of value pluralism'.[42]

Yet Raz's emphasis on the significance of cultural membership also makes him sensitive to demands for group rights. Like Kymlicka, Raz believes that cultural membership plays an important role in the well-being of its members. In the first instance an individual's identity is determined at least in part by their culture. Cultural membership 'is one of the prime facts by which people are identified' and 'one of the primary clues for people generally in interpreting the conduct of others'.[43] For Raz, the cultural group we belong to determines our horizons and opportunities and facilitates personal relationships. If a culture decays, is persecuted or is discriminated against, 'the options and opportunities open to its members will shrink, become less attractive and their pursuit less likely to be successful'.[44] Consequent-ly, Raz maintains that cultural groups should be supported in their attempt to ensure their continued existence and vitality. Here Raz advocates policies which offer legal protection to the customs and practices of different groups, allow for public support of cultural institutions and give public space to all cultural groups. Furthermore, parents should be allowed to educate their children in accordance with their own culture, provided the children are also encouraged to be familiar with and respect the history and traditions of other cultures in the country.

However, like Kymlicka, Raz believes that measures to promote cultural continuity must not be allowed to undermine individual autonomy. For both writers it is the contribution cultural membership makes to individual well-being and prosperity which makes it of value, and which sets the limits to the support cultural groups can expect in their attempt to perpetuate themselves. But, whereas Kymlicka argues that such a commitment to autonomy is compatible with the idea of state neutrality, Raz recognises that liberalism itself constitutes a distinctive cultural community. Given that our identity, goals and opportunities are to a significant extent shaped by our environment, Raz maintains that individuals who live in a liberal, autonomy-supporting society can only prosper if they lead an autonomous life. After all, the opportunities offered by such an environment are quite distinct from those available in a social environment that does not value autonomy. Within a liberal society a culture that undermines or seriously restricts the autonomy of its members is liable to impair the well-being of those who belong to it. Cultural groups can therefore only expect support as long as they respect the autonomy of their members. Consequently, Raz stresses that individual members have to be free to abandon their cultural group and that cultural groups should be open to change brought about by coexistence with other groups rather than attempt to preserve their culture in some pure form. As he acknowledges, this emphasis on individual autonomy and on cultural change and adaptation is likely to bring his conception of liberal multiculturalism into conflict with the very groups whose continued existence it aims to ensure. Nonetheless, Raz believes that the importance liberal multiculturalism attaches to toleration and respect, together with the fact that members of all cultural groups do share the same economic environment and belong to the same political society, will be sufficient to generate a common culture strong enough to ensure social stability.

Yet, despite his recognition of the inevitability of conflict, Raz appears ultimately to be too optimistic. On the basis of his own analysis, liberal multiculturalism only respects cultures insofar as their continued existence fulfils liberal purposes. Thus, while liberalism will stress respect and tolerance, such toleration will always be highly conditional. Consequently, there remains a potential for substantial conflict. The difficulties inherent here are evident in Raz's discussion of the status of non-autonomy-valuing subgroups in a liberal society. He maintains that such subgroups should be tolerated provided their culture is morally worthy and they enable their members to have adequate and satisfying lives. However, on his account of the relationship between individual well-being and the wider social environment, individuals can only thrive by pursuing an autonomous lifestyle. Hence, a Razian liberal will be inclined to maintain that in comparison to the opportunities provided by the dominant, autonomy-valuing culture, the life offered by such groups is impoverished and unrewarding. In this instance, Raz maintains such subgroups should be regarded as less satisfying and should be gradually assimilated. Therefore, ultimately most non-autonomous subgroups would be subject to assimilation.

Furthermore, Raz's own account of the pervasiveness of cultural membership suggests that, as 'ways of life', cultures may well have their own distinct political and economic practices and patterns of organisation. For example, numerous Muslim writers, such as S. Akhtar[45] and A. L. Tibawi,[46] have stressed the all-embracing nature of Islam. Since Islamic teaching aims to integrate political, social and economic life, Islam does not recognise the separation between religious and political affairs central to the liberal perception of the political arena. From this perspective liberalism's preoccupation with individual freedom threatens to rob religion of its social and political significance. As a theologico-political doctrine Islam therefore challenges some of liberalism's most fundamental assumptions about the relationship between revelation and politics.[47] This suggests that rather than offering a mechanism for social integration, the dominant economic and political practices of liberal societies could easily give rise to tension. After all, if cultures are 'ways of life', then the political and economic aspect of a culture will need to be acknowledged if that culture is to be able to flourish.

Unlike Kymlicka's attempt to ground group rights in a commitment to neutrality, Raz's openly perfectionist approach allows him to readily acknowledge the limits and character of a theory of group rights grounded in the liberal principles of autonomy and equality. However, ultimately Raz remains too optimistic about the possibility of generating a shared common culture grounded in liberal multiculturalism. In the final analysis his theory of group rights leads Raz to support policies of assimilation. Given that many non-liberal minorities are clearly committed to ensuring the long-term survival of their culture, such moves are liable to be met with fierce opposition.

Chandran Kukathas: Multiculturalism and Freedom of Association

In the light of the difficulties which surround Kymlicka's and Raz's attempts to develop a distinctly liberal theory of group rights via an appeal to the principles of autonomy and equality of respect, libertarians such as Chandran Kukathas have questioned the very need for a liberal theory of group rights. While, like Kymlicka, Kukathas endorses a version of liberal neutrality, he rejects the commitment to equality which shapes Kymlicka's response to the 'politics of difference'. For Kukathas the fact of human diversity ensures that equality remains unattainable. While diversity implies that people view and value equality differently, equality demands that we know which bundles of goods are to be equalised. As the difficulties which surround Kymlicka's approach suggest, even a more modest goal of eliminating certain important inequalities between groups remains problematic in the light of the diverse values and goals groups pursue and the complex character of intra-group relations. Thus Kukathas concludes that equality and diversity are incompatible, as attempts to ensure group equality inevitably lead to significant changes in the structure of diversity. To address the potential conflicts and tensions that inevitably arise due to human diversity, Kukathas proposes a conception of liberalism grounded in a fundamental commitment to individual liberty of conscience and, subsequently, freedom of association. In his opinion a robust account of an individual's right to freedom of conscience and association can accommodate many of the demands for self-government on the part of minority groups and cultural communities.

Kukathas maintains that liberals must retain their traditional commitment to the moral primacy of the individual, since groups by their very nature cannot provide an adequate basis for moral and political settlements. Groups are not fixed and unchanging entities. On the contrary, the formation of groups, and the boundaries between groups, reflect environmental influences and 'tend to shift with the political context'.[48] Thus, for example, the birth of new nation states frequently gives rise to new cleavages based upon new group identities. Furthermore, cultural groups are far from homogeneous and conflicts of interest within cultures are common. To grant groups rights would simply affirm present power structures and favour existing majorities. Thus, from a liberal perspective, minorities and cultural communities are best seen as associations of individuals. Hence, for liberals, 'collectives matter only because they are essential for the well-being of the individual.'[49]

According to Kukathas, this emphasis upon the individual does not imply that liberals will 'press for assimilation or integration of cultures or find communalism unacceptable'.[50] On the contrary, given the liberal regard for freedom of conscience, individuals must be free to associate with one another and live according to the communal practices they consider acceptable. Thus the practices of cultural communities should be respected 'not because the culture has the right to be preserved but because individuals should be free to associate: to form communities and to live by the terms of those associations'.[51] In line with his belief in the limited state, Kukathas maintains that a liberal polity is best regarded as an association of individuals and groups who live together under the law, but who pursue a wide variety of different ends and do not seek a deep social or political unity.[52] This emphasis upon freedom of association also implies that individuals must be free to leave a community should they no longer wish to live by the terms of the association. Although Kukathas accepts that most individuals are born into cultural communities and thus do not choose their cultural membership, he maintains that in as far as the members of an association recognise the terms of the association and the authority that upholds them as legitimate, cultural communities can be regarded as voluntary associations. While the preferences of members will undoubtedly have been shaped by the community they were born into, what matters is that people are free to act in accordance with the preferences they happen to hold, regardless of whether or not these preferences were formed endogenously.

As Kukathas acknowledges, such a robust defence of freedom of association may grant cultural communities a considerable amount of authority over individual members. Since his approach places no restrictions upon the character of the association, it does not require that communities adopt liberal values and norms. Cultural communities may choose to be quite illiberal. As long as members of a minority or cultural community wish to continue to live by their beliefs, the wider society has no right to interfere. Thus, for example, according to Kukathas, '[t]he wider society has no right to require particular standards or systems of education within such cultural groups or force their schools to promote the dominant culture'.[53] Furthermore, he insists that the costs and risk of exit to individual members do not affect their right to leave a community. Thus the right to exit is not diminished if the cost of exit, in terms of leaving behind family, friends, or property, is extremely high or the risk, due to lack of skills or knowledge, is great. However this is not to suggest that cultures as such have a right to perpetuate themselves. Although groups may exercise considerable control over their members, this authority rests upon the 'acquiescence of its members' and 'members have the inalienable right to leave – to renounce membership of the community'.[54] For Kukathas:

liberalism does not maintain that assimilation is in itself unacceptable or that the overwhelming of one (minority) tradition by another is wrong. Assimilation, no less than differentiation, is a part of the way of the world. If people elect to abandon their ways or their communities, in order to enter others or to slip into the mainstream of social life, that has simply to be accepted. It is accepted by liberalism even if it means the disappearance of communities that cannot survive defections. And it is accepted even though the defectors leave reluctantly: because the costs or pressures of minority life are too great.[55]

Kukathas maintains that this emphasis upon a substantive right to freedom of exit shifts the ethical balance between individual and group in the individual's favour, especially if the formal right of exit is accompanied by substantive opportunities to leave the group. Thus the right of exit limits the authority the group has over the individual. A commitment to freedom of exit implies, at the very least, 'the existence of a wider society that is open to individuals wishing to leave their local groups'.[56] For this condition to be met the principle of freedom of association must be upheld within the wider society. Since it is unlikely that in such a society other liberal freedoms would not also be valued, Kukathas believes that in all likelihood the wider society will be one that can be described as embodying a liberal political culture.

Although Kukathas offers an interesting defence of liberal individualism, it is, however, questionable whether his approach is compatible with either liberalism or genuine diversity. While liberals will fear that this approach grants too much power to the collective and fails to ensure that individuals are equipped to offer their informed consent, non-liberal minorities are liable to view Kukathas's conception of cultural groups as voluntary associations as a misconstrual of the value of cultural membership and a threat to the viability of at least some cultural communities.

The liberal critique

Unlike many liberals, Kukathas does not regard autonomy as vital to human flourishing. Consequently he believes that a liberal state should not interfere with illiberal practices which restrict or undermine individual autonomy. On the contrary, cultural groups should be 'left alone'. However, it is questionable whether such a laissez-faire attitude is compatible with Kukathas's emphasis upon individual rights and freedoms. Kukathas believes that cultural practices should be regarded as legitimate as long as individuals have consented to the terms of the association and the authority which upholds them. To ensure that consent is freely given, individuals must have an effective right of exit. Yet, illiberal cultural practices which restrict individual autonomy may well undermine consent. For example, on Kukathas's account, religious minorities would be free to pursue educational policies which aim to instil a firm faith commitment in its future members or which deny future members vital information about the religious beliefs of other groups. For Kukathas the fact that the subsequent preferences of the members of such religious communities are the product of socialisation and conditioning rather than autonomous choice does not undermine their freedom. However, while members of such illiberal minorities may well acquiesce in the values and norms that govern the community, it is difficult to see how under these circumstances members could be said to have consented. After all, for liberals consent typically requires deliberate and informed agreement.[57] From a liberal perspective the difficulties here are particularly acute in the light of the power differentials within groups, which may undermine the ability of some group members to express their dissent. As Kukathas's objections to group rights indicate, he is keenly aware that groups are not homogeneous. Yet, while he rejects the idea of group rights because such rights enshrine existing power relations, his readiness to tolerate illiberal practices leaves his account open to the same objections. As Okin notes,[58] if illiberal societies are 'left alone', powerful sections within the group may ensure that those who are regarded as inferior are socialised in a manner which secures their compliance. Furthermore, the powerful could use the dependency of the powerless to guarantee their 'acquiescence'. For example, a culture which denies women the opportunity to work outside the home, ensures that women are economically dependent upon men. If women are denied the opportunity to develop the skills necessary to succeed in the workplace – be it via a lack of education or work experience – their ability to express their dissent or to exit from the group is severely restricted. By denying that an individual's right to freedom of exit can be restricted via socialisation, or the high costs and risks of exit, Kukathas reduces consent to a merely formal requirement. Thus consent becomes mere acquiescence. In the light of these difficulties liberals may well conclude that Kukathas's approach grants the group too much control over individual group members. In the absence of a commitment to individual autonomy, the idea of freedom of association is simply too weak to ensure that liberal rights and freedoms, such as informed consent and a substantive right of exit, are respected.

'Deep diversity' and freedom of association

Kukathas maintains that by and large minority groups and cultural communities simply wish to be 'left alone' to pursue their own conception of the good life. Hence he believes that his emphasis upon freedom of association ensures that his approach can accommodate many of the demands voiced by cultural, religious and ethnic minorities. However, not only does the emphasis Kukathas places upon non-interference fail to reflect the nature of the demands made by many advocates of a 'politics of difference', his conception of cultural communities as voluntary associations misconstrues the value many groups attach to cultural membership and threatens to undermine the viability of at least some minority groups. The demands and aspirations of indigenous groups provide a good example of the difficulties inherent in Kukathas's approach. Rather than demand to be left alone many North American Indian communities have campaigned to retain or even extend special group specific rights which either grant group members additional rights or which restrict the rights of majority. Thus American Indian bands have sought to secure the survival of their culture by restricting property ownership in traditional homelands to group members or by conferring special voting rights upon members of the indigenous community. While such special rights are regarded by many minorities as vital to their survival, they cannot be accommodated within a libertarian framework based upon non-interference. Furthermore, the idea of freedom of association may be alien to the aspirations of such groups. For example, in 1969 the Trudeau government sought to dismantle the Canadian reservation system by abolishing the differential voting, property, mobility and residence rights effective in Indian territories. Rather than be tied to a reservation system, native Canadians would be free to associate voluntarily and thus preserve their way of life if they wished to do so. In this way the proposals aimed to ensure that all citizens enjoyed equal rights. Indians, however, were fiercely opposed to these measures, which they regarded as an attempt to forcibly integrate them into the wider Canadian society. Given that Indian communities will always be vulnerable to the decisions of the majority, the abolition of measures which coercively restrict the mobility, residence and political rights of both Indians and non-Indians would have undermined the viability of Indian ways of life.[59] Yet this would effectively deny Indians the right to freedom of conscience and freedom of association. After all, the disappearance of these communities would not be due to the choices of its members. Without group-specific rights and protections Indian communities would cease to exist even if their members remained firmly committed to their way of life. In circumstances such as these a response to multiculturalism based upon non-interference and freedom of association will result in the forced inclusion or assimilation of minority groups.

Liberty, Equality and Group Rights

The difficulties which surround the responses by Kymlicka, Raz and Kukathas to the question of minority rights suggest that liberal attempts to accommodate the demands voiced by advocates of a 'politics of difference' through an appeal to the liberal values of equality and individual freedom will remain problematic. Given the potential impact of group rights upon individual autonomy, many liberals will rightly regard group rights as a threat to individual self-determination. In the face of thick multiculturalism, advocates of diversity, however, are liable to view a preoccupation with individual autonomy as an attempt to impose liberal values upon non-liberal minorities and thus are likely to consider approaches such as those offered by Kymlicka and Raz as a potential threat to the long-term viability of non-liberal minorities. Yet, if individual well-being is as intricately linked to secure cultural membership as Kymlicka and Raz propose, the continued viability of non-liberal minorities will be vital to the sense of self-respect and well-being of their members. The objections raised to Kukathas's proposals suggest that these problems cannot be overcome by abandoning the idea of a group right in favour of a robust account of individual freedom of association. Not only is the idea of freedom of association too weak to guarantee important liberal rights and freedoms, it misconstrues the value many minorities attach to cultural membership and threatens to undermine the long-term survival of at least some minority groups.

Notes and References

1. Will Kymlicka, *Liberalism, Community and Culture* (Oxford: Clarendon, 1991) p. 137.
2. Will Kymlicka, *Liberalism Community and Culture*, and *Multicultural Citizenship* (Oxford: Clarendon, 1995).
3. W. Kymlicka, *Multicultural Citizenship*, p. 84.
4. Kymlicka employs the notion of a societal culture to distinguish between national and ethnic minorities. In Kymlicka's opinion, ethnic minorities lack societal cultures and thus are not entitled to self-government rights. However, as the discussion in Chapter 2 indicated, it is difficult to sustain

the argument that ethno-religious groups lack institutional embodiment or that ethnic groups do not qualify for self-government rights because they left their native culture voluntarily. Furthermore, not all national minorities will necessarily be able to provide their members with a societal culture. Rather than simply privilege national minorities, Kymlicka's argument is strengthened if it is taken to apply to all minorities which can provide their members with a societal culture.

5. W. Kymlicka, *Liberalism, Community and Culture*, p. 165.
6. Ibid. p. 167.
7. Ibid. p. 166.
8. Here Kymlicka offers the example of the 'Quiet Revolution' in French Canada, which radically transformed French Canadian culture in the 1960s. While the 'Quiet Revolution' amounted to a major shift in the norms and values of the French Canadian culture, it did not, in Kymlicka's opinion, undermine the cultural structure.
9. W. Kymlicka, *Liberalism, Community and Culture*, p. 169.
10. Ibid. p. 206.
11. Ibid. p. 135.
12. Ibid. p. 135.
13. W. Kymlicka, *Multicultural Citizenship*, p. 109.
14. For similar reasons Kymlicka is rather critical of the Muslim campaign against Salman Rushdie and his book *Satanic Verses*. In Kymlicka's opinion *Satanic Verses* was particularly offensive to Muslims because Rushdie had been raised as a Muslim and had rejected Islam. Thus according to Kymlicka, the *Satanic Verses* controversy should be seen first and foremost as a debate about apostasy, which is an intra-community matter. On Kymlicka's account of group rights measures which discriminate against apostates cannot be justified. (W. Kymlicka, 'Reply to Modood', *Analyse und Kritik*, Vol. 15, No. 1, 1993, pp. 92–6.) For an alternative interpretation of the Rushdie affair see T. Modood, 'Kymlicka on British Muslims', *Analyse und Kritik*, Vol. 15, No. 1, 1993, pp. 87–91.
15. C. Kukathas, 'Cultural Rights Again: A Rejoinder to Kymlicka', *Political Theory*, Vol. 20, No. 4, Nov. 1992, pp. 674–80, pp. 675–6.
16. Ibid. p. 674.
17. B. Walker, 'Plural Cultures, Contested Territories: A Critique of Kymlicka', *Canadian Journal of Political Science*, Vol. 30, No. 2, 1997, pp. 211–34, p. 217.
18. Ibid. p. 219.
19. Ibid.
20. G. Levey, 'Equality, Autonomy, and Cultural Rights', *Political Theory*, Vol. 25, No. 2, April 1997, pp. 215–48, p. 223.
21. D. C. Bricker, 'Autonomy and Culture: Will Kymlicka on Cultural Minority Rights', *The Southern Journal of Philosophy*, Vol. 36, No. 1, pp. 47–59, p. 52. Bricker's concerns are echoed by Tomasi, who concludes, that it is simply implausible to maintain that 'changes in a group's beliefs, values and institutions need not be changes – with respect to people's beliefs about value – in the group's history, language and culture' (J.

Tomasi, 'Kymlicka, Liberalism and Respect for Cultural Minorities', *Ethics*, Vol. 105, No. 3, April 1995, pp. 580–603, p. 592).

22. In the eyes of critics like Bricker, to suggest, as Kymlicka does, that the 'Quiet Revolution' in French Canada did not change the structure of French Canadian culture is to confuse historical continuity with an unchanged structure.

23. D. C. Bricker, 'Autonomy and Culture: Will Kymlicka on Cultural Minority Rights', p. 53.

24. J. Tomasi, 'Kymlicka, Liberalism and Respect for Cultural Minorities'.

25. R. Beiner cited in Z. Bauman, 'Communitarianism, Freedom and the Nation State', *Critical Review*, Vol. 9, No. 4, pp. 539–53, p. 551.

26. S. Moller Okin, 'Feminism and Multiculturalism: Some Tensions', *Ethics*, Vol. 108, No. 4, July 1998, pp. 661–84, p. 678.

27. W. Kymlicka, 'Reply To Modood', p. 95.

28. Council of Mosques, *The Muslims and Swann* (Bradford, 1986).

29. Islamic Academy, *Swann Committee Report* (Cambridge, 1985).

30. Ibid. p. 5.

31. Kymlicka, *Multicultural Citizenship*, p. 43.

32. As Tomasi notes: 'If an individual makes an important life choice – say, to sell his land to a (wealthy) white person and raise his family in a city near a major university – but is told he is forbidden to do so by law, then that person's self respect, the respect he has for the value of the choices he makes about how he wants to lead his life (and the personal hopes he has for his children's lives) may receive a direct and heavy blow.' (J. Tomasi, op.cit. p. 591).

33. For a detailed and informative discussion of the case see W. Janzen, *Limits on Liberty, The Experience of Mennonite, Hutterite and Doukhobor Communities in Canada* (Toronto: University of Toronto Press, 1990).

34. B. Barry, *Justice as Impartiality* (Oxford: Clarendon Press, 1995).

35. J. Chaplin, 'How Much Cultural and Religious Pluralism can Liberalism Tolerate', in J. Horton (ed.), *Liberalism, Multiculturalism and Toleration* (London: Macmillan, 1993) pp. 32–49, p. 45.

36. Ibid. p. 46.

37. C. Taylor, 'Multiculturalism and the "Politics of Recognition"', in C. Taylor and A. Gutman (ed.), *Multiculturalism and the "Politics of Recognition"* (Princeton: Princeton University Press, 1992).

38. W. Kymlicka, *Multicultural Citizenship*, pp. 167–8.

39. Ibid. p. 167.

40. M. Freeman, 'Parents, Children and Citizen', paper presented at the conference of MANCEPT (Manchester Centre for Political Thought) on *Multiculturalism and Citizenship*, Department of Government, University of Manchester, 13 November 1998.

41. Raz, *Essays in the Morality of Law and Politics* (Oxford: Clarendon Press, 1994) p. 114.

42. Raz, 'Multiculturalism: A Liberal Perspective', *Dissent*, Winter 1994, pp. 67–79, p. 73.

43. J. Raz, *Essays in the Morality of Law and Politics*, p. 116.

44. Ibid. p. 119.
45. S. Akhtar, *The Final Imperative* (London: Bellew Publishing, 1991).
46. A. L. Tibawi, 'Islamic Education: Its Traditions and Modernisation into the Arab National Systems', cited in J. R. Muir, 'The Isocratic Idea of Education and Islamic Education', *Papers of the Philosophy of Education Society*, (March 31–April 2), pp. 28–36.
47. Ibid.
48. C. Kukathas, 'Are there any Cultural Rights?' in W. Kymlicka (ed.), *The Rights of Minority Cultures* (Oxford: University Press, 1995) pp. 228–56, p. 232.
49. Ibid. p. 233.
50. Ibid. p. 237.
51. Ibid. p. 238.
52. C. Kukathas, 'Liberalism and Multiculturalism: The Politics of Indifference', *Political Theory*, Vol. 26, No. 5, Oct. 1998, pp. 686–99.
53. Ibid. p. 238.
54. C. Kukathas, 'Are there any Cultural Rights?', p. 239.
55. C. Kukathas, 'Liberalism, Multiculturalism and Oppression', in A. Vincent, *Political Theory: Tradition and Diversity* (Cambridge: University Press, 1997) pp. 133–53.
56. Ibid. p. 252.
57. Here the difficulties inherent in Kukathas's approach are akin to the objections raised by J. Cohen with regard to Walzer's conception of shared values. See Chapter 6, p. 155.
58. S. Moller Okin, 'Feminism and Multiculturalism: Some Tensions', p. 675.
59. For a detailed discussion of this case see W. Kymlicka, *Liberalism, Community and Culture*, pp. 142ff.

Chapter 6: Charles Taylor and Michael Walzer: Liberalism and the 'Right to Cultural Survival'

One of the key aspects definitive of the 'politics of difference' has been the demand that the state should seek to secure the survival of cultural and ethnic groups. This goal of cultural survival has been reflected in the emphasis many groups have placed upon collective goals such as the continued survival of their language, religion and customs and has frequently been associated with the demand by territorially based minorities for greater regional autonomy or, in cases such as Quebec, secession. What characterises such demands is the desire to employ the powers of the state to protect and promote the group's distinctive vision of the good life. Thus, for instance both the Catalans in Spain and the Quebecois in Canada have sought to establish a distinctive legal and political framework geared specifically to the protection of their language and culture.

Although the aim of 'cultural survival' has been central to the demands of many groups seeking recognition, this goal has proved particularly troublesome for liberals. While liberals such as Rawls, Habermas and Kymlicka view the 'politics of difference' principally in terms of differently constituted individual identities and, consequently, have emphasised the importance of individual autonomy and liberty, the vision of the liberal state associated with such responses to the 'politics of difference' ultimately remains incompatible with the goal of 'cultural survival'. In line with their emphasis upon individual autonomy liberals such as Rawls, Habermas and Kymlicka maintain that the state should not promote a distinctive vision of the good life. While the state should protect individual rights and freedoms, it should remain neutral vis-à-vis particular conceptions of the good, leaving individuals free to fashion their own lives. Thus even Kymlicka, who supports the idea of group-differentiated rights, grounds these rights in individual autonomy. Such a vision of the state must remain hostile to the desire of minority groups to enlist the support of the state to protect and promote their particular vision of the good life.

However, recently a number of liberal thinkers have questioned the assumption that liberalism must presuppose state neutrality. Probably the two most influential theorists to re-assess the relationship between liberalism and state neutrality are Charles Taylor and Michael Walzer.[1] In this context Taylor and Walzer have been particularly concerned with the demands of national and cultural groups for state support in the protection and promotion of cultural or national identity. In contrast to Rawls, Habermas and Kymlicka, who view the 'politics of difference' primarily in terms of differently constituted individual identities, Taylor and Walzer are first and foremost concerned with the aim of differently constituted political societies to protect their particular way of life. Given the close link between the goal of 'cultural survival' and the demand for greater self-determination on the part of territorially defined national and cultural minorities, their response to the 'politics of difference' has led Taylor and Walzer to develop a distinctive vision of the liberal national community. While liberals such as Rawls and Habermas see the state primarily as an association of autonomous individuals, Taylor and Walzer view the liberal state as a political community united by common meanings based upon a shared language, history and culture. For both theorists these common meanings play a vital role in the formation of individual identities. Thus, according to Taylor, individual identity is constructed dialogi-cally within the context of particular cultural communities. In a similar vein, Walzer views human beings as first and foremost culture producing creatures. Given the intricate link between individual identity and cultural membership, Taylor and Walzer maintain that respecting the individual implies respecting the individual's particu-lar culture. Consequently both theorists believe that a political community has a right to promote and safeguard its particular conception of the good. For Taylor and Walzer, therefore, the liberal state is not marked out by a commitment to cultural neutrality, but by a sense of tolerance and respect vis-à-vis the cultures and values of minorities. Consequently both Taylor and Walzer conclude that the liberal state can legitimately promote a particular conception of the good life, provided it respects the fundamental rights and liberties of all citizens, including those who 'do not share the public definition of the good'.[2]

While Taylor and Walzer attempt to offer a liberal defence of a 'right to cultural survival', a number of liberal critics have questioned whether the emphasis these two theorists place upon collective goods is ultimately compatible with key liberal commitments such as individual freedom and autonomy. In the eyes of critics, Taylor's and

Walzer's preoccupation with cultural identity not only potentially marginalises other sources of identity, but also underestimates the heterogeneity of cultural groups and the role internal power relations play in the formation of cultural identity. Thus for Habermas,[3] Taylor too readily sacrifices individual freedom and autonomy in order to ensure cultural survival. In a similar vein Dworkin[4] concludes that Walzer's readiness to endorse the given social meanings within a particular culture ultimately leads to political conservatism and moral relativism.

Not only are the 'liberal credentials' of Taylor's and Walzer's approach open to question, it is also doubtful whether their vision of a 'right to cultural survival' can capture the complex set of demands associated with the 'politics of difference'. Whereas Taylor and Walzer portray the struggle for cultural survival on the part of national minorities as paradigmatic of the demand for recognition in general, their conception of liberal, national communitites ultimately fails to capture important elements of both thin and thick multiculturalism. Like liberals, advocates of thin multiculturalism are liable to question the emphasis both theorists place upon cultural homogeneity and the recognition of existing identities. For example, while Taylor believes that multiculturalism requires the recognition of the specific identities of particular others, critics such as Nicholson[5] and Wolf[6] have been quick to point out that in the case of women and other traditionally marginalised groups such as Afro-Americans, it is precisely the recognition of their particular identity which is problematic. After all, historically women have been only too readily recognised and defined in terms of their gender. For Nicholson and Wolf, rather than focus upon the recognition of specific identities, a 'politics of difference' must seek to problematise the underlying assumptions, attitudes and prejudices of those who grant recognition.

Finally, both Taylor's and Walzer's response to fundamental value conflict remains problematic. Taylor's focus upon the particular case of Quebec, which in his own terms is best seen as a debate among liberals, leads him to underestimate the 'depth of diversity' and the far reaching implications of the demand for cultural survival. Thus Taylor premises his conception of a 'right to cultural survival' upon a narrow definition of culture, which fails to acknowledge the political and economic dimensions of cultural survival. Although Walzer's inherently pluralistic and radically particularistic account appears at first glance better placed than Taylor's 'politics of recognition' to capture the far reaching implications of genuine cultural diversity, Walzer's preoccupation with the political community as the arena in which the meanings and distributions of social goods are determined will be viewed with suspicion by at least some advocates of thick multiculturalism. As Kymlicka notes,[7] given this exclusive emphasis upon the political community, the level of protection enjoyed by cultural and ethnic minorities depends upon the character of a given political community. Hence Walzer's approach cannot offer firm safeguards for minorities.

In the light of the difficulties which surround Taylor's and Walzer's visions of a 'liberal, national community', this chapter will conclude that their approaches underestimate both the complexities of the 'politics of difference' and the tensions between a 'right to cultural survival' and key liberal commitments such as autonomy. Furthermore, the emphasis Taylor and Walzer place upon internal cultural homogeneity entrenches rather than resolves cultural disagreements, and thus could be said to generate a momentum for secession. Although Taylor explores the possibility of building a federal structure that can encompass more than one national community, such federations are liable to remain fragile in the face of the demands for 'autonomy' on the part of its constituent communities. Thus a world of internally quite homogeneous national communitites may not be well placed to promote a multicultural society. Therefore, while Taylor and Walzer offer an innovative response to the demand for a 'right to cultural survival' their approaches ultimately fail to engage with many of the fears and aspirations of both liberals and advocates of a 'politics of difference'.

Charles Taylor: The Politics of Recognition

Taylor develops his response to the 'politics of difference' in the context of his analysis of the rise of modernity and the development of modern conceptions of the self. For him the demand for recognition at the heart of the contemporary 'politics of difference' must be viewed within the context of a distinctly modern conception of individual identity based upon the ideals of authenticity and equal dignity. On Taylor's account, in pre-modern society individual identity was fixed with reference to the role a person occupied within the social hierarchy. This social hierarchy, which provided the basis for recognition in terms of 'honour' or preference, was in turn validated by reference to external horizons of meaning such as the Good or God. However, with the rise of modern science these cosmological and theological background-orders that legitimated the old hierarchical order were gradually rejected.[8] As the old order waned, the inherently inegalitarian concept of 'honour' was slowly displaced by the idea of equal human dignity, which emphasises the worth of those qualities and attributes which all human beings have at least potentially in common. This preoccupation with universal human potential gave rise to the demand for equal recognition; an ideal central to modern democratic politics. Not only did the collapse of the old social order provide the background conditions for the advance of the concept of equal dignity, it also gave rise to the ideal of authenticity. Whereas in pre-modern society individual identity was determined by reference to a pre-given external social order, the modern conception of authenticity rests upon a highly individualised conception of identity, which defines identity in terms of the goals of self-fulfilment and self-realisation. Thus the ideal of authenticity demands that the individual be true to herself, true to her own originality. While, according to Taylor, this vision of individual identity can be traced back to the eighteenth century and especially to Rousseau's notion of an inner moral voice, it is the Romantics such as Herder, who provided the first clear articulation of the ideal of authenticity.[9]

The ideal of authenticity

Although the ideal of authenticity invites us to choose our own identity, Taylor stresses that properly understood the idea of authencity does not imply a Sartrean vision of unconstrained freedom. On the contrary, if the choices the individual makes are to be meaningful, the individual must have access to a framework which allows her to determine what is and is not significant or important. If our self-chosen identity is not to be trivial, the object of our choice must have some value independent of our having chosen it. Yet, this in itself only shows that 'some self-transcending issues are indispensable', it does not establish that 'any particular one has to be taken seriously.'[10] To appreciate how an individual derives her 'horizons of significance', Taylor maintains it is necessary to examine the complex relationship between the individual and the wider community.[11] While human beings are self-interpreting animals, who construct their own identity, self-interpretation is not achieved monologically. To engage in self-interpretation, we must acquire language in the broadest sense, 'covering not only the words we speak, but also other modes of expression, including the languages of art, of gesture, of love and the like'.[12] It is language which provides us with patterns or frameworks that enable us to identify and interpret our feelings. For example, to identify my particular feeling as one of shame rather than embarrassment, I must have the concepts of shame and embarrassment in my vocabulary and I must be able to distinguish between their meanings. Language, however, is, by definition, a shared, social possession and conveyed intersubjectively. Since we acquire the language necessary for moral discrimination by engaging in dialogue with others, we establish what is of value through the shared experience of the significance of goods for those around us. While we can critically engage with the shared meanings we have learned from others and at times may choose to reject perceived evaluations, we could not engage in such critical enterprises in the absence of language. Therefore, while the ideal of authenticity invites the individual to choose her own identity, this choice takes place within the framework of the shared meanings that define our language community. For Taylor each cultural community is characterised by its own distinct moral language, with its own distinct conception of the good and its own perception of how the various goods worth pursuing should be organised.

In addition to language, the wider community also provides the setting in which we negotiate and affirm our identity. Here again Taylor emphasises the intersubjective or dialogical character of identity formation. Not only do we define our identity in a social space circumscribed by our relations to others – I am Mary's sister, a member of this University, an atheist as opposed to a believer – the attainment of a secure identity also requires that my identity be recognised by others. This recognition, however, has become deeply problematic with the rise of the modern ideal of authenticity. As long as the individual's identity is fixed by reference to established social hierarchies, recognition is automatically guaranteed. However, the self-defined, original sense of identity associated with the ideal of authenticity does not enjoy such a priori recognition, but has actively to seek recognition in exchanges with others. This raises for the first time the danger that recognition may be denied or identity misrecognised. As Taylor notes, given the intersubjective nature of identity, 'a person or a group of people can suffer real damage, real distortion, if the people or society around them mirror back to them a confining or demeaning or contemptible picture of themselves.'[13] Given that individual identity is constructed dialogically within the context of particular cultural communities, failure to grant due recognition to an individual's culture also constitutes a threat to his or her identity. Hence, on this account 'non-recognition of cultural difference is a form of latent violence'.[14] Thus in the 'age of authenticity' the demand for recognition has come to play an important role in both the private and the political sphere, giving rise to a distinctly modern identity politics. For Taylor, this identity politics has its roots in modern nationalist politics, which provides the model for the demands for recognition by feminists, cultural minorities, the gay movement etc.[15]

Not only has the idea of authenticity made recognition more significant, it has also raised the stakes so far as the idea of equal human dignity is concerned. According to Taylor the interplay between the ideals of authenticity and equal human dignity has given rise to the complex 'politics of equal recognition' characteristic of modernity. The ideal of equal human dignity demands that all people be treated as free and equal. Yet, once this ideal is combined with the idea of authenticity it points in at least two directions. While on the one hand it implies the 'protection of the basic rights of individuals as human beings', it gives rise, on the other hand, to the demand that 'the particular needs of individuals as members of specific cultures' be acknowledged.[16] It is therefore not surprising that the 'politics of equal recognition' has come to be associated with two rather different political ideals: a 'politics of universalism' and a 'politics of difference'. Whereas the 'politics of universalism' invokes the idea of equal human dignity in order to secure equal rights and entitlements for all citizens, the 'politics of difference' appeals to the ideal of authenticity in its demand that '[e]veryone should be recognised for his or her unique identity';[17] for what distinguishes her from everyone else. In contrast to the 'politics of universalism' which is committed to forms of non-discrimination that are blind to the ways in which citizens differ, the 'politics of difference' 'redefines non-discrimination as requiring that we make these distinctions the basis of differential treatment.'[18] Given the close link between identity and community membership, the 'politics of difference' implies not only that the particular identity of given individuals be accorded recognition, it also demands that actual evolved cultures be accorded equal respect. Since different cultural communities are characterised by their own distinct moral languages and have their own distinct perception of which goods are valuable and how to organise these goods, the advocates of a 'politics of difference' believe that the supposedly neutral, difference-blind principles of a 'politics of universalism' will ultimately merely reflect the values and meanings of the dominant culture in modern societies.

The politics of recognition

Yet, as Taylor notes, the majority of contemporary liberal theorising has remained firmly rooted within the 'politics of universalism'. The commitment to procedural equality and state neutrality which characterises much of contemporary liberalism is based upon a difference-blind conception of non-discrimination. In line with its regard for universal rights this type of liberalism emphasises the idea of equal human dignity, perceived in terms of universal human potential. Thus, rather than associate dignity with the particular form of life chosen, this strand of liberalism views dignity in terms of the universal human capacity to fashion ones own life. Human dignity is therefore defined in terms of autonomy. Consequently the state must not endorse any particular outcome of deliberation over and above others. Taylor believes that such a response to the 'politics of equal recognition' will inevitably remain hostile to the aspirations of the 'politics of difference'. While for the advocates of a 'politics of difference' recognition of actual identities and cultures requires differential treatment, this strand of liberalism, with its emphasis upon difference-blind neutrality, is profoundly hostile to the idea that the standard schedule of liberal rights might apply differently in different cultural contexts. Consequently the liberalism of universal rights remains opposed to the promotion of collective goals, such as the 'right to cultural survival'. After all, as Taylor notes, the demand for cultural survival is a 'collective goal, which . . . almost certainly will call for some variations in the kinds of laws we deem permissible from one cultural context to another.'[19] For liberals committed to the idea of universal rights the desire by cultural and national minorities, such as the Quebecois in Canada, to establish a distinctive legal and political framework geared to safeguarding their cultural heritage and identity, violates the 'principle of neutrality' and thus is discriminatory with regard to those citizens who do not belong to the group whose identity is granted protection. For Taylor, however, this appeal to the 'principle of neutrality' constitutes a failure to acknowledge the implications of the ideal of authenticity. Given the complex relationship between individual identity and cultural membership, a failure to recognise and safeguard the particular identity of existing cultural communities is actually incompatible with a commitment to equal respect. Indeed, like many advocates of the 'politics of difference', Taylor believes that the 'liberalism of universal rights', with its emphasis upon individual autonomy and liberty, is best regarded as the expression of a particular conception of the good. Thus to insist upon the 'principle of neutrality' constitutes a threat to genuine cultural diversity.

However, in Taylor's opinion, liberalism does not have to be marked out by a commitment to cultural neutrality. On the contrary, he maintains that a liberal society can legitimately promote the collective goods associated with a particular conception of the good life, provided it respects the fundamental liberal rights of all citizens and grants equal citizenship to all members of society, 'including all those who do not share public definitions of the good'.[20] Here Taylor draws a careful distinction between fundamental rights, such as rights to life, liberty, due process, freedom of religion, free speech etc. and the wide range of possible privileges and immunities, which may be granted by the state. While the liberal state must protect the fundamental rights of all citizens equally, privileges and immunities 'can be revoked or restricted for reasons of public policy'.[21] Indeed the liberal state should at times 'weigh the importance of certain forms of universal treatment against the importance of cultural survival, and opt sometimes in favour of the latter'.[22] Thus, for instance, on this account, the government of Quebec is entitled to safeguard the continuation of French Canadian language and culture. Hence laws stipulating that commercial signs be in French and that require that companies with more than fifty employees employ French, as well as the compulsory French language education of children of French speaking parents and immigrants, do not, according to Taylor, violate the fundamental rights of the English speaking community in Quebec. They merely restrict certain privileges and immunities. Thus a government may effectively safeguard the survival of a nation's culture, without violating the rights of those citizens who do not subscribe to this particular vision of the good. As Taylor acknowledges, this vision of a liberal national community does, of course, suffer strains. While '[a]ll are citizens without distinction, . . . the state has its raison d'être in a cultural nation to which not all citizens belong'.[23] For Taylor such tensions must be accepted as inevitable.

While Taylor seeks to defend a 'right to cultural survival' he does not believe that all cultures should automatically be regarded as of equal value. Indeed, for him, to insist upon the equal worth of all cultures is to rob the idea of worth of all meaning and would thus render recognition pointless. Therefore, while we should approach every culture on the presumption that it is of equal worth, 'it can't make sense to demand as a matter of right that we come up with a final concluding judgement that their value is great, or equal to others.'[24] In order to arrive at an informed judgement of worth, Taylor urges us to immerse ourselves in cultures other than our own, so that we can come to understand what that culture's contribution might consist of. This allows us to situate our own background valuations alongside those of different and previously unfamiliar cultures. On this basis we can achieve a 'fusion of horizons' by developing new vocabularies of comparison which allow us to articulate these contrasts. While 'such a fusion of horizons' may allow us to appreciate what is of value in other cultures, Taylor stresses that 'liberalism can't and shouldn't claim complete cultural neutrality'.[25] On the contrary, liberalism is a 'fighting creed' and as such incompatible with a wide range of other cultures. In the final analysis, even a difference-sensitive liberalism, which allows for the pursuit of collective goods, cannot tolerate cultures which do not respect the fundamental liberal rights of all citizens.

Cultural membership, autonomy and authenticity: the liberal critique

Although Taylor attempts to develop a distinctly liberal defence of a 'right to cultural survival', some critics have questioned the liberal credentials of Taylor's 'politics of recognition'. In the eyes of liberal critics such as Steven Rockefeller, an emphasis upon ethnic identity and cultural survival is liable to generate a separatist mentality that is 'inconsistent with the ideals of freedom, equality and the ongoing, co-operative and experimental search for truth and well-being'.[26] Yet for many liberals these ideals are definitive of a liberal society. Not only is the closure with respect to outsiders, which tends to accompany the consolidation of cultural identity, liable to impair the sense of solidarity which underpins the liberal commitment to equal dignity and universal rights, it may also threaten to undermine the freedom and autonomy of group members. As Habermas notes, policies such as the Quebec language laws, which seek to guarantee the long-term survival of a particular cultural community, extend well beyond what could be justified as 'just providing . . . a facility to already existing people'.[27] After all, the 'language laws' of Quebec not only ensure that francophones are able to use French in public, but actually restrict the availability of English language-based education and limit the use of English in certain spheres of life. Such measures clearly constrain the ability of francophones to choose freely to speak English. Yet if cultural survival is to be guaranteed such restrictions are vital. To ensure long-term survival a culture must systematically socialise future citizens into the language, values and norms definitive of that culture. This is most readily achieved if the choices of future citizens are restricted. However, such attempts to fix the identity of future generations are not readily compatible with the ideals of individual freedom and self-determination upon which liberalism is premised. As Ripstein observes, while keeping traditions alive is one of the most abiding of human aspirations, 'it is not clear that this is the sort of aspiration that liberals should be prepared to use the state to protect.'[28]

Here liberals are liable to be particularly fearful of the desire of non-liberal societies to preserve their traditional character. For example, while the long-term survival of certain religiously-based cultures may well require state intervention and protection to ensure that children continue to share the faith of their parents, liberals would surely not wish to use the powers of the state to enforce religious faith.[29] Taylor seeks to address such fears by distinguishing between 'fundamental rights' and 'privileges and immunities'. However, '[f]undamental liberal rights always require interpretation'.[30] In a truly multicultural society should the 'right to freedom of religion' be interpreted primarily in terms of the right of individuals to choose faith commitments autonomously or should it merely imply tolerance of the faith of others? Thus for Ripstein, while the distinction between 'fundamental rights' and 'privileges and immunities' 'is by itself impeccable, Taylor asks it to support a heavier load than it can bear.'[31]

A preoccupation with cultural identity may not only restrict the freedom of future generations, but may also prove oppressive vis-à-vis existing group members. Even if individual rights are respected, a 'politics of cultural survival' may lead to pressure being placed upon the individual to define herself primarily in terms of her cultural membership rather than a whole host of alternative criteria which may shape her identity. After all, our cultural identity constitutes only one influence upon our conception of the good life. In modern societies we all belong to many distinct and sometimes opposing groups. Thus our occupation, social status and choice of neighbourhood all contribute to our sense of self and conception of the good life. In the face of such a range of possible sources of identity, a preoccupation with cultural membership may lead to an undue emphasis upon this aspect of the self. Indeed, as Amelie Rorty[32] notes, in the context of the American multiculturalism debate members of the Jewish American and African American communities have been pressurised to define themselves primarily in terms of their cultural identity. These communities tend to expect their members actively to participate in promoting specific policies associated with Jewish or Black interests and to vote along ethnic lines. While individuals may choose to resist such pressures, such resistance often carries with it costly personal consequences in terms of losses of alliance and friendship.

Such pressures upon individual members of a community become particularly troubling once the contested nature of cultural identity is recognised. While Taylor is sensitive to the diversity of differently constituted political societies, his vision of particular cultures is remarkably homogeneous. For Taylor, the members of a cultural community share meanings and values and are collectively committed to the promotion of their particular conception of the good. Such an emphasis upon shared meanings and goals, however, appears to underestimate the extent to which cultural identity will always remain internally contested. As Houston[33] observes, part of the difficulty here stems from the manner in which Taylor tends to conflate the construction of individual identity and cultural identity. While the construction of individual identity presumes a constituting self prior to the dialogue with others, which generates a sense of unity and coherence, cultural identity lacks such a unifying centre. In the construction of cultural identity there simply is 'no neutral referee to choose a coherent logic between multiple competing narratives'.[34] The construction of cultural identity is therefore an inherently political process, characterised, in the words of Amelie Rorty, by powerful, intracultural struggles to determine the 'right of authoritative description'.[35] Therefore what is to be regarded as 'shared inheritance' is liable always to remain to some degree contested. Indeed, 'even cultures that define a significant part of their shared inheritance by a canonic text . . . are frequently divided by their interpretations of those texts'.[36] Such internal political struggles to define cultural identity suggest a potentially far less harmonious relationship between the individual and the cultural community. Given that 'cultural descriptions are politically and ideologically laden',[37] the danger remains that a 'politics of cultural survival' will simply privilege the conception of cultural identity advocated by the most powerful actors within a particular community. This, however, may well be tantamount to a lack of respect for the identity of those members of the community whose conception of the community's culture is being marginalised. Indeed, given the potential tensions between individual and community, a 'right to cultural survival' may not only threaten individual autonomy, but may also conflict with the ideal of authenticity. After all, the potential pressures upon group members to define themselves primarily in terms of their cultural identity, the contested nature of supposedly authoritative descriptions of cultural identity, and the desire to fix the identity of future generations are not necessarily compatible with the goals of self-fulfilment, self-realisation and originality central to the ideal of authenticity. Given the tensions inherent in the relationship between the individual and the wider cultural community the link Taylor tries to establish between the recognition of individual identity and the protection of cultural communities is by no means as strong or self-evident as he assumes.

Recognition, identity and oppression

The fear expressed by liberals regarding the contested nature of group identities and the power to determine authoritative descriptions, have also been central to the concerns expressed by a number of feminist critics of Taylor's conception of a 'politics of recognition'. For Taylor, the demand to have one's particular, distinctive cultural identity recognised, which has characterised modern nationalist politics, has provided a model for the identity politics of a wide variety of social groups, including feminists, the gay movement and cultural minorities. Critics, however, have questioned whether such an appeal to a modern need to have identity recognised can genuinely capture the aspirations of such a wide range of social movements.[38] While Taylor's preoccupation with modern nationalism leads him to view identity politics in terms of the recognition of the exising identities of particular others, critics such as Nicholson and Wolf[39] have been quick to point out that in the case of women and other traditionally marginalised groups such as African-Americans, it is precisely the recognition of their particular identity which is problematic. Historically, for instance, women have only too readily been recognised and defined in terms of their gender. As Wolf notes, for these groups the problem is not that powerful sectors of the community do not notice or do not want to notice their specific identity, 'but that this specific identity is put to the service of oppression and exploitation'.[40] Consequently, in the case of women, the demands for recognition do not primarily reflect a desire to have a particular way of life recognised, but stem from an analysis of the ways in which 'oppression was manifesting itself in terms of forms of descriptions and evaluations'.[41] For Nicholson, this focus upon the power to describe and evaluate has led feminists to develop a 'politics of recognition' which goes well beyond the simple acknowledgement of difference. Thus women have sought to explore the impact imbalances of power have upon the very practice of recognition. Not only do these imbalances of power force some groups to seek recognition while enabling others to grant it, power also allows some groups to claim universal validity for 'what are, in effect, historically specific perspectives'.[42] Such an analysis of the practice of recognition shifts the focus away from those who seek recognition to those who are in a position to grant it. The aim of such a 'politics of recognition' is not simply to gain recognition of a particular identity, but to highlight the specificity and limitations of the judgements of truth and worth of those who grant recognition.

For Wolf and Nicholson, therefore, Taylor's focus on modern nationalism has led him to ignore the most challenging aspect of the 'politics of difference': the demand that we recognise the limitations and contingency of 'our' own perspective. Accordingly any adequate conceptualisation of multiculturalism must be premised upon this desire to question perceived conceptions of 'our' perspective. Whereas Taylor 'frames the topic of multiculturalism as one about how a "we" should regard claims of previously excluded groups about the worth of their past contributions',[43] for Wolf a 'politics of recognition' should first and foremost be about recognising 'ourselves as a multicultural community'.[44]

'Deep diversity' and 'the politics of recognition'

Not only does Taylor's account fail to address some of the most challenging aspects of the demand for recognition, his vision of a multicultural society may also prove problematic – albeit for rather different reasons – for at least some instances of thick multiculturalism. Taylor develops his defence of a 'right to cultural survival' in the context of his discussion of the constitutional crisis in Canada surrounding the status of Quebec.[45] On Taylor's analysis this debate is best perceived as a dispute between two particular conceptions of liberalism. While English speaking Canada is wedded to the 'liberalism of universal rights', Quebec favours a conception of liberalism akin to his 'politics of recognition'. Although these two models of liberalism differ with regard to the status of certain collective goals, both recognise fundamental liberal rights and acknowledge the importance of individual freedom. The Canadian constitutional crisis is therefore best seen as an instance of thin multiculturalism. This focus upon thin multiculturalism has far-reaching implications for Taylor's conception of culture and the measures necessary for its preservation. The shared commitment to a broadly liberal political order, which characterises the Canadian debate, allows Taylor to define a 'right to cultural survival' almost exclusively with reference to the preservation of language. However, as Rorty observes,[46] this implies a peculiarly narrow definition of culture. As 'ways of life', cultures are not only characterised by their particular language but may also have their own distinct political and economic practices and patterns of organisation. Once these political and economic aspects of cultural membership are acknowledged, Taylor's goal of securing cultural survival for the dominant culture, while safeguarding the basic rights of all citizens, becomes more problematic. After all the political and economic attitudes and practices of a particular culture could have serious implications for a wide-ranging set of public policies. For instance, the preservation of a culture such as Irish American culture, which is deeply rooted in Catholicism, may have important implications for public policy in such morally and politically divisive areas as abortion and euthanasia. While liberalism assumes a separation of the political and the moral, religious perspectives such as Catholicism and Islam may not necessarily recognise such a distinction. Indeed, for Muslim writers such as Akhtar and A. L. Tibawi, recognition of Islam requires an explicit acknowledgement of the political, social and economic implications of Islamic teaching.[47]

Although Taylor does not discuss the status of non-liberal cultures at length, his brief reference to the controversy surrounding Salman Rushdie's *Satanic Verses* provides an indication of the potential difficulties here. While many Muslims did not endorse the fatwa, they nonetheless regarded the book as a profound insult to Islam and thus campaigned for it to be banned. For Muslims, like many other religious believers, blasphemous speech constitutes a disregard for and threat to their values, beliefs and identities. Such a position, however, could be seen to undermine the fundamental liberal commitment to freedom of speech. Confronted with the difficulties a robust defence of liberal freedoms may pose for non-liberal cultures, Taylor concludes that liberalism is 'the political expression of one range of cultures, and quite incompatible with other ranges'.[48] Ultimately for him the 'right to cultural survival' is limited by a respect for traditional liberal rights and freedoms. Consequently, once the wider political implications of cultural membership are acknowledged, Taylor's 'politics of recognition' remains inhospitable to the demands of many advocates of thick multiculturalism. Thus Taylor appears to be caught in a dilemma: while in the eyes of liberals and advocates of thin multiculturalism his approach fails to provide adequate safeguards for key liberal values such as autonomy and equality of moral worth, non-liberal minorities fear that his approach remains too wedded to liberal values to accommodate the depth and complexity of diversity characteristic of contemporary liberal societies. Ultimately Taylor's attempt to balance a liberal regard for individual rights and freedoms and the desire of minorities to safeguard the survival of their culture does not succeed.

Michael Walzer: Complex Equality and the Liberal Political Community

At first glance the inherently pluralistic and radically particularist account of justice which underpins Walzer's defence of a 'right to cultural survival' appears to be better placed than Taylor's account to capture the depth and complexity of diversity in contemporary liberal societies. Whereas theorists such as Rawls attempt to establish an impartial point of view from which disputes regarding justice can be adjudicated, Walzer contends that all accounts of justice are rooted in the values and judgements of specific cultures and that different communities will value different goods. Thus rather than engage in misguided attempts to find a universal principle of justice or medium of exchange, a substantive account of justice should seek to interpret the meanings of social goods within particular communities. For Walzer the distributions of social goods and, hence, the principles of justice, in a given society flow out of and are relative to the meanings a particular culture attaches to these goods. Consequently, '[t]here is no single set of primary or basic goods conceivable across all moral and material worlds'.[49] On the contrary, conceptions of justice are radically particular and liable to change over time in accordance with changes in the social meanings of particular societies. Beyond basic rights to life and liberty,[50] our rights 'do not follow from shared conceptions of social goods, they are local and particular in character'.[51] On such an account a society is just if 'its substantive life is lived . . . in a way faithful to the shared understandings of the members.'[52] Therefore, according to Walzer, [j]ustice requires a defence of difference – different goods distributed for different reasons among different groups of people'.[53] Since human beings are first and foremost culture producing creatures, the way a people 'conceive and create and then possess and employ social goods'[54] shapes the concrete identities of actual men and women. Therefore, respecting the identity of concrete individuals implies respecting the meaning that they attach to social goods. Thus respect for the individual requires respect for the values, judgements and principles of justice of their cultural communities.

Not only are the principles of justice particular, they are also pluralistic. Communities typically value a variety of social goods. Thus in Walzer's opinion:

there never has been a single criterion, or single set of interconnected criteria for all distributions. Dessert, qualification, birth and blood, friendship, need, free exchange, political loyalty, democratic decision: each has had its place, along with many others, uneasily co-existing, invoked by competing groups, confused with one another.[55]

Each of the various social goods valued within a particular society has its own specific meaning and is thus associated with its own distinctive distributive norm. Consequently, if the meanings of social goods are to determine their distribution, different social goods will be distributed according to different criteria. Hence in a just society the distributive spheres associated with each social good should be autonomous. That is to say one's standing in one sphere should not be allowed to influence one's standing in other spheres. For example, one's ability to secure a political office and generally succeed in the political sphere should not give one advantages in other spheres, such as access to medical care or entrepreneurial opportunities. Walzer contends that, provided the autonomy of the various spheres is protected, each citizen can benefit from the particular talents they have, and enjoy the rewards of their 'own accomplishments'. While there can be legitimate inequalities in holdings within each sphere, no particular good should be convertible across spheres. Hence inequalities within one sphere should not be multiplied across other spheres. Walzer refers to this situation as one of 'complex equality'. Given that different goods are distributed according to different criteria, different people will get ahead in the different spheres. However, since no one is able 'to convert their advantages from one sphere to another, none is able to dominante the rest'.[56] Although a just society demands that the distributive spheres associated with each social good are autonomous of each other, Walzer recognises that in most existing societies one good or set of goods is dominant and determines value in all spheres. A good is dominant 'if the individuals who have it, because they have it, can command a wide range of other goods'.[57] Should one individual or group be successful in laying claim to a dominant good they have, in Walzer's terms, monopolised that good and are thus in a position to exploit its dominance. For Walzer to claim the right to monopolise a dominant good constitutes an ideology.

While Walzer believes that principles of justice are relative to the meanings a particular culture attaches to the social goods it values, he does not aim to provide a conservative defence of the status quo. On the contrary, debate and social criticism are vital elements of a just society. However, to be legitimate social criticism must remain rooted within the values and ideals which inform a particular society. Thus Walzer's 'connected critic' does not stand outside her community but seeks to interpret social meanings from within. To be authoritative within the community the social critic must make reference to the values of the community. The 'connected critic' therefore aims to explore the internal tensions and contradictions within society in an attempt to highlight the extent to which society fails to live up to or fails to enforce its own values and ideals.[58] Although the shared meanings and convictions of a given society will always be open to a variety of interpretations, the aim of social criticism is to mark off deep and inclusive accounts of these values from shallow and partisan ones. Given that shared social meanings play an important role in the identity of a community and its members, it is clearly important for a community to live up to its shared convictions. Criticism therefore plays a vital role in the 'ongoing collective project of self-interpretation and each member of the community can take the role of the critic.'[59]

Justice and the political community

Since principles of distributive justice can only be established within the context of a community, Walzer's particularistic and pluralistic conception of justice clearly presupposes a bounded world. On Walzer's account it is the political community which provides us with this bounded world of common meanings. From this perspective the state is best conceived not as an association of individuals, but as a community based upon common meanings, which allows the citizens of the state to develop a sense of relatedness and mutuality. It is at the level of the political community that 'language, history and culture come together . . . to produce a collective consciousness';[60] a shared set of sensibilities and intuitions. The political community is therefore the arena in which we determine and distinguish between the different meanings of social goods and mark out the various distributive spheres. Political power is used to enforce common understandings 'of what goods are and what they are for' and to 'defend the boundaries of all the distributive spheres'.[61] If distributive justice requires a set of shared meanings, sensibilities and intuitions, it is vital that each political community is able to retain its distinctive character. Consequently the members of a political community have a collective right to try and ensure the survival of their particular culture. For Walzer, this goal of cultural survival can only be attained if there is a degree of closure at the level of the state. Hence the members of a given political community are entitled to take steps to perpetuate their particular culture; for instance, members of a political community must have the right to determine whether and what kind of strangers are to be admitted to the political community. Political communities are therefore best thought of as national clubs or families. While in terms of law states constitute national clubs with their own admission policy, the moral life of political societies resembles that of families. After all, like family members, citizens feel a moral bond to national and ethnic relatives.

Although Walzer's particularist and pluralist account of justice leads him to defend a 'right to cultural survival', he believes that a community's right to perpetuate its culture and to shape the population of the community is subject to three restrictions: the meaning of membership to the current members, the principle of mutual aid, and equal citizenship rights for all admitted to the community. Membership of the political community is itself a social good. Indeed given the role of the political community in determining and articulating shared meaning, membership of the political community could be said to be the most significant social good. Thus membership of the political community is to be distributed in accordance with the meaning this social good has for the existing members of the political community. In addition to such internal constraints, Walzer believes that all political communities have certain obligations in relation to the destitute, hungry, persecuted and stateless. After all, unlike clubs or families, states control a given territory and the resources associated with that territory. As Walzer notes, in most cases there is 'a wide range of benevolent actions open to the community which will only marginally affect its present members as a body'.[62] Therefore, at the very least states should be bound by the principle of mutual aid. However, at a collective level even such as minimal commitment has potentially far reaching implications.[63] Thus, for example, the right of exclusion depends upon the population density and the extent of unclaimed territory. Where there is superfluous land, a political community cannot simply exclude needy people. The members of such political communities must choose between yielding 'land for the sake of homogeneity'[64] or becoming a multiracial society for the sake of land. Finally, should a political community decide to admit strangers, it must offer those it admits the opportunity to become citizens. For Walzer, to deny the rights of citizenship to some residents of a political community is inevitably tyrannical, since it creates a disenfranchised class which is subject to rule by others. Yet in important ways these residents resemble other citizens: they live within the state's territory, work in the local economy and are subject to local laws. To have long-term residents in a community who are not citizens is, according to Walzer, incompatible with a fundamental commitment to equality. Consequently admission and naturalisation must be governed by the same standards.

The liberal political community

Walzer argues that his conception of the state as a political community dedicated to the promotion of particular shared meanings is compatible with liberal ideas. Here Walzer, like Taylor, wishes to distinguish his vision of the liberal national community from the liberalism of state neutrality advocated by contemporary liberals such as Rawls, Habermas and Kymlicka. According to Walzer, liberal nation states can legitimately take an interest in the survival of the majority nation. Nation states need not be neutral with regard to language, history, literature, calendar or minor mores. What distinguishes liberal nation states is their tolerance and respect for ethnic and religious difference and their readiness to allow 'all minorities an equal freedom to

organise their members, express their cultural values, and to reproduce their way of life in civil society and in the family'.[65] He labels
this form of liberalism Liberalism 2, while he refers to the liberalism of
state neutrality as Liberalism 1. On
Walzer's account, the liberalism of state neutrality constitutes a
particular historical expression of the liberal commitment to tolerance.
While liberal nation states, such as France or Norway, display a
considerable degree of cultural homogeneity, immigrant societies like
the United States and Canada are highly heterogeneous. Faced with
such a multitude of cultural minorities the state simply cannot
guarantee the survival of all particular identities. Given their heterogeneity, immigrant political communities have, according to Walzer,
chosen state neutrality from within a shared understanding of the
meaning of membership within their particular political community.
In other words these societies have chosen Liberalism 1 from within
Liberalism 2. Thus, contrary to the claims of Rawls, Habermas and
Kymlicka, the preference of immigrant societies such as the United
States and Canada for Liberalism 1 does not reflect an absolute
commitment to state neutrality, nor does it indicate a deep dislike of
particularist identities. Like all other conceptions of justice this choice
reflects the particular 'social conditions and the actual life choices of
these men and women'.[66] Thus, despite their apparent heterogeneity,
the citizens of immigrant societies such as the United States and
Canada share a common understanding of the meaning of citizenship
within their society.

While Walzer regards liberal states as communities united by
common meanings, he is not insensitive to the role disagreements play
within modern liberal democratic societies. However, although he
readily acknowledges the plurality of views which characterise
modern democratic societies, he maintains that such disagreements
should not be seen as indicative of a lack of shared meanings. After all
people may share a common culture and nonetheless 'interpret
meanings in somewhat different ways' or 'take different positions on
boundary disputes and on overlapping or entangled goods.'[67] Such
disputes within cultural traditions must be distinguished from
disputes between people who come from different cultural traditions.
Whereas disagreements within cultural traditions are characterised by
a shared framework of common terms of reference and a common
vocabulary, disputes between cultural traditions are indicative of
radically diverse patterns of distribution. As his discussion of
Liberalism 1 in immigrant societies such as the US and Canada
suggests, the pluralism and disagreements regarding the good life that
characterise modern liberal societies are by and large best regarded as
disputes within cultural traditions. As such these disputes can

potentially be resolved by establishing which of the various interpretations offers the deepest and most inclusive account of the underlying shared framework of values. Disputes between cultural traditions, however, are liable to remain profoundly problematic. In these instances '[p]olitics must . . . substitute for justice'.[68] Where the population is mixed, such political accommodation can take a variety of forms, ranging from a guarantee of equal citizenship to outright secession. While recently and coercively incorporated nations, as, for example, the Baltic states, have a clear right to have their independence and sovereignty restored, the case is less clear with regard to anciently incorporated nations such as the Maori in New Zealand or Native Americans. Although it is no longer possible to restore these nations to their former independent status, these groups can, according to Walzer, legitimately expect a degree of collective self-rule. However 'exactly what this might mean in practice will depend upon the residual strength of their institutions and on the character of their engagement in the common life of the larger society'.[69] Whereas territorially concentrated minorities, whose culture differs significantly from that of the majority, are at least entitled to a strong degree of local autonomy, marginally differentiated and territorially dispersed communities can rightfully expect no more than a 'genuinely equal citizenship and the freedom to express their differences in the voluntary associations of the civil society'.[70] However, Walzer stresses that 'majorities have no obligation to guarantee the survival of minority cultures'.[71] Indeed '[t]hey may well be struggling to survive themselves'.[72] For Walzer, therefore, the right to cultural survival is ultimately exercised at the level of the political community.

Shared understandings and universal values: the liberal critique

While Walzer attempts to offer a distinctly liberal defence of a nation's right to cultural survival, liberal critics have questioned whether the emphasis he places upon shared understandings and collective goods is compatible with key liberal commitments such as individual freedom, autonomy and equality. Liberal fears here are fuelled in part by Walzer's response to disagreements within and between cultural traditions. For liberal critics such as Dworkin,[73] Walzer's vision of a world divided into distinct, yet internally homogeneous, moral cultures seriously underestimates the complexity of moral agreement and disagreement. After all, the peoples of this world cannot be neatly distributed among various moral traditions. On the contrary, 'traditions can be defined at different levels of abstraction, and people who belong to a common tradition at one level of abstraction will divide at

another more concrete level'.[74] Thus, for instance, while liberals and
groups committed to a traditional religious way of life, such as 'born
again' Christians, may share many ideas about what justice is, they
disagree profoundly about the degree to which the state may
legitimately interfere in the moral lives of its citizens. As Dworkin
notes, such disputes cannot be resolved by an appeal to shared moral
traditions or underlying common values. For Dworkin, 'if society is
divided on some issue, the tradition runs out where the dispute
begins'.[75] On Walzer's account, in the absence of common values, such
disagreements can no longer be viewed as disputes within a cultural
tradition, but must then be treated as disputes between cultural
traditions. Hence in these instances, politics must substitute for
justice. Yet, in the face of the rise of a 'politics of difference' and the
widespread disagreements regarding the good life, which characterise
modern democratic societies, critics such as Dworkin believe that to
accept that politics must replace justice as soon as a shared tradition
runs out, is to venture on a course where 'justice all but disappears for
us.'[76]

Dworkin's fears in relation to justice can be seen as indicative of
wider liberal worries regarding Walzer's failure to bear in mind the
distorting effects of power relations. While Walzer maintains that the
principles of justice reflect the shared understandings of the community as a whole, he does not seriously consider the 'differing
bargaining positions among the plurality of social groups that
characterise all modern societies.'[77] Even if we assume that the values
embodied in the political order of a particular community are clear
and determinate, the members of this community may comply with
the institutional requirements of this community for a variety of
reasons. As Cohen notes, while consent 'to a political order can reflect
a commitment to preserving and advancing the way of life of that
order', it can also 'result from combinations of fear, disinterest, narrow
self-interest, a restricted sense of alternatives, or a strategic judgement
about how to advance values not now embodied in the political
community'.[78] Only if consent is a reflection of a free and informed
commitment to a particular way of life, is it meaningful to say that the
members share the values that characterise the political community.

Here the difficulties inherent in Walzer's approach become most
readily apparent in his discussion of hierarchical societies such as the
caste system. According to Walzer, such systems are characterised by
'an extraordinary integration of meanings. Prestige, wealth, knowledge, office, occupation, food, clothing, even the social good of
conversation: all are subject to the intellectual as well as the physical
discipline of hierarchy'.[79] In such societies there is no room for the
idea of autonomous spheres. On the contrary, a single value

determines the distribution of all social goods. Thus in a highly integrated hierarchical society the idea of complex equality is not feasible. As Walzer recognises, in such societies 'justice will come to the aid of inequality'.[80] Yet inequality tends to curtail dissent and thus renders the idea of consent at best problematic. As Okin notes,[81] in a social system such as a caste society, 'in which social systems overlap, cohere, and are integrated and hierarchical', the existing ideology is liable to dominate to such an extent that dissent is unlikely to develop. In non-hierarchical societies the ruling class may well feel compelled to present its interests as universal and applicable to all. Consequently in a non-hierarchical society the ideas presented by the ruling class may, if taken literally, have quite radical implications, thus opening the door for social criticism. However, in a highly integrated, hierarchical society the very definition of the good may explicitly exclude certain sections of society. Therefore, even if the ruling ideas are taken literally, they support rather than challenge existing inequalities. After all '[o]ppressors often claim that they, aristocrats or Brahmins . . . are fully human in ways that serfs or untouchables . . . are not',[82] and that consequently it is just to expect those who lack the capacity for a fully human existence to support and be subservient to those who are capable of it. In integrated, hierarchical societies the position of the ruling class is frequently further strengthened by the fact that those excluded lack the education and social tools necessary to develop an alternative perspective. However, even if for some reason those who are excluded find the wherewithal to question the dominant definition of personhood, it is unlikely that their voices would be regarded as authoritative. Indeed they may simply not be regarded as members of the relevant community. As Friedman notes, while

Walzer thinks a connected social critic can call us back to our shared understandings of the goods appropriate to the spheres of justice . . . one wonders what the critic can be calling us back *from*, if not an 'authoritative' culturally shared understanding, compared to which the critic's disagreement must be nonauthoritative. Everything depends on how the community is defined, for this determines whose opinion constitutes the 'common meanings'.[83]

Given that in a highly integrated hierarchical society the avenues for effective social criticism are rather limited, consent remains at best problematic. Hence, for Okin, we should be 'wary of concluding . . . that the hierarchy is rendered just by . . . agreement or lack of dissent'.[84] In the eyes of his liberal critics, Walzer's failure to explore the impact of power relations within societies leads him to present a rather conservative account of justice which merely enshrines the status quo and provides insufficient safeguards for the equality and liberty of all members of society. Thus, from a liberal perspective the relativism inherent in Walzer's defence of internal principles of justice is, in the final analysis, not compatible with a commitment to equality. Yet, for liberals, such a commitment to equality constitutes a vital aspect of a just society.[85]

Complex equality, internal standards of justice and the 'politics of difference'

Like liberals, many advocates of thin multiculturalism have emphasised the importance of equality. Indeed from the perspective of advocates of difference such as feminists, Walzer's conception of complex equality is potentially rather attractive. The notion of separate spheres allows for a diversity of distributions and thus opens the door for a recognition of difference and particularity, which can allow members of society to realise their unique potential. Furthermore, by insisting that inequalities in one sphere should not translate into inequalities in other spheres, the notion of complex equality challenges existing patterns of domination and exclusion. Thus, for instance, the idea of complex equality allows feminists to challenge the processes which ensure that the sex roles charcateristic of the domestic sphere are translated into inequalities in other spheres, including the spheres of work and politics. For Walzer the real domination of women stems not from their role within the family as such, but from the fact that the family 'reproduces the structures of kinship in the larger world' and 'imposes . . . sex roles upon a range of activities to which sex is irrelevant'.[86] However, as Okin notes, complex equality demands that the family 'contains no inequalities, at least among its adult members, that translate into inequalities in other spheres'.[87] Such a conception of equality clearly challenges the traditional liberal public/private dichotomy and has potentially far-reaching implications for the relations between men and women, both within and outside the family. For instance, not only can the idea of complex equality be employed to challenge the continued political under-representation of women in the political sphere,[88] Walzer's commitment to the autonomy of spheres ultimately also implies a re-assessment of the distribution of work within the family . After all, as long as women are the primary carers within the family and are held responsible for most of the domestic labour, it will be difficult for women to attain equality within other spheres such as political life or the world of work.

Yet despite the attractions of the idea of complex equality, advocates of a 'politics of difference' have questioned the egalitarian credentials of Walzer's approach. Like liberals, advocates of thin multiculturalism are liable to question the implications of Walzer's commitment to internal standards of justice for his vision of equality. However, while liberal objections focus upon Walzer's defence of traditional, hierarchical societies, advocates of thin multiculturalism are preoccupied with the impact of shared understandings and power relations within liberal societies. Although they endorse key liberal values, such as autonomy and the equality of the moral worth of all persons, they have also been rather critical of traditional liberal conceptions of these values. For example, much of feminist scholarship explicitly aims to challenge the historically dominant liberal conceptions of formal equality and universality. For feminist critics such as Pateman,[89] the vision of the individual as an abstract autonomous, unencumbered being which underpins the traditional liberal vision of universality and formal equality, has led liberals to ignore the particularities and contingencies of our existence. In the eyes of many feminists this failure to acknowledge the specificity of women's bodies and experiences has resulted in a discourse in which what constitutes a true individual is representative only of men's experience rather than women. Thus, according to Pateman, the tendency to regard the atomised individual as the norm has led liberal theorists either to view women and children as a deviant case or to ignore the interdependence between women and children. In the face of conceptions of personhood which effectively exclude women, an emphasis upon shared understandings has far-reaching implications for the position of women within liberal societies. Indeed, given the all-pervasive nature of patriarchy, Okin maintains that Walzer's emphasis upon internal standards of justice will support inequality not only in traditional hierarchical societies such as caste systems, but will also pose a real obstacle to the critical re-evaluation of traditional conceptions of formal equality and universality. After all from a feminist perspective gender hierarchy in many ways resembles the hierarchy of caste societies. Like caste societies, gender hierarchies are highly integrated, with a single value, masculinity, determining the distribution of a wide array of different social goods. Just as the dominance of the prevailing ideology in a caste system ensures that effective dissent is unlikely to develop, the all-encompassing and pervasive character of patriarchy ensures that 'the opportunity for competing visions of sexual difference or questioning of gender is seriously limited'.[90] Yet in the absence of such competing visions of gender relations it is difficult to envisage how effective internal – or in Walzer's terms connected – criticism can develop. In the absence of an appeal to traditional liberal conceptions of universal equality gender hierarchies, like other hierarchical societies, may prove very stable and resistant to change. The worries expressed by feminists with regard to Walzer's emphasis upon shared understandings and internal principles of justice, are liable to be shared by other traditionally marginalised groups, such as Afro-Americans, whose demands for recognition are also based upon a critical re-evaluation of the dominant conceptions of equality and universality.

The political community and the right to national self-determination

While thin multiculturalism undermines Walzer's egalitarian credentials, thick multiculturalism challenges Walzer's conception of the state as a political community united by shared meanings and common values. In this context it is important to distinguish between well-established, territorially-based national minorities and other cultural and ethnic groups whose values and way of life differ significantly from that of the majority. Walzer's emphasis upon shared meanings and internal standards of justice is clearly well placed to capture the desire by many national minorities for greater self-determination. Given that on Walzer's account a political community is entitled to take steps to protect its distinctive character, territorially well-defined minority nations, which have maintained their distinctive character and institutional framework should be supported in their desire to ensure their long-term survival. Thus, for example, Walzer's account lends support to the demands of the Quebecois in Canada or the Basques and Catalans in Spain. All three are territorially well-defined, have maintained their own distinctive language and culture, and possess an institutional framework capable of supporting self-government. Hence all three can claim to be distinctive political communities. For Walzer, the degree of independence that is to be granted to such national minorities will depend upon the aspirations of and the relationship between minority and majority, in particular the degree to which the culture of the minority differs from that of the majority. If minority and majority share significant values in common, a degree of regional autonomy may be sufficient to ensure the long-term survival of the minority. However, '[i]f the community is so radically divided that a single citizenship is not possible, then its territory must be divided too'.[91] For Walzer the decisive factor here is admission to and exclusion from the political community. Given his commitment to equal citizenship rights for all, Walzer must insist that immigration and naturalisation are decided at the level of the state. If minority and majority are sufficiently similar in terms of their make-up and aspirations as to agree a common admission policy, then the present boundaries of the state can be maintained. Should the minority, however, desire an admission policy which differs significantly from that of the majority, the minority should secede.

Although Walzer's emphasis upon differently constituted political communities lends support to the demand for greater self-determination on the part of many national minorities, who can lay claim to a well-defined territory, it is doubtful whether his account can capture the complex set of demands associated with the 'politics of difference'. While Walzer is keen to protect both the diversity of differently constituted political communities and the diversity of social goods pursued within a given political community, he pays remarkably little attention to the different groups which constitute a given political community. On the contrary, his emphasis upon shared understandings suggests a rather homogeneous conception of the political sphere. As Galston notes, Walzer's vision of the political community ultimately rests upon the assumption that 'moral, legal and political communities are congruent', so that 'the community of shared meanings is also the sovereign nation state'.[92] However, this vision of the nation state as a moral community is quite ill-suited to reflect the diversity which characterises modern multi-cultural societies. As his account of 'Liberalism 1' suggests, for Walzer the disagreements which accompany the diversity of conceptions of the good, characteristic of modern liberal societies, are best regarded as disputes with the liberal cultural tradition. Thus, on Walzer's account, the rich diversity and complexity which characterise modern liberal societies, simply reflect the diverse and often conflicting interpretations of the meaning of liberal values.

Such a characterisation of the 'politics of difference', however, clearly underestimates the degree of diversity within contemporary liberal societies. While the debates surrounding thin multiculturalism can be seen as premised upon a shared commitment to key liberal values such as individual freedom and the equality of the moral worth of all persons, instances of thick multiculturalism are characterised by a fundamental conflict of values. Thus, for instance, while some religious minorities, such as 'born again' Christians in America or some members of the Muslim community in the UK, have attempted to ensure that in the course of schooling their children are not exposed to views and values which challenge their religious commitments, many liberals view such demands as a threat to the aims of a liberal education, which seeks to encourage critical rationality and independence in an attempt to foster the development of an autonomous life-style. The difficulties here are illustrated quite clearly by debates surrounding the education of ethnic minority children in Britain discussed in Chapter 3. While most liberals regard personal autonomy as an integral aspect of human dignity and as such take it to be of paramount importance, some religious minorities fear that an autonomy-valuing education will undermine their children's faith commitments. After all, the critical open-minded ethos of an education geared towards the development of autonomy may well engender doubt in children about the validity if their faith commitments.

Unlike most national minorities, groups such as 'born again' Christians in America or members of the Muslim community in Britain are territorially dispersed and frequently lack a well-developed institutional framework. Thus, while in the case of most national minorities a radical conflict of values can ultimately be resolved via secession, this avenue does not constitute a viable option in many instances of thick multiculturalism. Consequently, such groups must seek a political accommodation within the boundaries of the existing political community. Yet, given that for Walzer the meanings of social goods are internal to cultural traditions, there is no reason to assume that cultural communities whose values differ fundamentally will be able to agree on shared meanings over values such as local autonomy or cultural diversity. Indeed Walzer acknowledges that such disputes between cultural traditions are liable to remain profoundly problematic and that in these instances '[p]olitics must . . . substitute for justice'.[93] Nonetheless, given his vision of the state as a political community based upon shared meaning and values, Walzer must insist that such disagreements are resolved at the level of the overall political community. Walzer's explicit aim here is to develop a common framework which will allow deeply divided societies to slowly develop a common life.[94] This, however, places minority communities whose values differ significantly from those of the majority community in a very vulnerable position. For instance, the long-term survival of indigenous communities often requires admission policies that are notably more restrictive than those suitable for the majority community. Thus in Canada a number of indigenous tribes have sought to place restrictions on the rights of non-indigenous people to settle, own property and vote in aboriginal territories.[95] As Walzer himself recognises, since in most instances it is no longer possible to restore aboriginal tribes to 'anything remotely resembling their former independence',[96] secession does not constitute a viable alternative for most aboriginal peoples. Hence on Walzer's account indigenous peoples must seek an accommodation within existing state boundaries. However, given that membership of the community must be distributed in accordance with the shared meaning this social good has in the wider political community, attempts by minority communities to develop their own admission policy would not be legitimate. Thus on Walzer's account, the degree of diversity and cultural autonomy available within a given society will depend upon the value the wider political community attaches to these goods. While the commitment to tolerance characteristic of liberal nation states implies a degree of respect for ethnic and religious differences, Walzer openly acknowledges that this may guarantee minorities no more than the 'freedom to express their differences in the voluntary associations of the civil society'.[97] Thus Kymlicka argues that the emphasis Walzer places upon the political rather than the cultural community gives rise to a situation in which the 'equality of individuals as members and co-creators of a culture is replaced by a fictitious equality of individuals as citizens of a self-determining state'.[98] If shared meanings and principles of justice are to be determined at the level of the political community, only the wider political community is granted a 'right to cultural survival'. In the final analysis an approach which emphasises common citizenship and the political sphere, cannot safeguard the way of life of traditional cultural communities whose values and needs differ significantly from those of the wider political community. As Veit Bader notes,[99] historically the nation state has been a cultural unifier and one of the strongest enemies of diversity. While the protection of diversity clearly requires some degree of closure, approaches such as Walzer's which seek closure at the level of the nation state, cannot meet the aspirations of culturally diverse minorities campaigning for recognition within contemporary liberal nation states.

Liberal Nationalism and the Dangers of Secession

Although Taylor and Walzer offer two distinctive attempts to provide a liberal defence of a 'right to cultural survival', both approaches encounter similar difficulties. Not only do both thinkers ultimately fail to take into account the complexity and degree of diversity in contemporary liberal societies, both also underestimate the tensions between a 'right to cultural survival' and key liberal commitments such as autonomy and equality. Nonetheless the vision of a liberal national community offered by Taylor and Walzer is liable to appeal to at least some national minorities currently campaigning for self-determination. However, this appeal is not without its difficulties. The main problems here centre upon the question of secession. Both Walzer and Taylor stress that secession only constitutes one of a wide variety of possible means of resolving disputes. Indeed Taylor, in line with his opposition to the break-up of the existing Canadian state, aims to show that the Canadian dispute is best seen as a disagreement between two strands of liberalism and thus can potentially be resolved without resorting to secession. Yet, despite such caution, Taylor's and Walzer's account of the state as a political community links cultural membership and sovereignty and thus lends support to the idea that every 'people' is entitled to its own nation state. Given the heterogeneity of most existing states, this rather encourages moves towards secession. Yet the break-up of existing states carries with it considerable risks. In the light of the very large number of potential nations, there may 'simply not be sufficient usable space and other resources for every culture to have its own autonomous territory'.[100] Furthermore, the fragmentation which would accompany widespread secession would in all likelihood threaten political stability and give rise to widespread confrontation. After all, secession not only challenges the jurisdiction of the state, but also involves claims to territory and resources. Here it is important to bear in mind that in most cases groups seeking to secede will also contain cultural minorities which may in turn feel threatened by the assertion of nationhood on the part of the present minority. Finally, it is doubtful whether the idea of comparatively homogeneous nation states is really compatible with the idea of promoting difference and diversity. Taylor's and Walzer's conception of cultural communities as separate, bounded and comparatively homogeneous rests, to a considerable extent, upon what Tully so aptly refers to as a 'billiard-ball' conception of culture, nation and society.[101] However, as Buchanan notes, 'only if the boundaries – political, intellectual, cultural and aesthetic – of the various societies are *permeable* will individuals in one society be able to enjoy the diversity among societies'.[102] In the face of such dangers even theorists such as Buchanan, who supports the idea of a moral right to secession, believe that such a right must be carefully circumscribed. For instance, for Buchanan[103] the goal of cultural preservation only succeeds in justifying secession, if 1. the culture in question is genuinely imperilled; 2. less disruptive ways of preserving a culture, such as minority group rights within the existing state are not available or are inadequate; 3. the culture meets minimal standards of justice; 4. the culture does not wish to establish an illiberal state that would threaten basic individual and political rights and which would deny the right to free exit, and 5. neither the state nor a third party can show a valid claim to the seceding territory.

Yet, despite their desire to protect the identity of differently constituted societies, neither Taylor nor Walzer offers a well-defined, carefully delineated account of the scope and limits of the right to secede. On the contrary Walzer quite readily endorses secession as a solution to profound moral conflict. Not only does Walzer fail to address the potential dangers of secession, his emphasis upon common citizenship and the political community makes his approach hostile to less disruptive ways of preserving a culture, such as minority groups rights within the existing state. Furthermore, Walzer's emphasis upon internal standards of justice does not allow him to set limits on the kind of state to be established. Yet, as Buchanan's criteria for secession suggest, liberals would at least wish to ensure that citizens of a newly established illiberal state would not be denied the right to free exit. In contrast to Walzer, Taylor's analysis of the Canadian constitutional crisis leads him to explore the idea of federal structures to accommodate different national communities within one state. However, given his vision of the state as a political community, it is difficult to see how such a federation could succeed. According to Taylor, the Canadian constitutional crisis can be resolved if the constitution recognises 'deep diversity' and acknowledges that members of minority nations belong in a very different way and are 'Canadian through being members of their national communities'.[104] Thus the federal state recognises the primary attachment of these citizens to their national community. Yet, as Horton notes,[105] if the primary identity of citizens is as members of their national community, it is difficult to see what common good the federation will secure. While an alliance can promote law and order, security and common provisions, and may well be of instrumental benefit to the various national communities that constitute it, Taylor himself recognises that 'securing common goods in this sense is not sufficient to make them a single people'.[106] In the absence of a genuine sense of common purpose over and above the purely instrumental, a federation which recognises 'deep diversity' will be difficult to maintain in the long-run. The reservations that surround Taylor's and Walzer's attempts to support national minorities in their struggle to preserve their distinctive culture suggest that if these approaches are to succeed, both theorists must still address difficult questions surrounding secession. In the final analysis not only are the 'liberal credentials' of the approach advocated by Taylor and Walzer open to question, it is doubtful whether their vision of a 'right to cultural survival' can address the complex demands and potential difficulties associated with both thin and thick multiculturalism. Thus, although the vision of a liberal national community advocated by Taylor and Walzer may appeal to some national minorities campaigning for self-determination, it cannot offer an adequate response to the wider questions posed by the 'politics of difference'.

Notes and References

1. C. Taylor, *The Ethics of Authenticity* (Cambridge, MA: Harvard University Press, 1991); 'The Politics of Recognition', in A. Gutmann and C. Taylor (eds), *Multiculturalism and the Politics of Recognition* (Princeton: Princeton University Press, 1992) pp. 25–73; 'Nationalism and Modernity', in R. McKim and J. McMahan (eds), *The Morality of Nationalism* (New York: Oxford University Press, 1997), pp. 31–55. M. Walzer, *Spheres of Justice* (Oxford: Blackwell, 1983); M. Walzer, 'Comment' in A. Gutmann and C. Taylor (eds), *Multiculturalism and the "Politics of Recognition"* (Princeton: Princeton University Press, 1992, pp. 99–103; *Thick and Thin* (Notre Dame: University of Notre Dame, 1994).
2. C. Taylor, 'The Politics of Recognition', in A. Gutman and C. Taylor (eds), *Multiculturalism and the "Politics of Recognition"*, p. 59.
3. J. Habermas, 'Struggles for Recognition in Constitutional States', *European Journal of Philosophy*, Vol. 1, No. 2, 1993, pp. 128–55.
4. R. Dworkin, 'What Justice Isn't', in *A Matter of Principle* (Oxford: Clarendon Press, 1996) pp. 214–20.
5. L. Nicholson, 'To be or not to be: Charles Taylor and the Politics of Recognition', *Constellations*, Vol. 3, No. 1, 1996, p. 1–16.
6. S. Wolf, 'Comment', in A. Gutman and C. Taylor (eds), *Multiculturalism and "The Politics of Recognition"*, pp. 75–85.
7. W. Kymlicka, *Liberalism, Community and Culture* (Oxford: Clarendon Press, 1989).
8. For a good account of Taylor's views on the rise of the ideals of authenticity and equal dignity see L. Vogel, 'Critical Notices: *The Ethics of Authenicity* and *Multiculturalism and The Politics of Recognition*, *International Journal of Philosophical Studies*, Vol. 1, Part 2, 1993, pp. 325–35.
9. See Chapter 1 for a discussion of the Romantic conception of originality and diversity.
10. C. Taylor, *The Ethics of Authenticity*, p. 41.
11. See C. Taylor, *Sources of the Self: the making of modern identity* (Cambridge: Cambridge University Press, 1989).
12. C. Taylor, 'The Politics of Recognition', in A. Gutman and C. Taylor (eds), *Multiculturalism and the "Politics of Recognition"*, p. 32.
13. Ibid. p. 25.
14. C. Houston, 'Alternative Modernities – Islamism and Secularism on Charles Taylor', *Critique of Anthropology*, Vol. 18, No. 2, 1998, pp. 234–40, p. 238.
15. C. Taylor, 'Nationalism and Modernity', in R. McKim and J. McMahan (eds), *The Morality of Nationalism*.
16. A. Gutman, 'Introduction' in A. Gutman and C. Taylor (eds), *Multiculturalism and the "Politics of Recognition"*, pp. 3–24.
17. C. Taylor, 'The Politics of Recognition', in A. Gutman and C. Taylor (eds), *Multiculturalism and the "Politics of Recognition"*, p. 38.

18. Ibid. p. 39.
19. Ibid. p. 60.
20. Ibid. p. 59.
21. Ibid.
22. Ibid. p. 61.
23. C. Taylor, 'Nationalism and Modernity', in R. McKim and J. McMahan (eds), *The Morality of Nationalism*, pp. 31–55, p. 52.
24. C. Taylor, 'The Politics of Recognition', in A. Gutman and C. Taylor (eds), *Multiculturalism and "The Politics of Recognition"*, p. 69.
25. Ibid. p. 62.
26. S. Rockefeller, 'Comment', in A. Gutman and C. Taylor (eds), *Multiculturalism and "The Politics of Recognition"*, pp. 87–98, p. 92.
27. J Habermas, 'Struggles for Recognition in Constitutional States', p. 131.
28. A. Ripstein, 'Recognition and Cultural Membership', *Dialogue*, Vol. 34 (1995), Part 2, pp. 331–41, p. 333.
29. See for instances the responses by members of the Muslim community in Britain to the recommendations by the Committee of Inquiry into the Education of Children from Ethnic Minority Groups discussed in Chapter 3.
30. A. Ripstein, 'Recognition and Cultural Membership', p. 336.
31. Ibid. p. 335.
32. A. Oksenberg Rorty, 'The Hidden Politics of Cultural Identification', *Political Theory*, Vol. 22, No. 1, Feb. 1994, pp. 152–66.
33. C. Houston, 'Alternative Modernities, Islamism and Secularism on Charles Taylor'.
34. Ibid. p. 238.
35. A. Oksenberg Rorty, 'The Hidden Politics of Cultural Identification', p. 158.
36. Ibid. p. 159.
37. Ibid. p. 158.
38. L. Nicholson, 'To be or not to be: Charles Taylor and the politics of recognition'.
39. S. Wolf, 'Comment', in A. Gutman and C. Taylor (eds), 'Multiculturalism and "The Politics of Recognition"; L. Nicholson, 'To be or not to be'.
40. S. Wolf, 'Comment', p. 77.
41. L. Nicholson, 'To be or not to be: Charles Taylor and the politics of recogition', p. 6.
42. Ibid.
43. Ibid. p. 11.
44. S. Wolf, 'Comment', in A. Gutman and C. Taylor, *Multiculturalism and "The Politics of Recognition"*, p. 83.
45. For a good account of Taylor's approach to the Quebec question see G. Laforest, 'Philosophical and political judgement in a multicultural federation', in J. Tully (ed.), *Philosophy in an Age of Pluralism* (Cambrdge: Cambridge University Press, 1994) pp. 194–209.
46. A. Oksenberg Rorty, 'The Hidden Politics of Cultural Identification'.
47. S. Akhtar, *The Final Imperative* (London: Bellew Publishing, 1991); A. L.

Tibawi, 'Islamic Education: Its Traditions and Modernisation into the Arab National Systems', cited in J. R. Muir, 'The Isocratic Ideal of Education and Islamic Education', *Papers of the Philosophy of Education Society* (March 31–April 2 1995), pp. 28–36.

48. C. Taylor, 'The Politics of Recognition', in A. Gutman and C. Taylor (eds), *Multiculturalism and "The Politics of Recognition"*, p. 62.

49. M. Walzer, *Spheres of Justice*, p. 8.

50. Walzer offers an account of the sources of this thin universalism in *Thick and Thin: Moral Argument at Home and Abroad*. While Walzer acknowledges that we share a universal core morality, he stresses that this does not suggest that people begin with a thin morality, which gradually thickens. On the contrary, '[m]orality is thick from the beginning, culturally integrated, fully resonant, and it reveals itself thinly only on special occasions, when moral language is turned to specific purposes' (p. 6). For Walzer this thin universalism stems from the recognition of a partial communality and reflects the fact that we have moral expectations not only about the behaviour of our fellow citizens, but also about the conduct of strangers.

51. M. Walzer, *Spheres of Justice*, p. xv.

52. Ibid. p. 313.

53. M. Walzer, *Thick and Thin: Moral Argumemt at Home and Abroad*, p. 33.

54. M. Walzer, *Spheres of Justice*, p. 8.

55. Ibid. p. 4.

56. D. Miller, 'Introduction', in D. Miller and M. Walzer (eds), *Pluralism, Justice and Equality* (Oxford: Oxford University Press, 1995) pp. 1–16.

57. M. Walzer, *Spheres of Justice*, p. 10.

58. Walzer, *Thick and Thin*.

59. S. O'Neill, *Impartiality in Context*, p. 69.

60. M. Walzer, *Spheres of Justice*, p. 28.

61. Ibid. p. 15n.

62. Ibid. p. 46.

63. Walzer, for instance, contends that a newly established state cannot expel a long-standing alien minority from the state's territory. The inhabitants have an attachment to the place and a reasonable expectation not to be forced to be transferred to another country.

64. Ibid. p. 47.

65. M. Walzer, 'Comment', in A. Gutman and C. Taylor (eds), *Multiculturalism and "The Politics of Difference"*, p. 100.

66. Ibid. p. 102.

67. M. Walzer, 'Spheres of Justice' p. 44.

68. Ibid.

69. M. Walzer, *Thick and Thin: Moral Argument at Home and Abroad*, p. 72.

70. Ibid. p. 73.

71. Ibid. p. 74.

72. Ibid.

73. R. Dworkin, 'What Justice Isn't', in *A Matter of Principle*.

74. R. Dworkin, '"Spheres of Justice": An Exchange', *The New York Review of Books*, 21 July 1983, pp. 43–6, p. 45.
75. Ibid. p. 46.
76. Ibid.
77. S. O'Neill, *Impartiality in Context* (Albany: State University of New York Press, 1997), p. 84.
78. J. Cohen, 'Spheres of Justice: A Defence of Pluralism and Equality', Book Review, *The Journal of Philosophy*, 83 (1986), pp. 457–68, p. 462.
79. M. Walzer, *Spheres of Justice*, p. 27.
80. Ibid. p. 313.
81. S. Moller Okin, *Justice Gender and the Family* (US: Basic Books, 1989) p. 64.
82. Ibid. p. 67.
83. J. Friedman, 'The Politics of Communitarianism', *Critical Review*, Vol. 8, No. 2, 1994, pp. 297–340, p. 311.
84. S. Moller Okin, *Justice Gender and the Family* p. 65.
85. Indeed for Dworkin a commitment to equality is the defining feature of liberalism.
86. M. Walzer, p. 240.
87. S. Moller Okin, *Justice, Gender and the Family*, p. 116.
88. S. Moller Okin, 'Politics and the Complex Inequality of Gender', in D. Miller and M. Walzer (eds), *Pluralism, Justice and Equality* (Oxford: Oxford University Press, 1995) pp. 120–43.
89. C. Pateman, 'The Theoretical Subversiveness of Feminism', in C. Pateman and E. Gross (eds), *Feminist Challenges* (Sydney: Alllen & Unwin, 1988) pp. 1–10.
90. S. Moller Okin, *Justice, Gender and the Family*, p. 66.
91. M. Walzer, *Spheres of Justice*, p. 62.
92. W. Galston, 'Community, Democracy, Philosophy: The Political Thought of Michael Walzer', *Political Theory*, Vol. 17, No. 1, February 1989, pp. 119 –30, p. 121. On this point see also V. Bader, 'Citizenship and Exclusion: Radical Democracy, Community and Justice. Or, What is Wrong with Communitarianism', *Political Theory*, Vol. 23, No. 2, May 1995, pp. 211–46
93. M. Walzer, 'Spheres of Justice: An Exchange', p. 44.
94. See M. Walzer, 'Spheres of Justice: An Exchange', p. 44: 'If the populations were mixed, as they most often are, then it might be (morally) necessary to work out a political accommodation. Politics must sometimes substitute for justice, providing a neutral frame within which a common life develops'.
95. W. Kymlicka, *Liberalism, Community and Culture* (Oxford: Clarendon Press, 1989).
96. M. Walzer, *Thick and Thin: Moral Argument at Home and Abroad*, p. 72.
97. Ibid. p. 74.
98. W. Kymlicka, *Liberalism, Community and Culture*, p. 227.
99. V. Bader, 'Citizenship and Exclusion: Radical Democracy, Community and Justice. Or, What is Wrong with Communitarianism'.

100. A. Buchanan, *Secession: The Morality of Political Divorce from Fort Sumter to Lithuania and Quebec* (Oxford: Westview Press, 1991) p. 55.
101. J. Tully, *Strange Multiplicity* (Cambridge: University Press, 1995).
102. A. Buchanan, *Secession*, p. 43.
103. Ibid. p. 61.
104. C. Taylor, 'Shared and Divergent Values', in *Reconciling the Solitudes* (Montreal: McGill-Queen's University Press, 1993) pp. 155–86, p. 183.
105. J. Horton, 'Charles Taylor: Selfhood, Community and Democracy', in A. Carter and G. Stokes (eds), *Liberal Democracy and its Critics* (Cambridge: Polity Press, 1998) pp. 155–74.
106. Ibid. p. 170.

Part IV: Value Pluralism and the 'Politics of Difference'

Value Pluralism and the 'Politics of Difference'

Since the Romantics, advocates of a 'politics of difference' have criticised the liberal Enlightenment tradition for the emphasis it places upon 'generality' and the need to transcend our particularistic attachments. Yet, while in the eyes of critics this Enlightenment vision of human excellence ultimately is hostile to the very notion of diversity, many prominent liberal attempts to accommodate the demands of a 'politics of difference' have remained firmly anchored within the Enlightenment school. Thus not only is the quest for impartiality on the part of theorists such as Rawls and Habermas based upon a commitment to universal reason, attempts by liberals like Kymlicka to ground a theory of group rights in equality of respect and individual freedom continue to be premised upon the Enlightenment principles of self-conscious reflection and individual self-determination. While the difficulties which surround the responses to diversity advocated by contemporary proponents of the Enlightenment tradition suggest that this strand of liberal thought may indeed by unable to accommodate the aspirations of advocates of diversity and difference, liberalism constitutes a complex and multifaceted family of beliefs. Indeed accounts of group rights, such as Taylor's 'politics of recognition', reflect a keen awareness of the limitations of Enlightenment cosmopolitanism. However, although the idea of a liberal political community advocated by writers such as Taylor and Walzer may appeal to some national communities campaigning for self-determination, it underestimates the degree of diversity within cultures and nation states. Not only do political communities tend to contain culturally diverse minorities, group identities themselves are frequently internally contested.

In the light of the difficulties which surround prominent liberal responses to the 'politics of difference' this section will examine the distinct approach to diversity inherent in the liberal value pluralism of writers such as Isaiah Berlin and Stuart Hampshire. This strand of liberal thought rejects the preoccupation with 'universal reason' which characterises the liberal Enlightenment project in favour of a vision of human excellence that echoes the Romantic regard for diversity. For value pluralists such as Berlin and Hampshire morality is characterised by numerous, conflicting values which cannot be combined in a single life or a single society. Consequently, human identities and cultures are by their very nature diverse; each expressing a distinct set of values and virtues. Given this inherent diversity, political life is characterised by the inevitable conflict among incommensurable cultures and values. Chapter 7 explores the implications of such a robust defence of 'diversity', while Chapter 8 considers the dilemmas difference and diversity pose for both liberals and their critics.

Chapter 7: Liberal Value Pluralism, Diversity and Conflict

While contemporary liberals have explored a variety of avenues in their attempts to respond to the 'politics of difference', most of this response has remained firmly rooted within the liberal Enlightenment tradition. With the notable exception of writers such as Taylor and Walzer, most contemporary liberals have continued to emphasise the Enlightenment principles of critical rationality, self-conscious reflection, self-determination and the search for universally acceptable fundamental principles and values. Thus not only is the quest for impartiality, which informs the work of Rawls and Habermas, underpinned by a commitment to universal reason, the vision of multicultural citizenship advocated by theorists such as Kymlicka continues to endorse the Enlightenment principles of self-conscious reflection and individual self-determination. Yet, since the emergence of the Romantic movement (see Chapter 1), advocates of diversity have criticised this Enlightenment ideal of human excellence for failing to acknowledge the significance of those characteristics which distinguish particular groups from others. In the eyes of critics the emphasis the Enlightenment tradition places upon 'generality' and the need to transcend our particularistic attachments ensures that this strand of liberal thought ultimately remains hostile to the notion of diversity. Indeed the difficulties which surround the responses to diversity advocated by contemporary proponents of the Enlightenment tradition, such as Rawls, Habermas and Kymlicka, suggest that Enlightenment liberalism may well be unable to accommodate the depth and complexity of diversity associated with the 'politics of difference'.

However, the Enlightenment project constitutes only one strand of the complex and multifaceted family of beliefs which makes up liberalism. In fact in evaluating liberalism it is vital to distinguish between two distinct principles of liberal thought: 'universal reason' and 'diversity'.[1] Whereas the liberal Enlightenment project is premised upon the principles of 'universal reason', the idea of 'diversity' has played an important role in liberal thought since early attempts such as John Locke's to respond to the 'political consequences of religious difference' in the wake of the Reformation.[2] This 'post-Reformation' liberalism has been characterised by the acceptance and management of diversity through mutual toleration. In practice these principles frequently aim at opposing goals. While the Enlightenment preoccupation with universal principles of reason leads its advocates to emphasise the need to transcend 'difference', 'post-Reformation' liberalism recognises diversity as an inescapable feature of human existence. 'Universal reason' and 'diversity' are therefore best seen as the expression of two competing strands of liberal thought.

At its most robust, post-Reformation liberalism regards diversity not merely as inevitable, but as positive. Thus for this strand of liberal thought diversity constitutes a vital aspect of human excellence. Such a defence of value pluralism has been central to the work of writers such as Isaiah Berlin and Stuart Hampshire.[3] From a value pluralist perspective morality is characterised by numerous, conflicting values which cannot be harmoniously combined in a single life or a single society. Consequently, human identities and cultures are, by their very nature, diverse; each expressing a distinct set of values and virtues. Given the extent of this inherent diversity, political life is characterised by the inevitable conflict among incommensurable cultures and values. For value pluralists such as Berlin and Hampshire, such conflicts have no uniquely rational solution, but can only be resolved provisionally within the context of specific political settlements. Therefore, the aim of political life ought not to be the pursuit of truth, but that of peace through the establishment and maintenance of an equitable modus vivendi. It is this commitment to a negotiated agreement which characterises value pluralist conceptions of the political such as Richard Bellamy's idea of 'justice as politics'. According to Bellamy, justice therefore consists first and foremost in 'the peaceful resolution of conflict through the process of balancing rival claims'.[4]

To recognise diversity as intrinsically valuable clearly has potentially far-reaching consequences for contemporary liberal democracies confronted by the demands of a 'politics of difference'. Given the emphasis value pluralists place upon negotiation and arbitration, such conceptions of liberalism will favour conceptions of democracy which stress the importance of public agreement as a means of justifying and legitimating political decisions. However, while value pluralists will welcome the procedural frameworks for the free and equal participation of all citizens developed by advocates of deliberative democracy such as Habermas, this strand of liberal thought rejects Habermasian notions of a rational consensus. On the contrary, value pluralism implies an agonal vision of the political, which acknowledges the inevitability of conflict.

Given its robust defence of 'diversity', liberal value pluralism is potentially rather attractive to advocates of both thin and thick multiculturalism. After all, a liberalism which recognises the inherent diversity of cultures and values not only acknowledges its own historical contingency, but also accepts that it cannot insulate itself from the dynamic of value conflict. Thus not only do value pluralists appreciate the profound diversity associated with thick multiculturalism, they are also keenly aware of the contested nature of the traditional conceptions of liberal values. Hence liberal value pluralism is sensitive to the desire of advocates of thin multiculturalism to reconceptualise the values of liberty and equality. However, while liberal value pluralism can accommodate the depth and complexity of the 'politics of difference', this strand of liberal thought is not entirely unproblematic from the perspective of both thin and thick multiculturalism. Indeed the emphasis value pluralists place upon the inevitability of conflict and the contingent nature of political agreements may at times threaten the standing of minorities.

This preoccupation with negotiation and political stability in the face of inevitable conflict may also trouble liberals. Given the wide diversity of possible ideological frameworks and the variety of existing cultures and cultural mixes, there is no reason to assume that liberalism will always be best-placed to secure peace and stability. As the outcome of a specific political agreement liberalism has no unique claim to reason, but, just like other conceptions of the good, has to prove its capacity to generate peace and stability within a specific political context. Thus, while liberal value pluralism as advocated by Berlin and Hampshire is clearly better placed than the currently dominant liberal Enlightenment tradition to respond constructively to the depth and complexity of diversity associated with the 'politics of difference', such a position is not without its dangers for both liberals and advocates of diversity.

Two Liberalisms

The principles of the Enlightenment undoubtedly have had a profound influence upon contemporary liberalism. Not only have many contemporary liberals continued to endorse the Enlightenment ideals of critical rationality, self-conscious reflection and self-determination, much of contemporary liberalism has remained preoccupied with the search for universally acceptable fundamental values and principles. Thus, just as the philosophers of the Enlightenment believed that critical rationality and conscious reflection would enable mankind to overcome national and cultural disagreements, contemporary liberals such as Rawls and Habermas have attempted to respond to the demands of the 'politics of difference' by searching for a neutral and impartial point of view grounded in universal reason, which can surmount difference and provide the basis for a common framework. In a similar vein, the commitment of Enlightenment thinkers to rational self-determination and individual freedom has continued to shape the vision of a liberal multicultural society advocated by proponents of liberal group rights such as Raz and Kymlicka. Hence, for both Raz and Kymlicka it is the contribution cultural membership makes to individual freedom and autonomy which makes it of value and which sets the limits to the support cultural groups can expect in their attempt to perpetuate themselves. Yet, since the Romantic critique of the ideals of 'generality' and 'uniformity', critics have rejected this Enlightenment vision of human excellence for failing to acknowledge the significance of those characteristics which distinguish particular groups from others. Hence, just as Romantics such as Herder set out to assert the value and pervasiveness of diversity in the face of the cosmopolitanism of the Enlightenment, contemporary advocates of a 'politics of difference' have been united in their attempt to highlight the political significance of our particular identities and allegiances.

However, while the emphasis upon 'universal reason', which characterises Enlightenment liberalism, may ultimately remain hostile to the aspirations of the advocates of difference and diversity, the Enlightenment project constitutes only one strand of the complex and multifaceted family of beliefs which makes up liberalism. Indeed in evaluating liberalism it is vital to distinguish between two distinct principles of liberal thought: 'universal reason' and 'diversity'. While the idea of 'universal reason' is central to the Enlightenment project, respect for diversity and difference has played an important role in the development of liberal thought since the Reformation. This regard for diversity can be seen to reflect the earlier Renaissance humanism of writers such as Montaigne, whose work is characterised by open-mindedness, sceptical tolerance, and a keen awareness of the limits of general theory.[5] In a similar vein, confronted with the religious strife which accompanied the Reformation, early liberals advocated the acceptance and management of diversity through toleration. John Locke, for example, in his famous *A Letter Concerning Toleration* defends tolerance of religious diversity in part on the grounds that religious belief cannot be coerced.[6] The relationship between such 'post-Reformation' arguments for the toleration of diversity and the

Enlightenment themes of 'universal reason' and 'autonomy' is clearly a complex and subtle one. The notion of faith as an expression of individual conscience – as something that 'one can only do for oneself'[7] – was a central tenet of the Reformation and underpins Locke's rejection of attempts to enforce faith as irrational. Thus Locke employs reason to establish the limits to toleration. Since it is not unreasonable to prohibit religious practices which threaten civil peace and endanger the state, intolerance on such grounds is acceptable. However, while the Enlightenment themes of 'universal reason' and 'autonomy' have clearly played an important role in classical liberal arguments for toleration, post-Reformation liberalism differs from the Enlightenment strand in its recognition that a diversity of values and beliefs and the ensuing tensions and conflicts constitute unavoidable features of human existence. Hence, whereas the Enlightenment tradition demands that citizens transcend their differences, post-Reformation liberalism views 'difference' as intractable. Furthermore, in practice, far from harmoniously complementing each other, the principles of 'universal reason' and 'diversity' frequently aim at opposing goals. For instance, the systematic promotion of critical rationality and open-mindedness is liable to undermine the long-term viability of religious groups whose life-style requires faith in divine revelation. Indeed it is precisely these fears which lie at the heart of the objections to the principles of a liberal education recently voiced by sections of the Muslim community in Britain and some groups of 'born-again Christians' in the United States.[8] Thus, the principles of 'universal reason' and 'diversity' are best seen as the expression of two competing strands of liberal thought.

Although the acceptance of profound diversity, characteristic of post-Reformation liberalism, can be defended via a variety of pragmatic or instrumental arguments, such as Locke's discussion of toleration,[9] a commitment to diversity is likely to be at its most robust if diversity is seen as an intrinsic value. Such a principled commitment to diversity echoes the Romantic vision of diversity as the very essence of excellence. Consequently, liberals committed to diversity as an intrinsic value have been sensitive to the concerns identified by the Romantics. It is these ideas and concerns which inform the rather distinctive liberalism of thinkers such as Berlin and Hampshire. Given the affinity between the Romantic critique of the Enlightenment and the worries expressed by many contemporary advocates of diversity, this strand of liberal thought appears to be well placed to respond positively to the challenges of a 'politics of difference'.

Diversity as an Intrinsic Value

The plurality of values

The idea of diversity and plurality as a positive good is deeply rooted within Western political thought and can be traced to 'the Heraclitean picture of the unavoidable and life-giving clash and friction of competing moral ideals and contrary visions of life'.[10] This vision of conflict as an essential and valuable aspect of the human condition is central to the defence of value pluralism offered by modern liberal thinkers such as Isaiah Berlin and Stuart Hampshire. For Berlin and Hampshire moral life is characterised by a plurality of values, which, due to their very natures, are bound to come into frequent conflict with one another. Thus, while ultimate values are objective and knowable, these values cannot be harmoniously combined in a single life or a single society. As Hampshire notes:

It is a general truth about human nature that the greatest, most admired, and most praiseworthy human beings are those who developed one or two of these abstractly described cardinal virtues to the highest degree, while altogether lacking others of them. It is also a general truth that some societies have specialised in the cultivation of some of these virtues, or in the cultivation of some vision of them, to the total exclusion of others.[11]

What is more, from a value pluralist perspective values are not only frequently uncombinable, they are incommensurable, that is to say they cannot be compared. Hence for value pluralists the conflict amongst ultimate values cannot be resolved by an appeal to the relative worth of each value or by attempts to find an overriding value. Values cannot be reduced 'to one value that serves as a common denominator to all the valuable ways of life'.[12] Here it is important to distinguish incommensurability from rough equality, indeterminacy and indifference. While regarding two options as of equal value implies passing a judgement about their relative value, incommensurability indicates that no judgement regarding their relative values can be made.[13] Nor does incommensurability imply indeterminacy in the sense of incompleteness or imperfection in our judgements of values. Neither does it signify indifference about the choices we have to make. As Raz notes, incommensurability is best defined in terms of a failure of transitivity. Thus, '[T]wo valuable options are incommensurable if (1) neither is better than the other and (2) there is (or could be) another option which is better than one but is not better than the other.'[14] Given that conflicting values cannot be compared, to choose one value over another always entails a sense of loss. Rather than give up a lesser pleasure for a greater one, what one loses is different in kind to the option one has chosen. To choose the life of a solitary artist in favour of the pleasures of family life simply amounts to choosing 'one way of life rather than another, both being good and not susceptible to comparison of degree'.[15] What is more, not only do these values differ in kind, the authority of what has been rejected cannot be denied.

This plurality of incommensurable values applies not merely to the relationship between the various goods which make up particular moralities or codes of conduct, but also extends to each of the goods and values in turn. Thus, for instance, the value of equality contains the incommensurable ideas of 'equality of opportunity' and 'equality of outcome'.[16] Furthermore, just as moral life is characterised by a plurality of incommensurable values, so human identities and cultures are, by their very nature, plural and diverse; each expressing a distinct set of values and virtues. Therefore, not only are clashes between ultimate values inevitable, conflicts between distinct and incommensurable cultures and identities constitute a permanent and unavoidable feature of human existence. This is not to suggest that cultures are immutable. Cultures clearly do respond to one another, be it in order to distinguish themselves from one another or, alternatively, accommodate each other. Besides, in complex modern societies individuals are frequently heirs to numerous and contradictory cultural traditions, giving rise to a complex interplay of values.

Although different individuals and societies develop and cultivate different values, Berlin and Hampshire stress that we are nonetheless capable of recognising what is of value in other life-styles and patterns of social organisation.[17] However, as Raz[18] notes, this appreciation of other ways of life always co-exists with a degree of rejection and dismissivness. Thus value pluralism inevitably gives rise to a sense of tension. Furthermore, while we can appreciate and recognise other forms of life, value pluralism does not imply that all life-styles are of equal value. According to Hampshire value conflicts should not be resolved by resort to brute force, domination and tyranny. Therefore some ways of life, such as Nazism, which deliberately aimed to 'eliminate all notions of fairness and justice'[19] in favour of physical conflict and violence, are absolutely evil.[20]

The 'drive for diversity'

The emphasis upon inherent diversity springs from the conception of human nature at the heart of value pluralism. In the eyes of Berlin and Hampshire humans are essentially self-creating and self-transforming beings. Hence our common humanity only partially determines our nature. Here Hampshire invites us to distinguish between our common human potentialities and the equally human drive for diversity, which leads to these common needs being realised and satisfied in many different ways.[21] Thus, while the structure of human thought is shaped by highly abstract categories or norms such as fairness, truth and so on, these can manifest themselves in a great variety of ways, each historically and culturally specific. Consequently the substantive content of these categories or norms can never be specified or fixed once and for all.[22] Thus, for example, while the recognition of some form of justice may be essential to all valuable forms of human association, different societies have developed a wide variety of frequently incompatible conceptions of justice. Since our common humanity does not determine our nature, the values we pursue will in part be a reflection of our particular historical, political and cultural heritage.

This embedded and encumbered vision of the self echoes the significance Taylor and Walzer attach to cultural membership. However, while Taylor and Walzer recognise a plurality of cultural and moral perspectives, they view each perspective as quite settled and internally coherent. Thus for Taylor and Walzer the plurality of competing values is predominantly a question of choosing between a plurality of moral traditions and cultures (see Chapter 6). This contrasts sharply with Berlin's and Hampshire's vision of values, moral perspectives and cultures as inherently conflictual and internally incommensurable. From a value pluralist perspective, value conflict cannot be restricted to the sphere of competing moral traditions. On the contrary, it affects all aspects of human life.[23] This emphasis upon a genuine diversity of values also distinguishes value pluralism from the views of writers such as Kymlicka, who sees self-creation primarily in terms of the liberal ideal of autonomy. Value pluralists, however, view autonomy as only one of the possible forms of self-creation. After all as Gray notes, the value pluralist's

conception of human nature as only partially determinate and accordingly culturally variable to a significant degree . . . is a very different animal from the conception of man as a species whose most distinctive activity, and the activity which is the precondition for all which is most valuable in human life, is the making of choices.[24]

The rejection of 'universal reason'

In the light of their conception of human nature, value pluralists such as Berlin have sought to somewhat distance themselves from the views and goals associated with the Enlightenment. While Berlin admires the Enlightenment[25] in as far as its attack upon dogmas, prejudices and superstitions mitigated suffering, prevented injustice and exposed ignorance,[26] his emphasis on the plurality of values leads him to reject the Enlightenment goal of gradual convergence upon a universally shared set of liberal values. As Garrard[27] notes, although Berlin admires the commitment of the Enlightenment philosophers to individual freedom, he believes that in the final analysis the notion of individual freedom is incompatible with the Enlightenment ideal of 'universal reason'. The attempt to make humanity conform to a single truth encourages an authoritarianism which at its most extreme gives rise to the Rousseauesque picture of forcing people to be free. It is this keen awareness of the tensions within the Enlightenment ideal which makes Berlin sensitive to the insights of the Romantics. Hence, whereas Berlin repudiates the irrationalism of the romantic epoch, he endorses the romantic conception of man's ends as unpredictable and frequently incompatible. Thus Berlin maintains that:

the romantics have dealt a fatal blow to the proposition that, all appearances to the contrary, a definite solution of the jigsaw puzzle is, at least in principle, possible, that power in the service of reason can achieve it, that rational organisation can bring about the perfect union of such values and counter-values as individual liberty and social equality.[28]

As John Gray notes, this rejection of 'universal reason' undermines the notion of rational choice, so central to the liberal Enlightenment tradition and its goal of establishing universal values. For value pluralists choices among incommensurable values are underdetermined by reason. Consequently there cannot be one value which in all cases prevails over others. Hence conflicts of values cannot be settled a prioi via an appeal to abstract principles of rational choice. Reason cannot 'advise us how to choose between options which are incommensurate'.[29] This is not to suggest that in particular cases reason has nothing to say about which value should prevail under these circumstances. Given a particular individual's commitments and circumstances it may well be rational to pursue one option rather than another. As Raz notes, while an action may well be rational in as far as it is based upon what a particular individual takes to be an undefeated reason, this does not necessarily imply that it is 'action for a reason which defeats all others'.[30]

Value conflict and the political sphere

The rejection of 'universal reason' clearly has important implications for the political sphere. In the absence of universal values and standards we cannot establish purely theoretically a generally applicable set of basic liberties and fundamental rights. On the contrary, value pluralism implies that the restraint of liberty and the establishment of basic rights are political rather than theoretical or jurisprudential questions. Value pluralism therefore entails the primacy of the political over the legal and theoretical. For value pluralists, political life is the domain in which the inevitable conflicts among different values can be negotiated. The aim of such negotiation is to find mechanisms which prevent this conflict from becoming a physical conflict – 'the Hobbesian war of "all against all"'.[31] As Hampshire notes, the basic procedures governing adjudication and negotiation, such as principles of fair discussion, are understood and applied across a wide variety of religious, moral and philosophical beliefs. Indeed, almost all societies have found it necessary to establish institutions and procedures 'for adjudicating between conflicting moral claims advanced by individuals or groups within a society', cabinets or councils to discuss various policy options, and diplomatic channels to negotiate conflicts of interests with neighbouring societies.[32] For Hampshire all these institutions and procedures 'involve the fair weighting and balancing of contrary arguments bearing on an unavoidable and disputable issue'.[33] All are therefore 'subject to the single prescription "*audi alteram partem*" ("Hear the other side")'.[34] In his opinion, it is this principle of adversarial argument which provides the paradigm for intellectual thought. Thus individuals transfer and duplicate the adversarial patterns of public and inter-personal life in their private deliberations. Given that all human beings at times encounter competing and incompatible demands, they are all familiar with the need to weigh up and balance contrary arguments and to draw conclusions from them. According to Hampshire, it is this general experience of having to weigh pros and cons, which provides the basis for a shared minimal conception of justice. It is therefore not surprising to find that there is a widespread agreement among cultures and conceptions of the good that at its most basic justice requires the establishment of a regular and reasonable procedure for weighing claims and counter claims. Such procedures ought to be fair and ensure that the conditions under which adversarial argument takes place do not grossly favour one side.[35]

The emphasis this shared minimal conception of justice places on negotiation implies the establishment of institutional mechanisms which enable the members of all value and belief groups to participate. on a fair basis in the deliberation of public issues and the formulation of public policy. However, while this minimal, shared conception of justice allows us to establish a procedural framework which facilitates conflict resolution, these '[u]niversal and abstract principles of justice will under-determine what counts as equal and fair dealing in the widely various contexts of negotiation'.[36] The shared procedural rules can therefore not generate substantive conclusions. Furthermore, the institutional character of the procedural framework is liable to vary according to historical and social circumstances. Since value conflicts have no uniquely rational solution, they can only be resolved provisionally within the context of specific historical settlements. Consequently, while there is widespread agreement that justice requires that all sides be given a fair hearing, 'the requirements of justice vary immensely in different places and at different times in virtue of local customs and rules'.[37] Thus, the shared political culture and values which help to contain conflict within a particular political community should be regarded as the product of a practical political agreement. Yet, since no society can hope harmoniously to combine all values, such political agreements will always be subject to challenge and revision. In the final analysis the procedures for conflict resolution in any state will never be perfectly fair or completely unbiased and thus will always be open to criticism. Hence for Hampshire 'justice is strife':

political prudence . . . must expect a perpetual contest between hostile conceptions of justice and must develop acceptable procedures for regulating and refereeing the contest. The contests are unending if only because what is generally thought substantively just and fair today will not be thought just and fair tomorrow . . . The rock bottom justice is in the contests themselves, in the tension of open opposition, always renewed.[38]

This emphasis upon negotiation and conflict also lies at the heart of Richard Bellamy's conception of 'justice as politics'. For Bellamy the core meaning of justice is to be found in the 'peaceful resolution of conflict through the process of balancing rival claims so as to arrive at an agreement acceptable to all parties'.[39] Agreement here does not depend on the nature of the decision itself, but on having one's interests and values taken into account. In this sense 'authoritative choice can be accepted as right choice even when one believes it to be incorrect'.[40] However, given that no society can combine all values and that values always remain open to a variety of interpretations, justice can never get beyond the political struggle to achieve and maintain an equitable modus vivendi. Value pluralism therefore implies a dynamic conception of the political community. This dynamic is driven not by a search for truth, but by a desire for peace, to be secured via the establishment of a dynamic modus vivendi.

Liberalism and Value Pluralism

The relationship between value pluralism and liberalism is a complex and subtle one. Clearly, core liberal ideals such as negative liberty, toleration and a limited state, which does not seek to impose a particular ranking of values upon its citizens, encourage diversity and thus acknowledge the plurality of values. However, value pluralism does not privilege liberalism. After all, non-liberal societies need not deny the truth of value pluralism. Recognition of the value of other ways of life does not imply that a particular society cannot insist upon the preservation of the specific ranking of incommensurable values which 'are embedded in and necessary for the survival of a particular way of life that is itself worthwhile.'[41] Indeed, given 'that not all values *can* be pluralistically combined and that some become very pale in too much pluralistic company',[42] pluralist liberal societies, in all their diversity, will only reflect a limited range of possible values. Hence from a value pluralist perspective illiberal societies which shelter worthwhile ways of life are a vital expression of the diversity of fundamental values. Such societies are therefore entitled to seek to preserve their way of life.

For John Gray, liberalism grounded in value pluralism is distinguished by its 'agonistic character, its acknowledgement of an irreducible diversity of rivalrous goods'.[43] Hence a commitment to value pluralism gives rise to a genuinely political conception of liberalism. Such a liberalism will not only acknowledge its own historical contingency, but will also accept that it cannot insulate itself from the dynamic entailed in value conflict. From a value pluralist perspective, liberalism is best seen as one particular cultural perspective characterised by its own specific ranking of values. Thus rather than seek universal justifications for the core values and principles that define a liberal society, value pluralist liberals will base their defence of liberalism upon the social milieu and historical circumstances which have given rise to liberal societies. From such a perspective liberalism is best seen as the expression of a particular practical political settlement, which gradually emerges from the long controversies surrounding religious toleration that accompanied the Reformation and its aftermath.

Not only does value pluralism favour a historicist defence of liberalism, it also gives rise to a liberalism which accepts the dynamic of value conflict. Apart from the inevitable conflict between itself and other ways of life, liberalism must, on this analysis, also realise that the very liberties at the heart of its theory are at times incommensurable. As Berlin notes, not only are the values of liberty and equality potentially incommensurable, they each in turn entail conflicting elements, leading, in the case of liberty, not only to tensions between positive and negative conceptions of liberty, but also to conflicts among different negative liberties.[44] For value pluralists such conflicts can only be settled within the political sphere. A liberalism informed by a commitment to value pluralism will therefore acknowledge the primacy of the political. Consequently, it will regard the nature and extent of basic liberties, the content of fundamental liberal rights and specific, substantive principles of justice as subject to political debate and agreement. Thus, the restraints on liberty and the precise content of fundamental liberal rights is liable to change over time and from place to place. Allegiance to liberalism should therefore not be conceived as allegiance to a particular set of abstract principles, but is best regarded as the expression of a specific shared culture. What remains distinctly liberal about this approach is the belief that all groups should have equal access and an equal right to be heard.

Liberal Value Pluralism and the 'Politics of Difference'

The rather robust defence of 'diversity' which characterises value pluralist liberalism makes this strand of liberal thought potentially well suited to accommodate the demands associated with both thin and thick multiculturalism. Its awareness of its own historical contingency and the conflicts and tensions which are inherent in core liberal values allows value pluralist liberalism readily to acknowledge the political significance of group membership. Given that our common humanity only partially determines our nature, the interpretation and ranking of the values we adopt will to some extent be a reflection of our social and cultural heritage. For value pluralists, therefore, the demands for recognition which have characterised the 'politics of difference' are simply an expression of the inevitable plurality of ultimate values. While such demands may conflict with existing interpretations of fundamental liberal rights, or may even entail a rejection of key liberal commitments, such antagonism and disagreement should not be seen as an extraordinary threat to well-established liberal societies, but should be viewed as instances of the unavoidable tensions between different cultures and value systems.

Value pluralism and thin multiculturalism

From the perspective of thin multiculturalism the emphasis a liberalism grounded in value pluralism places upon the complexity and plurality of the liberal tradition may prove particularly helpful. For example, this awareness allows value pluralist liberals to see the demands by liberal minorities such as the Quebecois as an expression of the inevitable tensions at the heart of liberalism. Given the incommensurability among, and the conflicting elements entailed within liberal values, the particular restraint upon liberty and the precise content of fundamental liberal rights is liable to vary from society to society. In the light of their distinct history and cultural heritage it is therefore neither surprising nor in itself objectionable that English- and French-speaking Canadians wish to interpret and rank these values in different ways.

This recognition of diversity and conflict within the liberal tradition ensures that value pluralist liberals will not only recognise the potential for conflict between different liberal societies, but also allows this strand of liberal thought to be sensitive to the desire of historically marginalised groups, such as women, to re-evaluate traditional liberal conceptions of liberty, equality and the public/ private distinction. While liberal societies are characterised by a fundamental commitment to these values, value pluralists accept that liberty and equality are open to a wide variety of conflicting and at times incommensurable interpretations. In a similar vein the boundaries between the public and the private can, and historically have been, drawn in a wide variety of different ways. For advocates of diversity such a fluid and pluralistic conception of the liberal tradition not only avoids the dangers associated with Rawls's attempt to draw a firm distinction between the political and non-political (see Chapter 3), it also suggests that value pluralist liberals will be aware of the tensions and conflicts within cultures in general. Hence value pluralist liberals will be receptive to the fears expressed by proponents of diversity with regard to the picture of cultural diversity implicit in the work of writers such as Taylor and Walzer. As the previous chapter suggested, Taylor and Walzer see diversity predominately in terms of distinct cultural perspectives. For critics this emphasis upon the internal coherence of cultural traditions gives rise to an unduly homogeneous picture and leads Taylor and Walzer to ignore the extent to which the dominant interpretation of a cultural tradition reflects existing power relations. However, once cultural traditions are recognised as inherently plural, the impact of power relations upon the character of a particular culture cannot be ignored.

Value pluralism and thick multiculturalism

Just as its awareness of the internal complexity of cultural traditions ensures that value pluralist liberalism is sensitive to many of the concerns expressed by advocates of thin multiculturalism, so the acknowledgement of a genuine diversity of values allows this strand of liberal thought to avoid the difficulties which tend to mar prominent liberal responses to the challenge of thick multiculturalism. From a liberal perspective the demands associated with thick multicultural-ism have tended to be problematic, because many of the measures regarded by minority groups as essential to the preservation of their culture and identity potentially place restrictions upon central liberal values such as the promotion of individual freedom and autonomy. For example, whereas Christian fundamentalists in America have sought the legal right to withdraw their children from those aspects of the school curriculum which they regard as incompatible with their beliefs, such demands are widely regarded as irreconcilable with the promotion of autonomy and tolerance central to a liberal education.[45] Similar difficulties surround the demands of many ethnic and national minorities. For instance the desire of some native groups to place restrictions on the sale of traditional homelands, may limit the freedom of individual members of the group to dispose of their property as they see fit.[46] Yet in the face of such demands liberals like Rawls, Habermas, Kymlicka and Raz have tended simply to reassert the significance liberalism attaches to individual liberty and auton-omy. Thus, for example, both Kymlicka and Raz stress that the promotion of cultural continuity must not be allowed to undermine individual autonomy. In contrast to this emphasis upon autonomy, the recognition of cultures and values as inherently diverse allows value pluralist liberals to acknowledge the fears of minorities who do not share the liberal commitment to autonomy, and makes this strand of liberal thought sensitive to the loss entailed in imposing liberal values upon such groups. From a value pluralist perspective autonomy constitutes only one possible form of self-realisation, and liberalism only one of a wide variety of worthwhile ways of life.

Value pluralism, conflict and deliberation

If liberalism accepts profound diversity and consequently acknow-ledges its own complexity and historical contingency, it clearly cannot simply impose its own values upon reluctant minorities. After all from a value pluralist perspective diversity constitutes a vital aspect of human excellence. Liberalism will therefore have to strive to accommodate the demands of a 'politics of difference'. Yet, how is a liberalism grounded in value pluralism to respond to the conflicts and tensions which inevitably accompany difference and diversity? Given the central role the widely recognised principles of adjudication, arbitration and negotiation play within a value pluralist conception of a procedural framework for conflict resolution, liberals who affirm the inherent diversity of values will favour conceptions of democracy and democratic citizenship which encourage participation and stress the importance of public argument as a means of justifying and legitimising political decisions. This emphasis upon participation and public argument is, of course, central to the ideal of deliberative democracy advanced by liberals such as Habermas (see Chapter 4). Indeed, given value pluralism's emphasis upon the contested nature and the historical contingency of the values characteristic of liberal societies, value pluralist liberals will clearly welcome Habermas's emphasis upon encouraging the participation of traditionally excluded groups and will share his concern that unless all citizens participate in public debate and express their specific needs, there is a real danger that the needs of socially disadvantaged groups will be misunderstood. However the nature, role and limits of public argument envisaged by value pluralist liberals differs significantly from that advocated by proponents of deliberative democracy such as Habermas. According to Habermas moral norms can be justified 'independent of the prejudices or biases of any particular tradition or culture'.[47] Hence for Habermas practical discourse aims to establish universally justified moral norms acceptable to all participants in discourse. Thus, ultimately, Habermas's model of deliberative democracy rests upon the idea that difference can be overcome in the course of rational deliberation and that a neutral and impartial view can be established. Yet from the perspective of value pluralist liberals this search for consensus which underpins Habermas's conception of deliberative democracy is fundamentally misguided. Given that ultimate values are uncombinable and incommensurable, value conflict is an inevitable and essential aspect of the human condition. Consequently no society can harmoniously combine all values. Whereas for Habermas deliberation is driven by the search for truth in the form of universal norms, value pluralists see debate and negotiation as a means to peace. While public deliberation must aim to defuse and manage conflict, it can never transcend it. Consequently, although the commitment to the principles of liberty and equality for all implies that liberal value pluralists will seek to ensure that all groups have a right to be heard, the principles and values which characterise liberal society must be recognised as the expression of a particular cultural tradition. Hence in liberal societies, like all other societies, political agreement will always be partial and subject to conflict and revision.

Such a robust defence of diversity and open acknowledgement of the limits of consensus may be rather attractive to those minorities whose aspirations cannot be readily accommodated within the liberal framework. Given the difficulties surrounding Habermas's approach identified in Chapter 4, it is apparent that the consensus liberals such as him seek can only be achieved if those conceptions of the good that do not share the liberal commitment to autonomy are excluded from practical discourse in the constitutional state. From a value pluralist perspective, however, non-liberal groups cannot be excluded from public debate simple because their values may undermine the present consensus. Confronted with vocal minorities demanding recognition, a liberalism grounded in value pluralism must accept that it cannot insulate itself from the dynamic inherent in such challenges. On the contrary value pluralist liberalism is likely to be sensitive to the possible need to re-evaluate the principles that underpin the existing political framework.

The danger of conflict

While such a dynamic and open-ended vision of political deliberation and debate undoubtedly has its attractions, it may nonetheless not be without its dangers from the perspective of both thin and thick multiculturalism. Although a genuine commitment to diversity as an expression of human excellence implies that it would be unsatisfactory to leave political decisions simply to the force of the greatest number, and thus provides a powerful motive for debate and deliberation, the emphasis value pluralists place upon the contingency of political agreements and the inevitability of conflict suggests that, in the final analysis, a group's capacity to influence the political system may be a function of its actual political power. While a vocal and well-organised minority frequently can have considerable impact, many minorities may find it difficult to muster the resources for an effective political campaign. Value pluralist liberalism may well be more sympathetic than other strands of liberal thought to the desire of non-liberal minorities to preserve and perpetuate their particular culture and way of life. However it is unlikely that it will always be possible to resolve value conflicts in a manner that is satisfactory to all concerned. In the case of comparatively small, territorially well-defined minorities such as the Amish and the Hutterites, value pluralist liberals may favour 'set-aside' deals which grant the minority special rights or exceptions. Such arrangements safeguard diversity without impinging significantly upon the wider society. However, even value pluralist liberals may find it difficult to accommodate the demands of larger and/or territorially dispersed minorities. After all, as Parekh aptly notes, political dialogue aims to yield decisions. Yet:

It is difficult to see how a decision can be reached other then by minorities accepting the society's established decisionmaking procedure and the values embedded in it. Minorities should, of course, be free to convince the majority, and the latter should enter into an open-minded dialogue with them. However, if the majority remains genuinely unpersuaded, its values need to prevail. In the absence of such finality, no decision is possible and the point of dialogue is lost.[48]

Since the principles of liberty and equality are definitive of a commitment to liberalism in general, in a liberal society the decision-making procedure and the values embedded in these procedures will clearly be shaped by these ideals. While a liberal society can be tolerant in terms of morality and religion, it cannot be agnostic as far as the political principles which give it its specific character are concerned. Therefore, while the principles of liberty and equality are open to a wide variety of different interpretations, and as thus will always remain contested, it is the shared concern with liberty and equality which provides the criteria whereby a liberal political community assesses the legitimacy of political demands. For liberals this shared concern typically implies a commitment to the separation of the state and church, civil and religious law and a distinction between the public and the private. Yet, it is precisely these preoccupations and distinctions which have been challenged by at least some of the minorities currently campaigning for recognition. For example, some Muslim critics, such as Akhtar,[49] have emphasised the pervasiveness of Islamic teaching and its implications in the economic and social sphere. Given that different cultures may well have their own distinct political and economic practices and patterns of organisation, at least some of the demands currently voiced by minorities campaigning for recognition will conflict with the political principles which give a liberal political community its specific character.

While non-liberal minorities may feel the impact of value conflict most keenly, the difficulties inherent in such conflicts are not restricted to instances of thick multiculturalism. Although advocates of thin milticulturalism will readily accept the fundamental political principles which govern a liberal political community, they may nonetheless express reservations about the degree to which a value pluralist stance privileges the particular conception of liberal principles favoured by the most powerful sections of society. For example, while feminists have sought to re-interpret existing notions of liberal citizenship, such reinterpretations are, on a value pluralist perspective, no less contestable than alternative conceptions of liberal citizenship. If the agreement which constitutes a particular political community is constructed in the context of diversity and conflict, and if all interpretations of the community's values are contestable, there will always be a danger that the most powerful social group will impose its values upon the political system. Thus groups such as women, who have traditionally been comparatively powerless may remain marginalised and excluded. Given that feminist scholarship[50] suggests that the traditional difference-blind interpretation of liberal scholarship is deeply ingrained in Western political thought, such continued marginalisation constitutes a real danger.

However the emphasis of value pluralism places upon the contingency of political agreements and the inevitability of value conflict may not only threaten the standing of minorities and traditionally powerless groups, it may also trouble liberals. For value pluralists the aim of political activity is the establishment of peace and stability rather than the pursuit of truth. Given the wide diversity of existing cultures and the variety of possible cultural mixes, we have no reason to assume that liberalism will always be best placed to secure peace and stability. As the outcome of a specific political agreement liberalism has no unique claim to reason, but, just like other conceptions of the good, has to prove its capacity to generate peace and stability within a specific political context. From the perspective of value pluralism, liberalism's capacity to successfully respond to the challenge posed by cultural pluralism will, in the final analysis, depend on its capacity to generate a stable political community. However, liberals have no reason to take such an outcome for granted. In this context it is important to bear in mind that while a recognition of the genuine plurality of values gives liberals a strong reason to accept certain compromises in pursuit of a modus vivendi with non-liberal groups, its partners in negotiation may not share this motivation.[51] Although there is widespread agreement among cultures regarding a minimal procedural conception of justice, not all cultures accept the idea of value pluralism or the liberal notion of equality of respect. Thus value pluralist liberals are faced with the danger that while they will seek an equitable modus vivendi based upon a sense of respect for other ways of life, this sense of respect may not be reciprocated by all non-liberal groups. For some groups dialogue and negotiation may simply be of instrumental value and as such constitute at best a necessary evil. As Tamir notes, such a situation places liberalism 'on the defensive as it asymmetrically opens itself to illiberal influences.'[52]

Liberal Value Pluralism and Conflict

Although liberal value pluralism is better placed than the currently dominant liberal Enlightenment tradition to respond positively to the depth and complexity of diversity associated with the 'politics of difference', such a position is not without its dangers for both liberals and advocates of diversity. While the open and dynamic conception of the political community central to a value pluralist perspective grants this position the flexibility to acknowledge and respond to a wide variety of different concerns and perspectives, it does not privilege any particular viewpoint and does not guarantee a specific outcome. Thus neither liberals nor advocates of diversity can be certain that their concerns will win out in the process of political debate and negotiation. Yet in the face of the difficulties which surround the more ambitious goals of Enlightenment liberalism such uncertainties may be inevitable in a society characterised by a genuine diversity of values.

Notes and References

1. This distinction draws upon W. Galston's article 'Two concepts of liberalism', *Ethics*, Vol. 105, April 1995, pp. 516–33, in which he differentiates between the principles of 'autonomy' and 'diversity'.
2. Ibid. p. 525.
3. I. Berlin, *Four Essays on Liberty* (Oxford: University Press); *The Age of the Enlightenment* (New York: Books for Libraries Press, 1970); *Against the Current* (Oxford: University Press, 1981); *The Crooked Timber of Humanity* (London: John Murray, 1990); S. Hampshire, *Innocence and Experience* (London: Penguin Books, 1989); 'Justice is Strife', *Proceedings and Addresses of the American Philosophical Association*, Vol. 65, No. 3, Nov. 1991, pp. 19–27; *Justice is Conflict* (London: Duckworth, 1999).
4. R. Bellamy, 'Pluralism, liberal constitutionalism and democracy: a critique of John Rawls's (meta) political liberalism', in J. Meadowcroft (ed.), *The Liberal Political Tradition* (Cheltenham: Edward Elgar, 1996), pp. 77–100, p. 93.
5. For a discussion of Renaissance humanism and its role in the development of modernity see S. Toulmin, *Cosmopolis, The Secret Agenda of Modernity* (New York: Free Press, 1990).
6. J. Locke, *A Letter Concerning Toleration* (Buffalo: Prometheus Books, 1990).
7. S. Mendus, *Toleration and the Limits of Liberalism* (London: Macmillan, 1989), p. 29.
8. For a detailed discussion of these objections see Chapter 3.
9. Variants of Rawls's notion of diversity as a fact of modern life could also provide the basis for a pragmatic defence of diversity.

10. S. Hampshire, 'Liberalism: The New Twist, *The New York Review of Books*, August 12 1993, pp. 43–7, p. 46. The idea that there is a plurality of values is also evident in the work of ancient sceptical thinkers, such as Carneades, who suggests that ultimate values might be incompatible with one another and that no solution could logically incorporate them all (see I. Berlin, 'Herder and the Enlightenment', *Vico and Herder: Two Studies in the History of Ideas*, London: Hogarth Press, 1976).

11. S. Hampshire, *Innocence and Experience*, p. 189.

12. J. Raz, 'Multiculturalism: A Liberal Perspective', *Dissent*, Winter 1997, pp. 67–79, p. 72.

13. J. Raz, *The Morality of Freedom* (Oxford: Clarendon, 1986).

14. Ibid. p. 325.

15. Ibid. p. 72.

16. For a discussion of the three levels of value pluralism in Berlin's thought see J. Gray, *Berlin* (London: Fontana Press, 1995) p. 43ff.

17. Individuals are often keenly aware of the opportunities they have forgone by following their chosen lifestyle. Thus, for example, a great artist who, in the pursuit of her art, has abandoned many normal human interests, such as, for instance, a stable family life, may nonetheless recognise the values inherent in these general human interests and may regard this as a price that had to be paid for the lifestyle she desired.

18. J. Raz, 'Multiculturalism: A Liberal Perspective'.

19. S. Hampshire, *Innocence and Experience*, p. 68.

20. For Hampshire ways of life which on principle reject all peaceful means of resolving conflicts should not be tolerated. While this will clearly exclude some ways of life, value pluralists like Hampshire regard diversity as an important and inevitable aspect of the political sphere. As such Hampshire's position differs sharply from that of Rawls, who wishes to confine diversity to the private sphere and who is subsequently prepared to exclude all ways of life which do not endorse the precepts of political liberalism.

21. Hampshire maintains that his position regarding human nature is 'close to Hume's: that opinions about substantial justice and the other virtues arise from, and are explained by, natural and widespread human sentiments greatly modified by very variable customs and social histories.' (*Justice is Conflict*, pp. 42–3). However, in contrast to Hume who holds that humanity has a tendency towards consensus, Hampshire holds that diversity and, subsequently, conflict are unavoidable.

22. J. Gray, *Berlin*.

23. For a discussion of the contrast between Berlin and Taylor see S. Macedo, *Liberal Virtues* (Oxford: Clarendon Press, 1991) p. 236ff.

24. J. Gray, *Berlin*, p. 25.

25. Berlin's interpretation of and attitude towards the Enlightenment is subject to controversy. For a discussion of various interpretations of Berlin's response to the Enlightenment see G. Garrard, 'The Counter-Enlightenment Liberalism of Isaiah Berlin', *Journal of Political Ideologies*, Vol. 2, 1997, pp. 281–96.

26. Indeed in *The Age of Enlightenment* (p. 29) Berlin refers to this period as 'one of the best and the most hopeful episodes in the life of mankind'.
27. G. Garrard, 'The Counter-Enlightenment Liberalism of Isaiah Berlin'.
28. I. Berlin, *The Crooked Timber of Humanity*, pp. 236–7.
29. J. Raz, *The Morality of Freedom*, p. 345.
30. Ibid. p. 339. A helpful account of the role of reason from a value pluralist perspective is offered by Berlin and Williams in their reply to Growder. See I. Berlin and B. William, 'Pluralism and Liberalism: a Reply', *Political Studies*, Vol. 42, No. 2, June 1994, pp. 306–9.
31. S. Hampshire, *Innocence and Experience*, p. 55.
32. S. Hampshire, 'Justice is Strife', p. 20.
33. S. Hampshire, *Justice is Conflict*, p. 21.
34. S. Hampshire, 'Justice is Strife', p. 20.
35. As Hampshire admits, in practice arbitration and negotiations in the political arena may at times be corrupt and thus fall short of the requirements of adversarial argument. 'But still the institutions of arbitration and negotiation are plainly designed for fair adversary argument' (Hampshire, 'Justice is Strife', p. 22).
36. Hampshire, *Innocence and Experience*, p. 75.
37. S. Hampshire, *Justice is Conflict*, p. 58.
38. S. Hampshire, 'Justice is Strife', p. 27.
39. R. Bellamy, 'Pluralism, liberal constitutionalism and democracy: a critique of John Rawls's (meta) political liberalism', p. 93.
40. Ibid. This view is echoed by Hampshire, who maintains that '[r]espect for process can, as a matter of habit, coexist with detestation of the outcome of the process, and this particularly in democracies' (*Justice is Conflict*, p. 50).
41. J. Gray, *Berlin*, p. 153.
42. B. Williams, 'Introduction' in I. Berlin, *Concepts and Categories* (London: Hogarth Press, 1978).
43. J. Gray, *Berlin*, p. 145.
44. For instance freedom of information may conflict with the right to privacy. In a similar vein the ideal of equality entails the incommensurable ideas of 'equality of opportunity' and 'equality of outcome'.
45. See the discussion of the case of Mozert v. Hawkins in S. Macedo, 'Liberal civil education and religious fundamentalism: the case of God v. John Rawls', *Ethics*, Vol. 105, April 1995, pp. 468–96. The difficulties this conflict poses for liberals such as Rawls is discussed in Chapter 3.
46. For a more detailed discussion of these difficulties see Chapter 5, pp. 117–18.
47. S. O'Neill, *Impartiality in Context: Grounding Justice in a Pluralist World* (Albany: State University of New York Press, 1997) p. 131.
48. B. Parekh, 'Minority Practices and Principles of Toleration', *International Migration Review*, Vol. 30, No. 1, 1996, pp. 251–84, p. 259.
49. According to Akhtar, Islamic teaching aims to integrate political, social and economic life and therefore does not recognise the separation between religious and political affairs central to the liberal perception of

the political arena. From this perspective liberalism's preoccupation with individual freedom threatens to rob religion of its social and political significance. As a theologico-political doctrine Islam therefore challenges some of liberalism's most fundamental assumptions about the relationship between revelation and politics (see S. Akhtar, *The Final Imperative,* London: Bellew Publishing, 1991).

50. C. Pateman, 'The Theoretical Subversiveness of Feminism', in C. Pateman and E. Gross (eds), *Feminist Challenges* (Sydney: Allen & Unwin, 1988) pp. 1–10.

51. Clearly non-liberal groups need not necessarily reject the idea of value pluralism. Recognition of the value of other ways of life does not imply that a non-liberal society cannot insist upon the preservation of their culture which is itself worthwhile.

52. Y. Tamir, 'Two Concepts of Multiculturalism', *Journal of Philosophy of Education,* Vol. 29, No. 2, 1995, pp. 161–72, p. 171. For Tamir this asymmetry is reflected in the divergent attitudes held towards the idea of cross-cultural exchange in Israel. While 'liberal Israelis, whether secular Jews, Muslims or Christians, endorse the idea of multiculturalism out of respect for others . . . their openmindedness is not reciprocated. Exposure to cultural exchanges is therefore not mutual; liberals expose their children to illiberal forms of life while defenders of illiberal cultures make a special effort to shelter their children from any form of cultural diversity' (p. 169).

Chapter 8: Liberalism and the 'Politics of Difference'

The 'politics of difference' clearly poses a complex, diverse and at times contradictory set of challenges for contemporary liberals. In their desire to assert the political significance of group membership, advocates of difference and diversity have not only highlighted the limitations of traditional liberal conceptions of impartiality and formal equality, but have questioned the force of the ideal of human excellence inherent in liberal values and commitments. Thus, whereas feminists and other thin multiculturalists maintain that genuine equality and individual liberty can only be attained if the scope and nature of individual rights and freedoms is redefined so as to account for the claims of difference and diversity, thick multiculturalism challenges the validity of the very values liberals and thin multi-culturalists share. At the heart of this disparate set of demands lie important questions regarding the conception of the self, the nature of diversity and the role of the political. It here that the 'politics of difference' challenges the Enlightenment liberalism which has con-tinued to dominate much of contemporary liberal thought. In place of the abstract unitary conception of the self central to the liberalism of the Enlightenment, the 'politics of difference' offers a vision of the self as firmly embedded in its particular characteristics and attachments. Rather than seek universal standards which allow us to transcend our particular attachments, the advocates of difference and diversity assert the significance of particular standards and local values. Consequent-ly, in place of the Enlightenment ideal of a 'homogenous' public framed by our common interest, the 'politics of difference' gives rise to a picture of the political as an arena in which differences are to be recognised and the ensuing tensions and conflicts are to be negotiated.

In their response to the 'politics of difference' contemporary liberals have shown considerable sensitivity to the concerns and aspirations of advocates of diversity. Not only do contemporary exponents of the liberal Enlightenment tradition acknowledge that modern liberal societies are marked by a diversity of opposing and irreconcilable philosophical and moral doctrines, many readily accept the limitations of the classical Enlightenment vision of the self. For example, for writers like Kymlicka and Raz secure cultural membership is vital to individual well being and the effective exercise of autonomy. In a similar vein, Habermas's context responsive account of impartiality accepts the complex relationship between the public and the private and hence remains sensitive to the impact of particular attachments and allegiances upon individual identity. As a consequence of these insights many contemporary liberals have been ready to depart from the Enlightenment ideal of universal citizenship and have reconceptualised individual rights and freedoms in the face of the claims of difference and diversity. Thus, whereas Habermas advocates greater political representation for traditionally marginalised or socially disadvantaged groups, Kymlicka and Raz support demands for group differentiated rights.

Yet, despite their willingness to acknowledge the impact of difference and particularity upon individual identity, most prominent contemporary liberals remain firmly wedded to the classical Enlightenment ideal of 'man as a species whose most distinctive activity, and the activity which is the precondition for all which is most valuable in human life, is the making of choice'.[1] Although the specific responses to the 'politics of difference' by Rawls, Habermas, Kymlicka and Raz differ notably, all retain a belief in the overriding value of autonomy and individual liberty. Not only is a commitment to autonomy central to Rawls's conception of a reasonable doctrine, it also delineates the limits of diversity in the accounts offered by Habermas, Kymlicka and Raz. For the latter writers autonomy provides both the rationale for and sets the limits to the support cultural groups can legitimately expect in their attempt to maintain themselves. At the heart of this continued commitment to the overriding value of autonomy lies a view of diversity and the role of the political which remains profoundly at odds with the aspirations of a 'politics of difference'. Just as classical Enlightenment thinkers such as Montesquieu retain the conviction that, despite the inescapable diversity of human life, different ways of life can be judged in terms of universal principles, contemporary proponents of the liberal Enlightenment tradition combine an acknowledgement of the facts of diversity with a continued commitment to critical rationality, autonomy and the 'general point of view'. While the belief in universality and the 'general point of view' is most apparent in the 'quest for impartiality' on the part of liberals such as Habermas and Rawls, it is also inherent in the continued commitment to the principle of neutrality by writers such as Kymlicka. By limiting the claims of diversity to those lifestyles which share the liberal belief in the overriding value of autonomy and individual liberty, contemporary proponents of Enlightenment liberalism remain wedded to the old Enlightenment project of building a homogenous public.[2] Consequently, many liberals have continued to emphasise the importance of shared interests, rational agreement and neutrality.

This continued 'quest for homogeneity' is by no means unique to the perspective adopted by contemporary proponents of the liberal Enlightenment tradition. Even theorists such as Walzer, whose highly particularistic and pluralistic account is informed by a keen awareness of the limitations of the Enlightenment ideals of critical rationality, autonomy and neutrality, ultimately fail to accept the profound diversity which characterises many modern liberal societies. While Walzer recognises that different political communities may display a wide variety of values, he perceives each community as internally quite homogeneous. Thus, for Walzer, within political communities values are shared instead of contested. In a sense, most prominent responses to the 'politics of difference' – be they defenders or critics of the Enlightenment tradition – have been informed by a 'flight from the political'. Rather than recognise the central role of the political arena as a domain in which conflicts among different values can be negotiated, the contemporary theorists considered here seek to minimise conflict and antagonism by setting firm limits to the claims of difference and diversity. Yet in the light of the difficulties which surround these responses, such a strategy appears misplaced. Whereas Habermas's context responsive account of impartiality, Kymlicka's and Raz's vision of liberal group rights, or Taylor's and Walzer's notion of a liberal political community can each accommodate certain aspects of the 'politics of difference', none of these approaches fully appreciates the complexity and diversity of the demands associated with the 'politics of difference'.

Given the difficulties and limitations of prominent responses to the 'politics of difference', liberals may well wish to reconsider the role diversity has played within liberal thought. After all, while the liberal Enlightenment project has been premised on the principle of 'universal reason', the acceptance and management of diversity through mutual toleration has played an important role in some strands of liberal thought since the Reformation. This regard for diversity and tolerance characteristic of liberal responses to the religious strife that accompanied the Reformation, echoes a Renaissance humanism which precedes the Enlightenment. For Renaissance humanists like Montaigne plurality, ambiguity and lack of certainty are not indicative of error, but constitute an inevitable part of being human. There simply 'may not be a rational way to convert to our point of view people who honestly hold other positions'.[3] While shared experience may gradually lead to some convergence, we cannot simply by-pass such disagreements. Instead, we must learn to live with diversity. Yet in the eyes of many of the philosophers of the Enlightenment this intellectual and practical tolerance was 'inconclusive, permissive and open to abuse'.[4] Thus in place of the open-mindedness, sceptical tolerance and emphasis on the limits of general theory which characterises the work of Renaissance humanists, the Enlightenment sought to establish a stricter ideal of rationality, which could transcend our inherited traditions. Hence the philosophers of the Enlightenment typically contend that provided we emancipate ourselves from the very diversity and contradictions of our traditional, inherited, local ways of thought, the slate can be wiped clean and rational solutions to problems and disagreements can be found.

However, it is precisely this stricter ideal of rationality that is challenged by the advocates of difference and diversity. Consequently rather than pursue the Enlightenment quest for the certainty of universal agreement, liberalism needs to recapture the emphasis upon plurality and ambiguity, which distinguishes early strands of modern thought. At its most robust, such a regard for diversity gives rise to a liberal value pluralism which looks upon diversity not only as inevitable, but as a positive and vital aspect of human excellence. In contrast to the continued belief in the overriding value of autonomy and individual liberty typical of contemporary Enlightenment liberalism, liberal value pluralists acknowledge the genuine diversity of possible forms of human self-creation. It therefore recognises the 'irreducible diversity of rivalerous goods'[5] and accepts that the common potentialities that characterise human beings can be realised and satisfied in many different and frequently incommensurable ways. This regard for diversity gives rise to a genuinely embedded vision of the self, which is well placed to capture the emphasis upon our unique characteristics that informs the 'politics of difference'. Consequently, this strand of liberal thought readily acknowledges its own historical contingency. Rather than seek to insulate itself from the dynamic of value conflict, liberal value pluralism recognises that liberalism, like all other cultural perspectives, will always remain contested. Therefore, apart from the inevitable conflict between itself and other ways of life, liberalism must realise the tensions between the very values at the heart of its theory. Hence it must accept that these values will always be subject to a wide variety of different interpretations. Whereas Enlightenment liberalism appeals to the powers of universal reason to transcend difference and particularity, liberal value pluralism emphasises the limits of reason in the face of diversity. Faced with incommensurable values, reason cannot 'advise us how to choose'.[6] Value pluralism therefore acknowledges the central role conflict, antagonism and power relations play within a genuinely diverse society. Consequently, it gives primacy to the political as the domain in which these conflicts among different values can be negotiated.

From this perspective the central challenge for liberals today is not to find grounds for universal rational agreement, but to develop a set of institutions which can effectively manage the conflict and antagonism that inevitably accompanies diversity. Yet the emphasis value pluralists place upon the contingency of political agreements and the inevitability of conflict, suggests that such a position is not without its dangers for either liberals or advocates of diversity. While the open and dynamic conception of the political community central to a value pluralist perspective grants this position the flexibility to acknowledge and respond to a wide variety of different concerns and perspectives, it does not privilege any particular viewpoint and does not guarantee a specific outcome. Thus neither liberals nor advocates of diversity can be certain that their concerns will win out in the process of political debate and negotiation. Nonetheless, for liberals there are good moral and prudential reasons for taking the demands for recognition seriously. Although liberal value pluralism does not imply that all cultures are of equal worth, the liberal commitment to equality of respect suggests that liberals cannot disregard the worth of other cultures to their members. As Taylor quite rightly notes, given a belief in equality of respect, liberals must approach any culture which has sustained a set of people for any length of time with at least a presumption of worth. Furthermore, to echo Rawls, securing political stability has to be a primary objective in a society characterised by a diversity of religious, philosophical and moral doctrines. In the face of the demands by non-liberal minorities for recognition, it is difficult to see how the liberal state could secure stability and win the loyalty and support of at least the majority of citizens, if the concerns of those conceptions of the good which do not accord with liberal commitments are simply excluded from public debate. Hence in the face of a genuine plurality of values and ways of life, liberals must seek an accommodation with those who differ.

Notes and References

1. J. Gray, *Berlin* (London: Fontana Press, 1995) p. 25.
2. Unlike many other contemporary liberals Raz does acknowledge the genuine plurality of values and hence recognises the potential for tension and conflict. However, while Raz admits liberalism's perfectionist streak,

he nonetheless remains optimistic about the possibility of generating a shared common culture grounded in liberal multiculturalism.

3. S. Toulmin, *Cosmopolis, The Secret Agenda of Modernity* (New York: Free Press, 1990) p. 30.

4. Ibid. p. 199.

5. J. Gray, *Berlin*, p. 145.

6. J. Raz, *The Morality of Freedom* (Oxford: Clarendon Press, 1986) p. 345.

Bibliography

Akhtar, S., *The Final Imperative* (London: Bellew Publishing, 1991).

Bader, V., 'Citizenship and Exclusion: Radical Democracy, Community and Justice. Or What is Wrong with Communitarianism', *Political Theory*, Vol. 23, No. 2, May 1995, pp. 211–46.

Bailey, C., *Beyond The Present And The Particular* (London: Routledge, 1984).

Barry, B., *Justice as Impartiality* (Oxford: Clarendon Press, 1995).

Barry, B., 'John Rawls and the Search for Stability', *Ethics*, Vol. 105, July 1995, pp. 874–915.

Bauman, Z., 'Communitarianism, Freedom and the Nation State', *Critical Review*, Vol. 9, No. 4, 1995, pp. 539–53.

Bell, D., *Communitarianism and its Critics* (Oxford: Clarendon, 1993).

Bellamy, R., 'Pluralism, liberal constitutionalism and democracy: a critique of John Rawls's (meta) political liberalism', in J. Meadowcroft (ed.), *The Liberal Political Tradition* (Cheltenham: Edward Elgar, 1996) pp. 77–100.

Benhabib, S., 'The Generalized and the Concrete Other: The Kohlberg-Gilligan Controversy and Feminist Theory', in S. Benhabib and D. Cornell (eds), *Feminism as Critique* (Cambridge: Polity Press, 1987) pp. 77–95.

Benhabib, S., 'Liberal Dialogue Versus a Critical Theory of Discursive Legitimation', in N. Rosenblum (ed.), *Liberalism and the Moral Life* (Cambridge, MA: Harvard University Press, 1991) pp. 143–58.

Benhabib, S., *Situating the Self* (Cambridge: Polity Press, 1992).

Benhabib, S., 'The Debate over Women and Moral Theory Revisted', in J. Meehan, *Feminists Read Habermas: Gendering the Subject of Discourse* (London: Routledge, 1995) pp. 182–203.

Berlin, I., *Four Essays on Liberty* (Oxford: Oxford University Press, 1969).

Berlin, I., *The Age of the Enlightenment* (New York: Books for Libraries Press, 1970).

Berlin, I., *Vico and Herder: Two Studies in the History of Ideas* (London: Hogarth Press, 1976).

Berlin, I., *Concepts and Categories* (London: Hogarth Press, 1978).

Berlin, I., *Against the Current* (Oxford: Oxford University Press, 1981).

Berlin, I., *The Crooked Timber of Humanity* (London: John Murray, 1990).

Berlin, I. and Williams, B., 'Pluralism and Liberalism: a Reply' *Political Studies*, Vol. 42, No. 2, June 1994, pp. 306–9.

Blackham, H. J., *Reality, Man and Existence* (London: Bantam Books, 1965).

Blum, L., Gilligan and Kohlberg, 'Implications for Moral Theory', *Ethics*, Vol. 98, April 1988, pp. 472–91.

Bricker, D. C., 'Autonomy and Culture: Will Kymlicka on Cultural Minority Rights', *The Southern Journal of Philosophy*, Vol. 36, No. 1, 1998, pp. 47–59.

Buchanan, A., *Secession: The Morality of Political Divorce from Fort Sumter to Lithuania and Quebec* (Oxford: Westview Press, 1991).

Caney, S., 'Anti-perfectionism and Rawlsian Liberalism', *Political Studies*, Vol. 43, No. 2, June 1995, pp. 248–64.

Caro, D., *Nietzsche contra Nietzsche* (Baton Rouge: Louisiana State University Press, 1989).

Chambers, S., *Reasonable Democracy, Jürgen Habermas and the Politics of Discourse* (Ithaca and London: Cornell University Press, 1996).

Chaplin, J., 'How Much Cultural and Religious Pluralism can Liberalism Tolerate', in J. Horton (ed.), *Liberalism, Multiculturalism and Toleration* (London: Macmillan, 1993) pp. 32–49.

Cooke, M., 'Authenticity and Autonomy: Taylor, Habermas, and the Politics of Recognition', *Political Theory*, Vol. 25, No. 2, April 1997, pp. 258–88.

Cohen, J., 'Spheres of Justice: A Defence of Pluralism and Equality', Book Review, *The Journal of Philosophy*, 83, 1986, pp. 457–68.

Cohen, M., et al (ed.), *Equality and Preferential Treatment* (Princeton, NJ: Princeton University Press, 1977).

Council of Mosques, *The Muslims and Swann* (Bradford: Council of Mosques, 1984).

Craig, E. (ed.), *Routledge Encyclopedia of Philosophy* (London: Routledge, 1998).

Crocker, L. G., *The Age of the Enlightenment* (London: Macmillan, 1969).

Dinnerstein, D., *The Mermaid and the Minotar: Sexual Arrangements and Human Malaise* (New York: Haper Colophon, 1976).

Durie, E. T., 'Justice, Biculturalism and the Politics of Law', in M. Wilson and A. Yeatman. (eds), *Justice & Identity* (Wellington: Bridget Williams Books, 1995) pp. 33–44.

Dworkin, R., 'Liberalism', in M. Sandel (ed.), *Liberalism and its Critics* (Oxford: Blackwell, 1984) pp. 60–79.

Dworkin, R., *Taking Rights Seriously* (London: Duckworth, 1978).

Dworkin, R., '"Spheres of Justice": An Exchange', *The New York Review of Books*, 21 July 1983, pp. 43–6.

Dworkin, R., *A Matter of Principle* (Oxford: Clarendon Press, 1996).

Elshtain, J. B., *Public Man, Private Woman* (Princeton, NJ: Princeton University Press, 1981).

Evans, R., *The Feminists* (London: Croom Helm, 1977).

Ferguson, M., *First Feminists: British Women Writers 1578–1799* (Bloomington: Indiana University Press, 1985) pp. 402.

Flax, J., 'Race, Gender and the Ethics of Difference', *Political Theory*, Vol. 23, No. 3, August 1995, pp. 500–10.

Frazer, E. and Lacy, N., 'Politics and the Public in Rawls's Political Liberalism', *Political Studies*, Vol. 43, No. 2, June 1995, pp. 233–47.

Frazer, E., 'Feminism and liberalism', in J. Meadowcroft (ed.), *The Liberal Political Tradition* (Cheltenham: Edward Elgar, 1996) pp. 115–37.

Freeman, M., 'Parents, Children and Citizen', paper presented at the conference of MANCEPT (Manchester Centre for Political Thought) on *Multiculturalism and Citizenship*, at the Department of Government, University of Manchester, 13 November 1998.

Friedman, J., 'The Politics of Communitarianism', *Critical Review*, Vol. 8, No. 2, 1994, pp. 297–340.

Fukuyama, F., *The end of history and the last man* (London: Hamish Hamilton, 1992).

Fullinwider, R. K., 'Citizenship, Individualism and Democratic Politics', *Ethics*, Vol. 105, April 1995, pp. 497–515.

Galeotti, A. E., 'A Problem With Theory: A Rejoinder to Moruzzi', *Political Theory*, Vol. 22, No. 4, November 1994, pp. 673–7.

Galston, W., 'Two Concepts of Liberalism', *Ethics*, Vol. 105, April 1995, pp. 516–34.

Galston, W., 'Community, Democracy, Philosophy: The Political Thought of Michael Walzer', *Political Theory*, Vol. 17, No. 1, February 1989, pp. 119–30.

Garrard, G., 'The Counter-Enlightenment Liberalism of Isaiah Berlin', *Journal of Political Ideologies*, 2, 1997, pp. 281–96.

Gilligan, C., *In A Different Voice* (Cambridge, MA: Harvard University Press, 1982).

Gray, J., *Berlin* (London: Fontana Press, 1995).

Gray, J., 'Agnostic Liberalism', *Social Philosophy and Policy*, 12, September 1995, pp. 110–35.

Gutman, A., 'Introduction', in A. Gutman and C. Taylor (eds), *Multiculturalism and the "Politics of Recognition"* (Princeton, NJ: Princeton University Press, 1992) pp. 3–24.

Habermas, J., 'Justice and Solidarity: On the Discussion Concerning "Stage 6"', *Philosophical Forum*, Vol. 21, Nos 1–2, Fall–Winter, 1989–90, pp. 32–52.

Habermas, J., *Moral Consciousness and Communicative Action*, translated by C. Lenhardt and S. Weber Nicholsen (Cambridge: Polity Press, 1992).

Habermas, J., 'Struggles for Recognition in Constitutional States', *European Journal of Philosophy*, Vol. 1, No. 2, 1993, pp. 128–55.

Habermas, J., 'Reconciliation through public use of reason: remarks on John Rawls's Political Liberalism', *The Journal of Philosophy*, Vol. XCI, No. 3, March 1995, pp. 109–31.

Habermas, J., 'Multiculturalism and the Liberal State', *Stanford Law Review*, Vol. 47, No. 5, 1995, pp. 849–53.

Habermas, J., *Between Facts and Norms* (Cambridge, MA: MIT Press, 1996).

Habermas, J., 'Three Normative Models of Democracy', in S. Benhabib (ed.), *Democracy and Difference: Contesting the Boundaries of the Political* (Princeton, NJ: Princeton University Press, 1996).

Habermas, J., 'The European Nation State: On the Past and Future of Sovereignty and Citizenship', *Public Culture*, Vol. 10, No. 2, 1998, pp. 397–416.

Halstead, J. M., 'Should Schools Reinforce Children's Religious Identity?', *Religious Education*, Vol. 30, No. 3–4, 1995, pp. 360–77.

Halstead, M., 'Voluntary Apartheid? Problems of Schooling for Religious and Other Minorities in Democratic Societies', *Journal of Philosophy of Education*, Vol. 29, No. 2, 1995, pp. 257–72.

Hampshire, S., *Innocence and Experience* (London: Penguin Books, 1989).

Hampshire, S., 'Justice is Strife', *Proceedings and Addresses of the American Philosophical Association*, Vol. 65, No. 3, November 1991, pp. 19–27.

Hampshire, S., *Justice is Conflict* (London: Duckworth, 1999).

Hare, R. M., 'Autonomy As An Educational Ideal Chairman's Remarks', in S. C. Brown (ed.), *Philosophers Discuss Education* (London: Macmillan, 1975) pp. 36–42.

Harris, A., 'Race and Essentialism in Feminist Legal Theory', *Stanford Law Review*, 1990, Vol. 42, pp. 581–616.

Honig, B., *Political Theory and the Displacement of Politics* (New York: Cornell University Press, 1993).

hooks, b., *Ain't I A Woman* (London: Pluto Press, 1981).

Horton, J., 'Charles Taylor: Selfhood, Community and Democracy', in A. Carter and G. Stokes (ed.), *Liberal Democracy and its Critics* (Cambridge: Polity Press, 1998) pp. 155–74.

Houston, C., 'Alternative Modernities – Islamism and Secularism on Charles Taylor', *Critique of Anthropology*, Vol. 18, No. 2, 1998, pp. 234–40.

Hueglin, T. O., 'Regionalism in Western Europe', *Comparative Politics*, Vol. 18, No. 4, 1986, pp. 439–58.

Ingram, A., 'Rawlsians, Pluralists and Cosmopolitans', in D. Archard (ed.), *Philosophy and Pluralism* (Cambridge: Cambridge University Press, 1996) pp. 147–61.

Islamic Academy, *Swann Committee Report* (Cambridge: The Islamic Academy, 1985).

Janzen, W., *Limits on Liberty, The Experience of Mennonite, Hutterite and Doukhobor Communities in Canada* (Toronto: University of Toronto Press, 1990).

Jones, P., 'Two Conceptions of Liberalism, Two Conceptions of Justice', *British Journal of Political Science*, Vol. 25, 1995, pp. 515–50.

Kant, I., *The Moral Law*, translated by H. J. Paton (London: Routledge, 1989).

Kant, I., *Political Writings* (Cambridge: Cambridge University Press, 1991).

Kukathas, C., 'Cultural Rights: Again A Rejoinder to Kymlicka', *Political Theory*, Vol. 20, No. 4, Nov. 1992, pp. 674–80.

Kukathas, C., 'Are there any Cultural Rights?', in W. Kymlicka (ed.), *The Rights of Minority Cultures* (Oxford: Oxford University Press, 1995) pp. 228–56.

Kukathas, C., 'Liberalism and Multiculturalism: The Politics of Indifference', *Political Theory*, Vol. 26, No. 5, October 1998, pp. 686–99.

Kukathas, C., 'Liberalism, Multiculturalism and Oppression', in A. Vincent, *Political Theory: Tradition and Diversity* (Cambridge: Cambridge University Press, 1997) pp. 133–53.

Kymlicka, W., *Liberalism, Community and Culture* (Oxford: Clarendon Press, 1989).

Kymlicka, W., 'Two Models of Pluralism and Tolerance', *Analyse und Kritik*, Vol. 13, 1992, pp. 33–56.

Kymlicka, W., 'Reply to Modood', *Analyse und Kritik*, Vol. 15, No. 1, 1993, pp. 92–6.

Kymlicka, W., *Multicultural Citizenship* (Oxford: Clarendon Press, 1995).

Laforest, G., 'Philosophical and political judgement in a multicultural federation', in J. Tully (ed.), *Philosophy in an Age of Pluralism* (Cambridge: Cambridge University Press, 1994) pp. 194–209.

Levey, G. B., 'Equality, Autonomy, and Cultural Rights', *Political Theory*, Vol. 25, No. 2, April 1997, pp. 215–48.

Locke, J., *A Letter Concerning Toleration* (Buffalo: Prometheus Books, 1990).

Locke, J., *Two Treatises of Government*, edited by P. Laslett (Cambridge: Cambridge University Press, 1993).

Love, N., 'Disembodying Democracy: Habermas's Legalistic Turn', *1998 Annual Meeting of the American Political Science Association*, Boston, 3–6 September 1998.

Lovejoy, A. O., *Essays in the History of Ideas* (Baltimore: Johns Hopkins Press, 1943).

Lovejoy, A. O., *The Great Chain of Being* (New York: Harper & Row, 1960).

McCarthy, T., 'Kantian Constructivism and Reconstructivism: Rawls and Habermas in Dialogue', *Ethics*, Vol. 105, October 1994 pp. 44–65.

Macedo, S., *Liberal Virtues* (Oxford: Clarendon Press, 1991).

Macedo, S., 'Liberal Civil Education and Religious Fundamentalism: The Case of God v. John Rawls', *Ethics*, 105, April 1995, pp. 468–96.

MacIntyre, A., *After Virtue* (London: Duckworth, 1985).

McIntyre, J., 'Multi-Cultural and Multi-Faith Societies: Some Examinable Assumptions', in E. Hulmes (ed.), *Occasional Papers 3*, (Oxford: The Farrington Institute for Christian Studies, 1981).

Madison, J., *The Federalist No. 10*, in A. Hamilton, J. Jay and J. Madison, *The Federalist*, edited by Max Beloff (Oxford: Basil Blackwell, 1948).

Margalit, A. and Raz, J., 'National Self-Determination', in W. Kymlicka (ed.), *The Rights of Minority Cultures* (Oxford: Oxford University Press, 1995) pp. 79–92.

Mendus, S., *Toleration and the Limits of Liberalism* (London: Macmillan, 1989).

Mendus, S., 'Time and Chance: Kantian Ethics and Feminist Philosophy', *Morrell Discussion Paper* (York: Department of Politics, University of York, 1990).

Mendus, S., 'Loosing the Faith: Feminism and Democracy', in J. Dunn (ed.), *Democracy the Unfinished Journey* (Oxford: Oxford University Press, 1992) pp. 207–19.

Mill, J. S., *On Liberty* (London: Penguin Books, 1985).

Miller, D. and Walzer, M. (eds), *Pluralism, Justice and Equality* (Oxford: Oxford University Press, 1995).

Moruzzi, M. N., 'A Problem With Headscarfs', *Political Theory*, Vol. 22, No. 4, November 1994, pp. 653–72.

Mouffe, C., 'Citizenship and Political Identity', *October*, Vol. 61, 1992, pp. 28–32.

Mouffe, C., *The Return of the Political* (London: Verso, 1993).

Muir, J. R., 'The Isocratic Idea of Education and Islamic Education', *Papers of the Philosophy of Education Society*, March 31–April 2, 1995 pp. 28–36.

Nicholson, L., 'To be or not to be: Charles Taylor and the Politics of Recognition', *Constellations*, Vol. 3, No. 1, 1996, pp. 1–16.

Nietzsche, F., *Daybreak* (Cambridge: Cambridge University Press, 1982).

Nussbaum, M. C., 'Human Capabilities, Female Human Beings', in M. C. Nussbaum and J. Glover (eds), *Women, Culture and Development* (Oxford: Clarendon Press, 1995) pp. 61–104.

Okin, S., *Justice Gender and the Family* (US: Basic Books, 1989).

Okin, S., 'Political Liberalism, Justice and Gender', *Ethics*, 105, October 1994, pp. 23–43.

Okin, S., 'Inequalities between the Sexes in Different Cultural Contexts', in M. C. Nussbaum and J. Glover (eds), *Women, Culture and Development* (Oxford: Clarendon Press, 1995) pp. 275–97.

Okin, S., 'Politics and the Complex Inequality of Gender', in D. Miller and M. Walzer (eds), *Pluralism Justice and Equality* (Oxford: Oxford University Press, 1995) pp. 120–43.

Okin, S., 'Feminism and Multiculturalism: Some Tensions', *Ethics*, Vol. 108, No. 4, July 1998, pp. 661–84.

Oksenberg, Rorty A., 'The Hidden Politics of Cultural Identification', *Political Theory*, Vol. 22, No. 1, February 1994, pp. 152–66.

O'Neill, S., *Impartiality in Context: Grounding Justice in a Pluralist World* (Albany: State University of New York Press, 1997).

O'Sullivan, N., 'Difference and the Concept of the Political in Contemporary Political Philosophy', *Political Studies*, Vol. 45, No. 4, September 1997, pp. 739–54.

Owen, D., 'Kant Critique and Enlightenment', *unpublished paper* (University of Southampton: Department of Politics, 1998).

Parekh, B., 'The Concept of Multi-Cultural Education', in S. Modgil et al (ed.), *Multicultural Education – The Interminable Debate* (London: Falmer Press, 1986).

Parekh, P., 'Education for a Multicultural Society', *Papers for the Philosophy of Education Society of Great Britain*, March 31–April 2 1995, pp. 1–10.

Parekh, B., 'Cultural Pluralism and the Limits of Diversity', *Morrell Conference on Toleration, Identity and Difference*, 18–20 September 1995, University of York, York, UK.

Parekh, P., 'Moral Philosophy and its Anti-pluralist Bias', in D. Archard (ed.), *Philosophy and Pluralism* (Cambridge: University Press, 1996) pp. 117–34.

Parekh, B., 'Minority Practices and Principles of Toleration', *International Migration Review*, Vol. 30, No. 1, 1996, pp. 251–84.

Parry, G., 'Political Liberalism and Education', in I. Hampshire-Monk and J. Stanyer (eds), *Contemporary Political Studies 1996*, Vol. 3 (Exeter: Short Run Press Ltd.) pp. 1697–708.

Pateman, C., 'The Theoretical Subversiveness of Feminism', in C. Pateman and E. Gross (eds), *Feminist Challenges* (Sydney: Allen & Unwin, 1988) pp. 1–10.

Phillips, A., *Democracy and Difference* (Cambridge: Polity Press, 1993).

Phillips, A., *The Politics of Presence* (Oxford: Clarendon Press, 1995).

Rawls, J., 'Kantian Constructivism in Moral Theory', *Journal of Philosophy*, Vol. 77, No. 9, 1980, pp. 515–77.

Rawls, J., *A Theory of Justice* (Oxford: Oxford University Press, 1986).

Rawls, J., *Political Liberalism* (New York: Columbia Press, 1993).

Raz, J., *The Morality of Freedom* (Oxford: Clarendon, 1986).

Raz, J., *Ethics in the Public Domain* (Oxford: Clarendon Press, 1996).

Raz, J., 'Multiculturalism: A Liberal Perspective', *Dissent*, Winter 1994, pp. 67–79.

Ripstein, A., 'Recognition and Cultural Membership', *Dialogue*, Vol. 34, Part 2, 1995, pp. 331–41.

Rockefeller, S., 'Comment', in A. Gutman and C. Taylor (eds), *Multiculturalism and "The Politics of Recognition"* (Princeton, NJ: Princeton University Press, 1992) pp. 87–98.

Rousseau, J. J., *The Social Contract* (London: Penguin Books, 1968).

Ruddick, S., *Maternal Thinking: Towards a Politics of Peace* (London: Women's Press, 1989).

Sandel, M., *Liberalism and The Limits of Justice* (Cambridge: Cambridge University Press, 1982).

Scheffler, S., 'The Appeal of Political Liberalism', *Ethics*, 105, October 1994, pp. 4–22.

Sharifi, H., 'The Islamic as opposed to the Modern Philosophy of Education', in S. M. al-Naquib al-Attas (ed.), *Aims and Objectives of Islamic Education* (Jedda: Hodder and Stoughton, 1979).

Spelman, E. V., *Inessential Woman* (Boston: Beacon Press, 1988).

Stolzenberg, M. N., '"He Drew a Circle That Shut Me Out" Assimilation, Indoctrination, and the Paradox of a Liberal Education', *Harvard Law Review*, Vol. 106, No. 3, January 1993, pp. 582–667.

Swann, M., *Education for All*, HMSO, February 1985.

Tamir, Y., 'Two Concepts of Mutliculturalism', *Journal of Philosophy of Education*, Vol. 29, No. 2, 1995, pp. 161–72.

Taylor, C., *Sources of the Self: the making of modern identity* (Cambridge: Cambridge University Press, 1989).

Taylor, C., *The Ethics of Authenticity* (Cambridge, MA: Harvard University Press, 1991).

Taylor, C., 'Multiculturalism and the "Politics of Recognition"', in C. Taylor and A. Gutman (eds), *Multiculturalism and the "Politics of Recognition"* (Princeton, NJ: Princeton University Press, 1992).

Taylor, C., 'Nationalism and Modernity', in R. McKim and J. McMahan (eds), *The Morality of Nationalism* (New York: Oxford University Press, 1997), pp. 31–55.

Taylor, C., *Reconciling the Solitudes* (Montreal: McGill-Queen's University Press, 1993).

Tomasi, J., 'Kymlicka, Liberalism and Respect for Cultural Minorities', *Ethics*, Vol. 105, No. 3, April 1995, pp. 580–603.

Toulmin, S., *Cosmopolis, The Secret Agenda of Modernity* (New York: Free Press, 1990).

Tully, J., *Strange Multiplicity* (Cambridge: Cambridge University Press, 1997).

Van Dyke, V., 'The Individual, the State, and Ethnic Communities in Political Theory', in W. Kymlicka (ed.), *The Rights of Minority Cultures* (Oxford: Oxford University Press, 1995) pp. 31–56.

Vogel, L., 'Critical Notices: The Ethics of Authenicity and Multiculturalism and The Politics of Recognition', *International Journal of Philosophical Studies*, Vol. 1, Part 2, 1993, pp. 325–35.

Walker, B., 'Plural Cultures, Contested Territories: A Critique of Kymlicka', *Canadian Journal of Political Science*, Vol. 30, No. 2, 1997, pp. 211–34.

Walzer, M., *Spheres of Justice* (Oxford: Blackwell, 1983).

Walzer, M., '"Spheres of Justice": An Exchange', *The New York Review of Books*, 21 July 1983, pp. 43–6.

Walzer, M., 'Comment' in A. Gutmann and C. Taylor (eds), *Multiculturalism and the "Politics of Recognition"* (Princeton, NJ: Princeton University Press, 1992) pp. 99–103.

Walzer, M., *Thick and Thin* (Notre Dame: University of Notre Dame, 1994).

Warnke, G., 'Discourse Ethics and Feminist Dilemmas of Difference', in J. Meehan, *Feminists Read Habermas: Gendering the Subject of Discourse* (London: Routledge, 1995) pp. 247–61.

White, J., *The Aims of Education Restated* (London: Routledge, Keagan and Paul, 1982).

Williams, B., 'Introduction' in I. Berlin, *Concepts and Categories* (London: Hogarth Press, 1978).

Wilson, M., 'Constitutional Recognition and the Treaty of Waitangi: Myth or Reality', in M. Wilson and A. Yeatman (eds), *Justice and Identity*.

Wokler, R., 'Enlightenment', in M. A. Riff (ed.), *Dictionary of Modern Political Ideologies* (Manchester: Manchester University Press, 1987).

Wolf, S., 'Comment', in A. Gutman and C. Taylor, *Multiculturalism and "The Politics of Recognition"* (Princeton, NJ: Princeton University Press, 1992) pp. 75–85.

Wollstonecraft, M., *A Vindication of the Rights of Woman* (London: Everyman, 1995).

Wootton, D., *Modern Political Thought: Readings from Machiavelli to Nietzsche*, (Cambridge: Hackett, 1996).

Young, I. M., 'Polity and Group Difference: A Critique of the Ideal of Universal Citizenship', *Ethics*, Vol. 99, January 1989, pp. 251–74.
Young, I. M., *Justice and the Politics of Difference* (Princeton: Princeton University Press, 1990).
Young, I. M., 'Gender as seriality: thinking about women as a social collective', in L. Nicholson and S. Seidman, *Social Postmodernism: Beyond identity politics* (Cambridge: Cambridge University Press, 1995) pp. 187–215.
Young, I. M., 'Communication and the Other: Beyond Deliberative Democracy', in M. Wilson and A. Yeatman, *Justice and Identity* (Wellington: Bridget Willimans Books, 1995) pp. 134–52.